Living (and Teaching) in an Unjust World

LIVING (AND TEACHING) IN AN UNJUST WORLD

New Perspectives on Multicultural Education

EDITED BY
WENDY GOODMAN

HEINEMANN
Portsmouth, NH

Heinemann
A division of Reed Elsevier Inc.
361 Hanover Street
Portsmouth, NH 03801–3912
www.heinemann.com

Offices and agents throughout the world

The editor and publisher wish to thank those who have generously given permission to reprint borrowed material:

Portions of "Questions of Power and the Power of Questions" by John Pryor were previously published in *Investigating Formative Assessment: Teaching, Learning and Assessment in the Classroom* by Harry Torrance and John Pryor, published in 1998 by Open University Press (Philadelphia). Reprinted by permission of Open University Press, Buckingham, United Kingdom.

Library of Congress Cataloging-in-Publication Data
Living (and teaching) in an unjust world : new perspectives on multicultural education / edited by Wendy Goodman.
      p. cm.
   Includes bibliographical references.
   ISBN 0-325-00381-5 (paper)
   1. Multicultural education—United States.   I. Goodman, Wendy.

   LB1099.3 .L58 2001
   370.117—dc21

                                                                                       2001026412

Editor: William Varner
Production service: bookworks
Production coordination: Lynne Reed
Cover design: Jenny Jensen Greenleaf
Manufacturing: Steve Bernier

Printed in the United States of America on acid-free paper
05   04   03   02   01   DA   1   2   3   4   5

Dedication

This book is dedicated to all the good educators working hard to promote democracy in diversity regardless of policies of adversity—as exemplified by Susan and Frankie.

If my book had the power to change the world:

- *For Rachel—I would wish that standardized tests would be replaced with Libraries, Art, Music, Drama and PE in every school every day*

- *For Aaron—I would exchange bell-shaped grading practices, especially at the university level, with evaluation based on learning and effort*

- *For Joshua—I would retire any teacher who holds students responsible for his/her own lack of professionalism*

- *For Bob—I wish a long life of learning*

I want to thank all the contributing authors for their endless patience with the publishing process. I want to acknowledge the thousands of students, young and not-so-young, who allowed all of us to learn along with them.

CONTENTS

0334642

INTRODUCTION:

Multicultural Education—Shifting Perspectives

As you read these words, ethnic genocide continues in parts of Africa and Europe. Palestinians are denied sovereignty. Swiss banks still profit from Nazi plunder. In the United States, police departments and customs officials profile certain travelers as potential bad guys. Klan members are murdering again. Navajo and Hopi dispute boundaries. And there looms the possibility of militarizing the U.S.-Mexico border.

When I embarked on this project, I saw a need to rethink multicultural education. I envisioned an anthology of classroom articles that would help the reader dip below the surface of multicultural Education. The working title of this book, "Beyond Burritos," was my way of identifying that goal. A response to those who limit multicultural education to tastebuds and textiles. A resource for conscientious educators who are no longer satisfied to teach the "Culture of the Quarter" or "Country of the Week." I wanted to provide a resource for teachers who live and teach in the real world where family structure is fluid, varied, and changing; where students live in mansions, duplexes, projects, or cars; where parents work in factories, fast food franchises, farms, or universities. A world where every learner is a lifelong learner and every student is valued.

So, I sent out a call for papers. I received responses from educators around the globe seeking to explore multicultural issues and concerns.

Perhaps it is the timing. Perhaps it is the forum. Whatever the cause, the authors of the articles submitted for this anthology take the reader into issues of multicultural education far deeper and broader than I had anticipated.

A reader of this book will go on a journey into educational systems exploring the just and unjust issues of schooling, beyond teaching about culture to facilitating self-discovery. And, if the reader's experience is similar to mine, while viewing classrooms as a mirror of larger society, the reader will conclude that multicultural education:

has its foundations in democratic classrooms

is most easily facilitated through empowering learners

is the path to true equity in education

begins with self-reflection

As editor, I have chosen to put the chapters together in couplets and triads. I have done so both to facilitate the reader's growth process and to emphasize that there are many paths to similar goals. Rather than read the chapters sequentially, I suggest you choose a set, read them both (or all three), and then take the time to reflect on the similarities and differences you find. Consider the applicability of each theme to your teaching/learning environment and to you, as an individual.

Overview of the Book

Debra Goodman—Living (and Teaching) in an Unjust World

The book begins with a piece by Debra Goodman, "Living (and Teaching) in an Unjust World." Debra's article chronicles the tough reality of education today. She asks, "How can a teacher cultivate an antiracist or multicultural perspective?" and explores "how school practices and structures conserve inequality." The chapter ends with a brief look at "the language of possibility."

The rest of the book explores that "language of possibility."

■   ■   ■

Deborah Horan—Listen to the Rhythm: Crossing Multicultural Boundaries

Deborah provides the fresh voice of a knowledgeable new teacher: "As a first-year teacher, I had been overwhelmed as I walked out of student teaching and immediately into a new school. . . . After three months immersed in a bilingual second-grade classroom, I was amazed to discover the positive impact music integration could have not only on literacy but also on classroom dynamics. . . ." In her honest portrayal, Deborah, challenged with a highly diverse multicultural classroom, shares her discovery that students learn more when learning is fun, engaging, varied, challenging, and diverse just like the greater world in which we live.

Wendy Goodman—Discovering the First Grade Curriculum in The Empty Pot

"All we have to do now is learn all about China, work through the first-grade curriculum, make sure all the kids learn to read and write, do it all in English and Spanish, and have an opera ready to perform in three months. Oh, we also need lesson plans for tomorrow!" I had not set out to teach a "multicultural" lesson to my students but I did learn one myself. I found that in learning about others, we make discoveries about ourselves. As we make discoveries about ourselves, we become empowered as learners. Empowered learners are more open to new concepts and ideas, which makes it easier to learn.

John Pryor—Questions of Power and the Power of Quesitons

"Of all the settings that teachers can find themselves working in, the inner city is usually acknowledged to be the most challenging. In fact it is usually spoken of in more explicitly negative terms. . . . My intention is to move beyond the stereotypes, which portray not only the inner city itself but also the people who inhabit it in a totally negative light. Instead, what I wish to do is to present an account of a short section of teaching and learning in a school in one of the least affluent parts of London, U.K., which exemplifies not just the difficulties of students and teachers in such settings, but also the way in which aspects of the context that may be seen as problematic can also contribute to a richness of experience and indeed a quality of learning that is often absent in other classrooms.

■   ■   ■

Cindee Karns—Turning over the Wheel: Discovering the Strength in Diversity

Cindee uses an analogy of navigating a river to teaching in eighth grade. "The rhythm of the school year feels normal and easy to my eighth-graders as they enter my classroom. They feel confident and assured that they definitely know what they are doing in school, until I hand over the wheel. They're usually reluctant just like I am in the boat. This year was no different." Cindee chronicles her solution to a call for "immediate action promoting tolerance and acceptance." "From my years of experience as a classroom teacher and as a parent, I knew that kids thrive at figuring out the impossible. I wondered if I could get my eighth-graders to identify diversity, figure out how to use it to their advantage, and then celebrate it."

Ana Inés Heras and Eileen Craviotto—Mediating Different Worlds: Bicultural Students at School

An old school reopened with a mission "to provide homelike learning environment for all children attending the school; to consider that families and teachers alike are the children's educators; and to educate all children, without making a distinction because of their socioeconomic or linguistic backgrounds." Ana and Eileen share their collaboration in that process where an emergent theme was that of children as cultural mediators. "From our perspective, it is important to consider the formation of bicultural identity as a process where both conflict and harmony co-occur, and are in constant interaction."

■   ■   ■

Thomas Caron—Literacy Liberation with Trade Books in Social Studies

Tom shares a research project that addresses the pressures of curriculum and testing and the push to "package" knowledge and concepts so that children can remember facts and score well on tests. "These very children need to navigate in a growing and changing world of information exchange with a quick and critical. Environments rich with literature and challenge, filled with insights and questions, flush with contrasts and comparisons, a wealth of literature and talk, emotional and cognitive response, are what is needed to provide the necessary base for children learning."

Katharine Davies Samway—We Never Read Any Book about Laos: Culturally Relevant Books in Literature Study Circles

Katharine takes a glimpse into a fifth/sixth-grade classroom and, through quotes from literature discussion and student journals, provides a powerful picture of the role books can play in Multicultural Education. We "learned more about each other, were able to teach others about our respective cultures, and were able to further develop understanding and respect for ourselves and each other."

■   ■   ■

Leslie Patterson and Shelia Baldwin—A Different Spin on Parent Involvement: Exploring Funds of Knowledge within a Systems Perspective

"Our questions have gradually shifted from 'What's wrong with these parents?' to 'What's wrong with our perceptions and understandings about the lives of these families?' We have gradually begun to see the complexity in home/school connections . . . that inquiry and conversation can be powerful tools for opening the boundaries between home and school." Shelia and Leslie describe dramatic changes in perceptions that lead to decisions that can lead "ultimately to significant programmatic changes and to changed lives."

Ann Edmonds—The Wheel of Advocacy: International Students in Middle America

Ann shares a successful model of school change focused on success of every student in its diverse population. "Far more than special events, visiting artists, or immigrant fairs, daily, intentional noticing differences and similarities is a powerful tool for multicultural learning."

■   ■   ■

Owen van den Berg—Affirming Difference While Building a Nation: Teaching Diversity in Neo-Apartheid America

Set against the backdrop of his personal experiences in South Africa, this article details the experience of one professor and his twenty-five undergraduate students (future teachers) of "undiverse" backgrounds in a course called "Cultural Diversity." He decides, "not to focus so much on the cultures of faraway, exotic places, or on trying to teach 'techniques of multicultural education' . . . but rather concentrate on encouraging the students to explore their own personal cultures, to identify the levels of difference and diversity that existed within their group, and then to proceed from there to deep discussion."

Dean Cristol—Becoming a Multicultural Educator: Talking the Talk and Walking the Walk

Dean takes a serious look at diversity education in preservice teaching. Three case studies of preservice teachers are utilized. "As a teacher educator, I must remember that multicultural education is a complex philosophy that must be first understood by the educator before integrating it into an educational system. Developing preservice teachers' multicultural perspectives is an intricate undertaking, which involves more than course work, internships, and student teaching."

María Angeles Fernández Castro—International Students, International Teachers: A Multicultural Dilemma

In this chapter, María Angeles provides a look into schools where teachers, rather than students, come from a 'foreign culture.' As teachers learn the local culture, they face the "challenge and responsibility to provide students with worldwide credentials that enable them to work in multi-cultural societies with an appropriate corpus of knowledge; and also to understand, tolerate, and perhaps adopt unfamiliar values, perceptions, and attributes."

■   ■   ■

Jill Gladstein—Using Critical Questioning to Investigate Identity, Culture, and Difference

The goal of this chapter is to show the reader how students explore the complexity of concepts of identity, culture, and difference. "I hope that by sharing my experiences in the ESL classroom, other teachers will see the need for students to continue their exploration of the topics of identity, culture, difference. It is through this exploration that the students learn about themselves, their own culture, and about the culture they are trying to acquire."

Nancy Gallavan—Sparking the Conversation: Teachers Find Cultural Connections and Communities of Learners

A fine balance between Nancy's narrative and student reflective journals provides a window into growth and change. "This Cultural Artifact assignment exemplifies one successful approach used in my multicultural education course. . . . Students not only engage actively in a personalized learning experience, they begin to construct an inclusive and useful definition for the meaning of culture. They explore their own rich and individual cultural heritages and histories. They discover and frequently enrich their understandings for the range of cultural diversity that thrives in the people around them.

They start to value cultural diversity and the importance for creating cultural connections among their own students and communities of learners within their own classrooms."

■ ■ ■

Joan Wink—Finding the Freedom to Teach and Learn, and Live

Joan invites readers to join her as she shares her experience. "I cannot adjust to the dogma underlying the current climate in education. Therefore, I will have to find creative forms of maladjustment to survive and thrive. Incidentally, if you would like to join me in creative maladjustment, you will find that a sense of humor is very handy. It also helps to be a bit nimble." This chapter enables readers to find ways to teach and value diversity in the face of adversity.

1 Living (and Teaching) in an Unjust World

Debra Goodman

I drive to school past charred houses, boarded up businesses, Chet's Gun Shop, and isolated store fronts decorated with bars and grates. I buy gas through a Plexiglas window and I have to pay in advance. On the empty streets near the school, I pass women shivering in short skirts or hot pants, scanning cars for early morning customers. I turn into the school parking lot at the rescue mission, where men are out raking the yard and sweeping the street as payment for a night's lodging.

The school doors are locked to keep out intruders and visitors must ring a bell. I get the computer from a locked storeroom down the hall, pull out the tape player from a padlocked closet. My classroom is furnished with mismatched tables, an assortment of chairs, and shelves scrounged or made from crates and boards. I have purchased many of the books and materials myself.

The bell rings at 8:30 and the students run in from all directions—coming from breakfast, morning latchkey, or the school doors. They hurry into the room to sign up for learning centers. They check out new clothes and talk about weekend activities as they look over the day's agenda and check on the hamsters.

I stand in the doorway greeting the children as they enter the room. The boys' urinals don't have running water and the stink drifts into the hallways. There is never any toilet paper, soap, or paper towels. Mrs. Beal, who cleans after school, is responsible for the entire second floor including four bathrooms and fifteen classrooms. She brings her own cleaning supplies and rags because the board does not supply materials she feels she needs.

As I walk in the room, there is a buzz of talk and activity. The art committee is setting out materials for the day. Some children are in the classroom library returning books or browsing for new reading materials. In the Science Center, a small group looks over the latest issue of Ranger Rick. Lisa shows me a story she has been working on over the weekend.

I look over the center sign up sheet and the attendance sheet and I notice that Linda is absent again.

"Does anyone know what's happened to Linda?"

"Mrs. Goodman, she got tooken."

"She what?"

"She got tooken. Social services came and got her."

I make a mental note to call protective services. They're always so surprised that a teacher would care. As if Linda isn't a part of our classroom family. As if she wouldn't want to pick up her work and say good-bye. I am also struck by the strong sense of community in the housing projects. All the neighborhood kids know what's happened to Linda.

We start out our class meeting with a mini-lesson on strategies for research and note-taking. I use my own research question as a demonstration. After each research group gives a brief progress report, we move into work time. I have a "small" group this year, only 29 students. (My friend who teachers first grade started out the year with 38 until "reorganization" on the sixth week of school.) Still 29 is an awkward number requiring seven work areas and seven groups. I want four to five in a group for committees, research, writing groups, or other group projects. It's not easy to divide my five-hour day or five-day week by seven.

After seeing that everyone is settled, I sit at the conference table. Catherine shows me a three-page letter written to her and her brother. In the letter, her uncle tries to explain why he shot Catherine's stepfather. Catherine was a new student in our fifth-grade class. In her journal, she wrote eloquently and fluently, working out her short but traumatic life story. Her uncle shot and killed her stepfather during a family fight. Her much-loved stepfather was dead, and her uncle was in jail. He eloquently pleads with his niece and nephew for their understanding. While his reasoning was disturbing and upsetting to Catherine and to me, his writing was well organized, clear, and mechanically correct.

As I talk with Catherine, laughter drifts from the Lego table, where Natasha and Daniel are making up stories to go with their elaborate constructions. Simone sits nearby in the research area reading about Jackie Robinson, occasionally stopping to take notes. Patricia sits at the writing table, frowning and smiling as she continues her story. And so my day goes.

There are many ways of telling the multifaceted stories of our classroom lives. There are tales of the tragedy of discrimination and neglect. Children in my classrooms are homeless. They have fathers and brothers in prison. They have seen a cousin shot down by a stray bullet. Their auntie is dying of AIDS. They have asthma and other health problems. They are going to a school in a district that generates half the per pupil spending of many nearby suburbs.

There are also the slice of life stories. Children in my classroom grow up in caring extended families. They live in a community with resources and connections. Their parents are articulate and literate. They enjoy friends, the popular culture of TV and music, stylish clothes, and good times. They are like the children of the suburbs, except perhaps less pretentious and more mature. Many already know how to clean the house, wash the dishes, and take care of babies. I often tell these stories of hope and possibility, not mentioning the locked school doors and the smells drifting through the hall.

However, it is important to bring these stories together in order to understand urban teaching. We are living, and teaching, in an unjust world. A world that many Americans never have to see or to face. But it is just down the road; across the bridge; on the other side of town. It is right beside the freeway on the way downtown, hidden above the subterranean passage from suburbs to concerts, festivals, ballgames, and restaurants. We can ignore the world American children are growing up in, but it is still there.

In the book *Affirming Diversity*, Sonia Nieto describes the sociopolitical context of multicultural education. "Multicultural and bilingual education developed as a response to inequality in education based on racism, ethnocentrism, and language discrimination" (Nieto 1996, p. 2). If school curricula already reflected our pluralistic society, we would not need "multicultural" education. Instead schools and curricula reflect a society with a history of discrimination and oppression based upon race, sex, class, culture, religion, and sexual orientation.

Inequality within our society or our classrooms cannot be addressed by "color blindness," or simply by learning about "different" cultures. For this reason, many educators have moved away from the term *multicultural* and talk about antiracist or "social justice" curricula. Multicultural education should not be viewed as a curriculum, but as an underlying perspective toward learning, teaching, and curriculum.

> "Multicultural or anti-racist education is fundamentally a perspective. It's a point of view that cuts across all subject areas, and addresses the histories and experiences of people who have been left out of the curriculum. Its purpose is to help us deal equitably with all the cultural and racial differences you find in the human family. It's also a perspective that allows us to get at explanations for why things are the way they are in terms of power relationships, in terms of equality issues. (Lee 1994, p. 20)

In a correspondence regarding the title of this book, author Owen van den Berg expressed his South African perspective.

"My problem with the title is in using the word 'multicultural.' When the apartheid government eventually allowed some contact between the races, it was on the basis of 'multiculturalism'—so for instance, a white soccer team could play against a black soccer team ("multicultural sport") but neither team was allowed to be mixed! Opposed to this were the people who wanted "non-racial" sport—anybody could compete alongside or against anybody—and many teachers lost their jobs because their school authorities tried to force them to organize and participate in "multicultural sport" and punished them if they organized "non-racial" sport.

How can a teacher cultivate an antiracist or "nonracial" perspective? It is not enough to want equality and fairness. We must first address the forces and structures that create inequality.

I grew up reading stories that explored the complexity of life and the issues of racial and cultural politics in America. Stories like *Native Son, The Dollmaker,* and *I Know Why the Caged Bird Sings.* These stories placed a human face on the tragedy of racial and economic oppression in America. They invited dialogue and thoughtful analysis. These stories are seldom told today. On the contrary, there is a tendency to assume that we can achieve equality by ignoring differences and treating all children as if they are the same. Sometimes, in the face of inequality, we deny its very existence.

Several years ago, in a discussion of the American civil rights movement, my highly capable and caring student teacher asked the children if they thought things had changed since the civil rights movement. Several African-American students in the class said, "No." They told stories of going to suburban shopping malls and being treated like shoplifting suspects. They talked about being questioned by police, or eyed suspiciously when they visited white neighborhoods. My student teacher, usually careful to allow children to discuss their views freely, began to argue with the students. They must have misunderstood, or perhaps they read too much into the situation.

My student teacher's response to the reported experiences of African American students provides insight into some of the complexities of this issue, particularly for European American teachers. In the media and popular opinion, we are experiencing what Jonathan Kozol calls a "hardening of feelings toward poor people." He quotes the commanding officer of the police in Central Park, New York: "We have to cut off the head of the enemy and the enemy is the homeless." (Kozol 1995)

In this climate, stories are woven into a cycle of blame that casts inner-city families as the perpetrators of their own oppression. Instead of poverty programs we hear about welfare fraud. Instead of civil rights movements we hear about immigrants taking "American" jobs. Instead of gun control and drug rehabilitation programs we hear about street crime and get-tough policies. The negative language of these urban horror stories preys on our fears. The characters in these stories are called street thugs, welfare queens, criminals, drug abusers, or illegal aliens (Kozol 1995). Four common assumptions harden our feelings and desensitize us toward the oppression of the poor and racial minorities.

Common (mis)assumptions about poverty and education:

- Everyone in America has the same opportunities. The poor get used to welfare, and don't lift a finger to help themselves.

- America's public schools have "failed" to educate America's children properly. As a result, young people are not prepared for the workforce, which leads to a life of poverty, welfare, violence, and crime.

- Differential treatment of poor or minority children is not due to discriminatory funding or schooling practices, but to waste and mismanagement in urban school districts and badly trained teachers.

- Poor children do not succeed in school because they are linguistically and culturally disadvantaged. These disadvantages are due to their environment, dysfunctional families and lack of role models. They won't get good jobs because they are illiterate and uneducated.

Ira Shor (1987) describes the "real potential of teaching" as the possibility of "confirming or challenging socialization into inequality." Carole Edelsky (1991) expresses these opposing forces as "conserving" or "transforming" movements within education. Transformative forces seek to "challenge socialization into inequality" by challenging the discriminatory assumptions and practices imbedded in our society, and reflected in our schools and classrooms. In the following pages I will challenge the preceding assumptions.

Everyone in America has the same opportunities. The poor get used to welfare, and don't lift a finger to help themselves.
America is known as the "land of opportunity" where anyone can get ahead if they only work hard enough. This might be true if

children in America all started out with the same resources and opportunities. In addition, this assumption ignores a legacy of active oppression and discrimination based on race, class, gender, and ethnicity. It also ignores the struggles against discrimination and oppression that have been necessary to overcome inequality.

The view of history that ignores discrimination or people's movements is perpetuated in the schools by a narrowing of history to names, dates, and events of politicians and famous or "important" people. A colleague once asked me to respond as a Jewish American to a documentary on the history of Jews in America. I didn't notice any overt inaccuracies in the documentary. However, there was no discussion of the ongoing political struggles against anti-Semitism. There was no mention of the sweatshops and the active role of many Jews in union organizing and civil rights campaigns. For me, the struggle for justice and human rights is an important part of Jewish-American history, and a part of my Jewish cultural identity as well.

This "whitewashing" of history is reinforced by sociological and educational jargon that ignores the political and social structures that conserve inequality. Euphemisms such as marginalized, disenfranchised, disadvantaged, at-risk, and LEPs (limited English proficient) imply that poor children and their families have the problems and obscure how our society is organized to perpetuate oppressive conditions for many children (Macedo 1997). In the United States, our system of local funding based on property taxes allows the owners of large corporations and the residents of wealthy and privileged communities to avoid taking responsibility for public services, recreation facilities, and schools for poor communities.

Jonathan Kozol (1991) describes the community of East St. Louis, a largely African American town surrounded by factories and chemical plants. The city is "clouded by the fumes that pour from vents and smokestacks." Manufacturing has caused lead and chemical poisoning of the soil and water where children play. Incidence of infant mortality, asthma, and other health conditions is extremely high. However, the chemical plants destroying this community don't pay any taxes toward schools, hospitals, waste disposal, or other services in East St. Louis. They have created small towns outside of the East St. Louis borders, legal fictions that allow them to avoid responsibility for the problems they have caused.

My colleague, Toby Curry, shared Kozol's *Amazing Grace* (1995) with teachers and students in our inner-city school in Detroit. We noticed parallel's between Kozol's descriptions of New York City's South Bronx and Detroit's Cass Corridor community where we worked. Our school neighborhood, a few miles from the largest incinerator in North America, is a popular site for illegal trash or chemical dumping. The small city park we use as a playground is littered with broken glass and used needles. Kozol's descriptions of the health conditions of South Bronx families led us to question our own students. We discovered a high rate of asthma among children in our community, and the second highest incidence of AIDS in our state. A discussion of the AIDs virus prompted tearful sessions with sixth- and seventh-graders as six members of the class had lost relatives to this disease.

Tax structures, government funding systems, and budgets are increasingly designed to protect corporations and wealthy communities, and minimize programs for the poor. Programs that have the potential to provide some relief from inequities (such as welfare, ADC, public education, community colleges, and mental health services) have been cut by conservative governments at the state and federal level. Ironically, urban districts such as East St. Louis or Detroit pay proportionately higher property taxes than suburban districts in those states as local residents try, with their limited resources, to fund schools and services for their children.

During the last eight years, programs needed to challenge inequality (such as affirmative action, national health insurance, food for children in poverty, access to affordable child care, public transportation, fully funded and supported public schools, support for higher education, drug rehabilitation, and so on) have been slashed and eroded. At the same time, deregulation and tax cuts for major corporations, have led to the widest income gap between rich and poor people in this country's history. Stories about lethargy and laziness of poor people today obscure these economic realities.

America's public schools have "failed" to educate America's children properly. As a result, young people are not prepared for the workforce, which leads to a life of poverty, welfare, violence, and crime.

In recent years the push to improve public education has been increasingly built upon attacks on public schools and public school teachers. Bess Altwerger (1998) analyzed a series of articles in the *Baltimore Sun,* and outlines the following strategies in undermining support for public schools.

1. Destroy public confidence in teachers

2. Destroy confidence in public schools

3. Make kids look like savages

4. Feed the press lies about current knowledge and research

5. Blame teacher educators

6. Provide a solution: phonics programs, private education, vouchers

7. Link to godliness (making alliances with the religious right)

8. Push legislation and teacher exams

Media campaigns against public schools prey on racism and fear. One article in the *Baltimore Sun* describes wild, out-of-control children and the classroom teacher's comment that "it's not their fault." Pictures of African American children are prominently displayed. In Altwerger's analysis this gross racism is a mere side effect of a campaign aimed at privatizing public education. The "solution" to this media-created problem is phonics, censorship, vouchers, high-stakes testing charter schools, public funds for private schools, and privatization of public schools. This "solution" protects the interests of the privileged, while providing opportunities for corporations to profit from public education. It also creates two school systems, one for those with money and one for those without.

In *Savage Inequalities* Kozol describes funding practices that deliberately reinforce social injustice by social class and race.

> "There is a certain grim aesthetic in the almost perfect upward scaling of expenditures from the poorest of the poor to the richest of the rich within the New York City area: $5,590 for the children of the Bronx and Harlem, $6,340 for the non-white kids of Roosevelt, $6,400 for the black kids of Mount Vernon, $7,400 for the slightly better off community of Yonkers, over $11,000 for the very lucky children of Manhasset, Jericho and Greatneck. In an ethical society, where money was apportioned in accord with need, these scalings would run almost in precise reverse. (Kozol, p. 123)

Poorly funded urban districts are often just next door to posh suburban districts. The lack of adequate public funding has created a situation where underfunded schools seek "corporate sponsors," who privately fund a variety of special projects and services. This private funding allows business leaders (rather than educators) to make decisions about school curriculum and programs. At the same time, as incentive to stay in urban communities, these corporations often receive tax breaks against the property taxes paid by homeowners in the same school community.

The particular scapegoats attacked by the anti–public school smears are multicultural or humanistic education; process writing and whole language; bilingual education and heritage language programs. These curricula are singled out because of the tendency toward teaching critical thinking, teaching social justice, and teaching that challenges inequities and inequalities.

Generalized attacks on public schools obscure the "savage inequalities" that allow some children to succeed while others fail. However, they are based on faulty premises. In fact, there is no general decline or failure in America's public education system. In *Manufactured Crisis*, Berliner and Biddle (1996) examine statistics that have been used to show a decline in public education. One problem is that test scores often group large discrepant populations together. When SAT scores, which "fell" during the late 1960s and early 1970s, are disaggregated according to race, culture, and class, this brief decline in scores disappears. This "decline" reflects that "students from a broader range of backgrounds were then getting interested in college, which should have been cause for celebration, not alarm." SAT scores of Blacks, Asians, Native Americans, Mexican Americans, and Puerto Ricans have all increased between 1976 and 1993.

The political agenda against public education becomes clear in the reactions to studies showing that there *is no decline* in achievement. An ETS study of the National Assessment of Educational Progress showed "very little change over the past two decades" in achievement scores in math and reading. Lamar Alexander and others responded that the scores were "not nearly good enough for the 1990s" (Berliner and Biddle, p. 14)

In an exhaustive and thorough analysis of measures of "reading performance Kaestle et al. (1991) come up with the following general conclusions:

- According to the U.S. census, the number of Americans who considered themselves "illiterate" decreased from 20 percent of Americans in 1870 to 0.6 percent of Americans in 1979.

- The median educational level of adults in the United States rose from 8.6 to 12.5 years of schooling between 1940 and 1980. Since "reading achievement" levels have remained stable at each grade level, the "level" of literacy in the United States has increased considerably.

- The definition of "functional illiteracy" has changed dramatically since the term emerged in the 1930s. First defined as at least three years of school, current "illiteracy measures" define "functional illiteracy" as an eigth- or even twelfth-grade "reading level."

While the authors do not find any decline in literacy, they do find discrepancies in scores of racial and cultural minorities, and the poor. "Even if schools today are performing about as well as they have in the past, they have never excelled at educating minorities and the poor." The assertion that public schools are failing is a smoke screen covering real problems of inequity, discrimination and racism in American schools.

Predictably, children in urban communities are the most hard hit by recent attacks on public schools. In Chicago, a state takeover of the public schools brought a move toward "tougher standards" and more rigid and basic education. Get-tough policies, such as ending "social promotion," have produced misleading test score results partially due to a 10 percent decrease in student enrollment due to dropouts. (Schmidt 2000) In districts such as Chicago, Detroit, and Brooklyn, N.Y., decisions on retention are being made solely on test score results. Thousands of inner-city children, primarily Latino and African American, are being held back or forced to take summer school classes regardless of their grades or teachers' judgements.

Differential treatment of poor or minority children is not due to discriminatory funding or schooling practices, but due to waste and mismanagement in urban school districts and badly trained teachers.

It is initially difficult to understand how overt economic discrimination can be allowed to continue in America's public schools. There is a prevalent misperception that poor districts and the students within those districts are beyond help. Myths about American schools mask oppressive practices, as revealed in the table on p. 11 based on discussion in *Manufactured Crisis* (Berliner and Biddle 1996).

Though easily debunked, these myths obscure the issues of homelessness, unemployment, and racial and cultural discrimination. America's problems are blamed on its public schools; injustices blamed on school employees, teachers, parents, and students. The manipulative nature of such attacks are clear as government positions shift. The 1980s' predicament of "the overeducated American" turned into an attack on "mediocrity" overnight.

> With few exceptions, the official reports explained away the real issues in the teacher shortage and the decline of education, choosing instead "blaming-the-victim" formulas such as student-teacher "mediocrity," the need for "excellence," and higher "standards," the softness in a "cafeteria-style" high school curriculum, and the "breakdown" of discipline in school and the family. In reality, the current crisis was invited by budget cuts in public schools and colleges, which left class

MYTHS	FACTS
■ Money is not related to school achievement.	■ The United States ranks ninth among sixteen countries in per pupil spending (just after Canada), fourteenth in spending compared to per capita income.
■ America spends a lot more money on education than other countries. ■ Costs in education have recently sky-rocketed wastefully.	■ Many countries provide national health care while health care and other benefits for U.S. school employees are paid by the school districts.
■ American schools are top-heavy and spend too much money on administration.	■ U.S. public elementary and secondary schools average 14.5 employees per administrator compared to 3.6 to 9.3 employees per administrator in other employment areas (including business).
■ American schools are generally incompetent. They do not produce workers with good technical skills.	■ America's teachers are highly educated. More than 50 percent of teachers had master's degrees in 1991.
■ Those who enter teaching have little ability and receive a poor academic education.	■ An elementary teacher takes "about 70 percent of his or her course work outside the school or college of education." There is an increase in five-year education programs, with a full-year teaching internship following college graduation.
■ American workers are not productive and schools are at fault. Industries must pay vast amounts for remedial training of workers.	■ Most business "training" funds go toward high-level technology. Only a small percent go toward remedial education.

size too large, school buildings shabby, instructional materials in short supply, education programs unable to afford careful mentoring of student teachers, and new blood not coming into aging academic departments. (Shor, p. 9)

Political responses to "the problems" of American education focus on instruction and evaluation rather than underlying inequities. President Clinton's call for volunteer reading teachers and national testing did nothing to respond to inequities in funding for schools and communities. Children, parents, and teachers are being held responsible for the problems of social injustice in this sort of Band-Aid approach to school reform.

Rather than addressing social inequities, school reformers—some well meaning—cry for higher standards and accountability. Journalists spread the alarm running banner headlines, "50% of City Students Below Average!" Districts and states have implemented more commercial testing, pushing teachers to increase student scores and pouring limited public education funds into private coffers. From the president on down, there are cries for national testing of children and their teachers. These practices have resulted on increased pressure on teachers, and a narrowing of curricula and classroom and school learning experiences. Worse, in spite of common understandings that these tests have built-in cultural and class biases, the new emphasis on testing has returned us to an era of deficit views of poor and urban children—blaming children and families for the inequities that have caused these problems.

Poor children do not succeed in school because they are linguistically and culturally disadvantaged. These disadvantages are due to their environment, dysfunctional families, and lack of role models. They won't get good jobs because they are illiterate and uneducated.

Sonia Nieto (1996) discusses three theories that attempt to explain the high level of "school failure" among racial and linguistic "minorities" in the United States:

- A deficit theory focuses the blame for failure on students and their families.

- An economic and social reproduction theory proposes that schools reproduce the economic and social structures of society.

- A cultural incompatibilities theory suggests that school failure is caused by incongruities between the culture of the home and culture of the school.

Deficit Theories

Gloria Ladson-Billings (1994, p. 8) traces the "language of deprivation" in the educational community. In the 1960s, children were labeled "culturally deprived" and "disadvantaged." Although the goal was to improve "student and teacher effectiveness, the use of such terms contributed to a perception of African-American students as deprived, deficient, and deviant." In the 1980s and 1990s, the popular term is "at-risk." "The language of deprivation had changed, but the negative connotations remained" (Ladson-Billings, p. 9).

Within this perspective, experiences and abilities in a different home language or dialect are disregarded or viewed as a detriment rather than a resource. "From their outlook poor reading and writing scores by Black English speakers are understood to be the direct result of these students' inability to abandon their own delimiting dialect." (Gilyard 1991) The complex literate identities that children bring to school are ignored when they are called by acronyms such as LEPs (limited English proficiency) or LD (learning disabled).

Deficit theories have been disproven by studies that document the wide range of genre and function in literacy practices of families and communities. Shirley Brice Heath (1983) describes the poor black community of Trackton, where babies are held on the laps of adults who sit reading the newspaper on their front porches, and calling comments about the news over to their neighbors. Luis Moll (1994) describes what he calls the "funds of knowledge" in the Latino community, which include community resources about school, church, auto repair, cultural history, health and medicine, and other areas of expertise. Taylor and Dorsey-Gaines (1988) describe how African American children in an inner-city community are "growing up literate" with the support of family and neighbors.

Economic and Social Reproduction

An alternate theory for the "failure" of non-mainstream children is the argument that "schools reproduce the economic and social relations of society and therefore tend to serve the interests of the dominant classes." In this theory the fact that "70 percent of students in urban schools were dropping out was understood not as a *coincidence* but actually as an *intended outcome* of the educational system. In other words [. . . these students] were doing just exactly what was expected: They were succeeding at school failure" (Nieto, p. 234).

This perspective is supported by examining how school structures such as tracking and grouping can result in practices where children have different educational experiences within the same classrooms or schools. Dyson and the teachers in the San Francisco East Bay study groups list reputations, expectations, grade levels, retentions, report cards, and standardized tests as factors in differential treatment of students. "Sociocultural and linguistic differences can be institutionally framed as correlates of academic deficiencies, from the very start of a child's school life" (Dyson, p.11). Discriminatory practices in school begin in the earliest grades. Patrick Shannon (1989) describes how tracking or ability grouping discriminates against children in "low" reading groups.

In "high-ability" groups:	In "low-ability" groups:
Teachers seldom interrupt students when working with "high" groups.	Teachers interrupt students in lower-ability groups during oral reading between two and five times more frequently.
Seventy percent of reading is done silently.	Seventy percent of reading is oral.
Students in high groups were often asked to read texts that were easy for them.	Students in lower groups were asked to read texts that were difficult for them.

Especially disturbing is Shannon's description of selection process for ability grouping. "What is most often found is that differences in dress, deportment, manners, language, and language use are interpreted as intellectual deficits" (Shannon, p. 102).

While social and cultural reproduction is a key element of children's schooling experiences, it can't completely explain children's success or failure in school. As Nieto (p. 325) states, "The purposes of the dominant class are not perfectly reflected in the schools but are resisted and modified by the recipients of schooling."

Cultural Incompatibility

Another explanation for "school failures" focuses on the culture of the classroom when school and home cultures as at odds with each other. "The more consistent that home and school cultures are, the reasoning goes, the more successful students will be, in general terms. The opposite is also true: The more that students' experiences, skills, and values differ from the school setting, the more failure they will experience" (Nieto, p. 235).

Cultural incompatibility is often linked with power issues enacted in the classroom. In a study of a dual-language bilingual program, Edelsky, working with Sara Huddelson, found that English-speaking children seldom learned very much Spanish. In this setting, English-speaking children were often in the role of language teacher, while the Spanish-speaking children were always in the role of learner.

> The gross inequality of power between two languages (and two groups of people) that guarantees that one set of young children will always be language teachers and the other set language learners, that one set will be congratulated for making almost no progress while the other is disparaged for making tremendous (but not 'total') progress—the situation is not one that any program can change. (Edelsky, p. 28)

This study illustrates the complex issues involved in how we view and describe student failure and achievement. Spanish-speaking children learned a great deal of English, but were considered "failures," while English-speaking children were applauded if they knew colors or numbers in Spanish. Even when progressive educators discuss these issues, "school achievement" and "school failure" are generally defined by scores on standardized test scores. Edelsky deplores this practice. "Even though tests are hopelessly biased, even though they are conceptually invalid, even though they are used to support social stratification, tests and test scores are nevertheless appealed to—with a straight face—in work that is supposed to promote change" (p. 5).

Standardized tests scores, which have been used to show the economic and racial gaps between learners, have also been attacked for cultural and linguistic bias. Edelsky describes the "pitfalls" of transformative research and/or teaching including "unexamined acceptance of prevailing conceptions of language instruction and evaluation, especially written language" and "a focus on failure, along with an absence of concrete examples of liberatory practice" (Edelsky, p. 3).

Beyond Failure and Moving Towards Liberatory Practice

While deficit views of learners and learning are widely rejected, these views continue to influence school curriculum and policy. Reid Lyon, a psychologist with the National Institute of Mental Health, bases his arguments for phonics and direct instruction on assertions that kindergarten children in inner cities don't know how to hold a book. Twenty children in Barbara Lauchlan's whole language kindergarten classroom in inner-city Detroit, interviewed by this author, knew a lot about reading and writing. These children all knew how to hold a book. They also knew about title pages, authors, and illustrators, where to start reading and how to proceed through a book. The kindergarteners expected that the text in books would make sense. The children described literacy experiences imbedded in the daily lives of their families.

From Lauren's kindergarten interview

"I take a book and I open it and I make the story up and I read it. And sometime I don't know how to read, or it's bedtime. My mommy reads a story to me and then we'll watch TV and then go to bed. Every night I read something."

Almost all the children identified themselves as readers, although only a few could construct meaning from an unfamiliar text. They described learning to read as a fairly simple social process; someone reads to you and then you read to yourself. Most of the children said they learned to read at home, from their parents. For these three children, the school literacy experiences in a whole language classroom were so familiar and comfortable, they felt like home literacy experiences. On the other hand they all insisted that books are read from top to bottom and left to right because of experiences reading "big books" with their teacher.

As five- and six-year-old beginning readers, these children surprised me by describing a range of strategies for reading and writing. Although Lauren was not yet reading independently, she described eight different reading strategies including: reading a familiar book, looking at a book and making up the words, and asking your mother to read to you. Marco, one of the least proficient readers in the group, described six different strategies including "pick an easy book":

From Marco's kindergarten interview

I don't be reading the hard books because . . . cause I don't know how to read 'em. So I be picking out the books. And then when she [the teacher] say, "When you get done with your journal, then you go look at the book." So I pick an easy book.

What impressed me about these discussions is that young children are not only learning how to read but how to be a reader. Conducting and analyzing these interviews allowed me to get to know these children as learners. It is unnecessary to check off progress or judge a child against a standard. It is enough to discover the child's wisdom, and his or her current areas of inquiry and build from this strong language base constructed in early experiences with family and community.

Nieto (1996, p. 230) points out that "characteristics students bring with them to school including their race, ethnicity, social class, and language, also often have a direct impact on their success or failure in school." However, there is no causal effect between these characterics and school failure. "Instead it is the school's perception of students' language, culture, and class as inadequate and negative, and the subsequent devalued status of these characteristics in the academic environment, that help to explain school failure."

Changing the school's perception's of student's language culture and class changes the discussion from explaining "school failure" to the stories of learners. As we investigate the stories of learners, we begin to glimpse the "multiple layers of communication that are part of their contextual worlds."

> Even when we speak of literacy as a social process, we rarely look beyond the literacy event and the linguistic transactions that take place. So much of the process remains buried in the multiple layers of communication that are part of our contextual worlds. We forget that to be literate is a uniquely human experience, a creative process that enables us to deal with ourselves and to better understand one another. (Taylor and Dorsey-Gaines 1988, p. 200)

At the beginning of this chapter, I described how Catherine brought in a three-page letter written by her uncle to explain why he shot Catherine's stepfather. I described how Catherine used her journal to cope with the grief and pain of her eleven years of life. That year, Catherine also survived an apartment fire where her family lost many possessions. The police suspected arson, and Catherine and her mother were subpoenaed to testify in court. I received letters from Catherine's mother explaining the situation and excusing her absences from school.

Like most families in the United States, Catherine's family life involves negotiating a wide range and variety of social literacy events. Some of these events were painful. Catherine could not begin to respond to her uncle's letter and she had great fears about testifying in court. Literacy events could be healing, as when Catherine wrote to me in her journal. Like most of the children in my classroom, the adults in Catherine's life negotiated these literacy events skillfully. However, their literacy competency did not bring them economic success.

Patti Stock (1995) describes a study of high school writing in Saginaw. Teachers were trying to discover elements of "failing" papers, but instead noticed that "the papers our failing students had written were composed of common thematic materials of violence and oppression, and sometimes even of hopelessness and despair." Stock describes leaving these meetings "wondering how students had mustered sufficient courage—if not sufficient literacy—to write about the troubling events of their lived lives. Reflecting on the events they described, I could not help but conclude that although students were not ordinarily occupied with writing or talking about these events in school, they certainly must be preoccupied with them when they sat in schoolrooms" (Stock 1995). If the curriculum of the school fails to address the "lived lives" of these students, we may have one explanation for their "failure" to learn to write well. As Edelsky points out, "The various interwoven socio-politico-historical contexts children live through are the contexts that show them what writing is, the contexts *through* which they write, the contexts they change (in)" (Edelsky, p. 42).

It is meaningless to provide a "multicultural education" without addressing issues of inequity in our society and how these issues are played out within the classroom. However, it is important to describe teaching and learning in all their complexity, without reducing them to the "success" or "failure" of individuals or groups.

> Much research in language and education provides both summaries and also richly detailed pictures of these failures, so much in fact that it is the "scientific" mainstay, however unintentionally, of a "failure industry." As McDermott has said, millions of people are "measuring, documenting, remediating, and explaining" these failures. What is conserving about all the activity is that it puts an analytic distance on failure and offers no countering "language of possibility" (Aronowitz and Giroux 1985) (Edelsky, p. 6).

Language of Possibility

What is the role of the classroom teacher when high levels of literacy and learning may not help our students to be economically successful? One response is to recognize literacy and learning support our students in creative processes that enable us "to deal with ourselves and to better understand one another." As educators we can't assume responsibility for changing the world by changing our classrooms. We can provide opportunities for children to bring their home worlds into the classroom and become articulate and critical learners. In addition, we can become learners with students striving to understand and challenge injustice in our society. Posing problems (Freire 1994) with our students is the crux of multicultural teaching and establishing a social justice curriculum.

Rather than study student failure, Gloria Ladson-Billings (1994) asks what makes children successful in school. *The Dreamkeepers* focuses on eight teachers that both principals and parents selected as "effective with African American children." This group included five African American and three white teachers who had been teaching from 12 to 40 years. While the eight teachers used a range of approaches and methodologies, Ladson-Billings identified six common elements of what she calls "culturally relevant teaching."

1. Students whose educational, economic, social, political, and cultural futures are most tenuous are helped to become intellectual leaders in the classroom.

2. Students are apprenticed in a learning community rather than taught in an isolated and unrelated way.

3. Students' real-life experiences are legitimized as they become part of the official curriculum.

4. Teachers and students participate in a broad conception of literacy that incorporates both literature and oratory.

5. Teacher and students engage in a collective struggle against the status quo.

6. Teachers are cognizant of themselves as political beings.

Culturally relevant teaching involves learning from students and becoming advocates for students. "Teachers make the students' culture a point of affirmation and celebration. This means they have to work actively against the constant and repeated denigration" of oppressed students (Ladson-Billings, p. 12). In addition to celebrating the culture and community of students, teachers document students' abilities and strengths, helping the student and the class to see themselves as knowledgeable and capable.

Susan Austin's inner-city, whole language classroom illustrates the apprenticeship in a learning community that Ladson-Billings describes. I observed these first- and second-graders "learning by overhearing" as they worked in small groups with many opportunities to observe and interact with other learners. When I asked Victor what he did if he was reading and he came to something he didn't know, he countered, "And the 'kids-on-the-rug' don't know it either?" The "kids on the rug" referred to the practice of asking friends for help when reading to the class. Victor's comment led me to understand that, in this community, what one knows we all know. Observing other children and asking for help is not considered "cheating" in this classroom structure.

I also observed Susan actively working to help students become "intellectual leaders" in the classroom. She always called on children who raised their hands and children came to expect and understand that their comments were valued. She particularly highlighted the comments of children who were not known to be intellectual leaders in the classroom. And whenever a student said something particularly clever, Susan would ask, "How did you know that?" or "How did you figure that out?" Susan's question prompted the student to share their thought processes, making their implicit understandings explicit to the class.

Rita Tenorio describes teaching kindergarten in Milwaukee. "In my 20 years of teaching I have learned that, contrary to what adults often believe, young children are not "color-blind." Instead they have an unstated but nonetheless sophisticated understanding of issues of race and power." (Tenorio, p. 24). Tenorio describes how moving toward whole language "helped me understand that my curriculum, while framed in a multisensory approach that included both academics and play, lacked choice." Whole language allowed her to see the flaws in her curriculum, which she had considered "fair and equal." Providing choices and focusing on students' own interests and stories established more opportunities for diverse perspectives. Stories provide multiple opportunities to extend classroom language.

In Vivian Paley's kindergarten classroom children dictate stories and then these stories are read and dramatized in front of the class. Literature books are often dramatized. The stories are further extended through art work and class murals. Parents are invited to come in and tell their stories. Paley writes her own stories, often addressing social issues such as racism or exclusion in a fairy tale format. These stories are discussed and often the characters and plots become part of the children's own stories and dramatic play.

Cai and Sims-Bishop (1994) describe the importance of introducing "the literature of a parallel culture." These stories, written from the perspective of a member of that culture, are important in the identity of children within a culture, and for the growth in understanding of other children. "The literature of a parallel culture opens the group's heart to the reading public, showing their joy and grief, love and hatred, hope and despair, expectations and frustrations, and perhaps most importantly, the effects of a racist society. Voices from the heart, once heard, can change other hearts" (p. 68).

Stock's *Dialogic Curriculum* (1995) describes high school English classes where students dialogue with their personal stories, with each other, with teachers, with published authors, and with themselves as they interact with their own writings. In this context students' lives become the starting point for learning. Students gain a renewed appreciation for the expertise and knowledge in their classroom and community. Students begin to see written texts as the thoughts and stories of other authors like themselves. As students share, teachers extend their personal stories and discussion with text sets that invite students to engage in a wide range of fiction and nonfiction.

While teachers may be comfortable with shifting classroom structure to create more student involvement, we are less comfortable viewing teaching as a political activity. There is a common assumption that politics should be kept out of the classroom. However, classroom teachers can never be politically neutral. Allowing children to choose their writing topics, for example, invites a variety of issues and problems that affect children's lives outside of school. Even a teacher who consciously attempts to be politically "neutral" makes hundreds of political decisions—from the books in the classroom library, to the posters on the wall, and to attitudes toward holidays. Is Valentine's Day celebrated but not International Women's Day? Do students learn about Spanish Conquistadors building missions and not Diá de La Raza?

> It's not only a case of what the teacher does, but what the teacher doesn't do. If a teacher decides not to discuss social movements, such as the movement against the War in Vietnam or labor organizing during the Great Depression, the subtle yet clear message is that social activism is not worthy of study, let alone something that students should consider a civic responsibility. It also disequips children from understanding that ordinary people make a difference in shaping events. (Shor, p. 47)

The term "banking education" was coined by Paulo Freire to describe a view of curriculum where learners are the passive recipients of knowledge deposited in their empty heads. This traditional approach has led to indoctrination of children with the views prevalent within the society. I can remember arguing with my eighth-grade teacher about the racism and anti-Semitism of the crusades, which our textbook called a "vigorous fight for a good cause."

.   Culturally relevant teaching recognizes the teacher is a "political being." However, this recognition also comes with a shift to classroom structures where children's experiences are valued and incorporated into the curriculum. Freire calls for a problem-posing curriculum where students are encouraged to investigate problems in their lives and communities, and teachers assist in helping students to find underlying causes and patterns. In whole language curriculum, there is a cry for an inquiry approach where children select topics and questions for study. These approaches are democratic, allowing for a variety of views and responses, rather than political indoctrination. "A progressive teacher, in contrast to a reactionary one, is always endeavoring to reveal reality for his/her students, removing whatever keeps them from seeing clearly and critically" (Freire, p. 212).

Classroom policies such as open discussion, providing choices, and self-selected topics provide a more democratic classroom structure where students have a more active role in their own learning. These structures allow students to bring their real-life experiences into school. However, Tenorio points out that it's not enough to bring out the understandings and experiences that children bring to school. "When it came to changing the curriculum and countering tracking, the key to success was reinforcing and building upon the knowledge students brought with them to school. Yet on issues of race, if I merely supported the children's natural 'instincts' and knowledge, I would end up reinforcing stereotypes and prejudices." Tenorio describes how she uses kindergarten children's experiences to raise some of the underlying issues and problems.

> For me the most "teachable moments" in multicultural/antiracist teaching have come in responding to children's negative remarks. First I put a stop to the behavior and make clear that it is inappropriate. Then I try to explain why it is inappropriate and acknowledge the "victim's" feelings. Often the remark is unrelated to the conflict at hand, and I try to help the parties focus on the real problem. The child who told her classmate that "there are no Black queens" for instance, needs to understand not only that her remark is incorrect, but also that she has insulted her friend. Next she had to see the real issue was that she wanted to wear the rhinestone crown and sequin dress which were part of the playhouse scenario. Beyond that moment, it's good to have discussions of the queens throughout African history, perhaps using a piece of literature like *Mufaro's Beautiful Daughters,* by John Steptoe. (Tenorio, p. 28)

Ira Shor reminds us that, "If we do not teach in opposition to the existing inequality of races, classes, and sexes, then we are teaching to support it. If we don't teach critically against domination in society, then we allow dominant forces a free hand in school and out."

Culturally relevant teaching involves teachers as learners with our students. When teachers position ourselves as learners with our students, a range of issues can be explored and critiqued together. Students are curious about the origins and explanations of inequities and inequality. How was slavery justified? Why are people prejudiced?

How come African Americans put up with Jim Crow laws? Together teachers and students seek out possible responses and solutions.

When students have opportunities to articulate the issues and lived experiences of their lives, they are learning to think critically and act on their own behalf. Within these learning experiences, teachers have many opportunities to highlight strategies for research, literacy, and mathematics. But more important, a problem-posing curriculum can engage students with people and literature that illuminate the complex human stories of our lives and communities.

I stand talking with my colleagues as the children leave the building at the end of another long day. Mr. Grant and I chat about writing workshop and share some of the children's work. I return the computer to the locked closet, the tape-recorder to the locked cupboard in my room. I stand for a moment thinking about the centers and work for a few hours planning for the next day.

As the sky outside begins to darken, I lock the classroom door and leave with bags bulging with memos, journals, research folders, and books. I check outside the parking lot window and watch a man who is washing his hands in a large puddle. He scampers around to the playground when I walk out the door.

I pull out of the parking lot. Across the street, in an empty lot, a fire burns in a trash can. People huddle close by on boxes and broken furniture. At the rescue mission men are lined up waiting for a hot meal, hoping for a place to spend the night. Most stare down at their shoes without talking, but one man stares at me intently every day.

I always wonder who he is.

References

BERLINER, B., and Biddle, B. (1996). *Manufactured Crisis: Myths, Fraud and Attack on America's Public Schools.* Dallas: Addison-Wesley.

CAI, M. and SIMS-BISHOP, R. (1994). "Multicultural Literature for Children: Towards a Clarification of the Concept." pp. 57–69 in A. H. Dyson, and Genishi, Celia (Ed.), *The Need for Story.* Urbana, IL: National Council of Teachers of English.

CUMMINS, J. (1996). Foreward. In S. Nieto (Ed.), *Affirming Diversity: The Sociopolitical Context of Multicultural Education,* (2d ed.). White Plains, NY: Longman.

DELPIT, L. (1995). *Other People's Children: Cultural Conflict in the Classroom.* New York: New Press.

DYSON, A. H. (1997). *What Difference Does Difference Make?: Teacher Reflections on Diversity, Literacy and the Urban Primary School.* Urbana, IL: National Council of Teachers of English.

EDELSKY, C. (1991). *With Literacy and Justice for All: Rethinking the Social in Language and Education.* New York: The Falmer Press.

FREIRE, P. (1994). *Pedagogy of the Oppressed.* New York: Continuum.

———. (1987). "Letter to North American Teachers." In I. Shor (Ed.), *Freire for the Classroom: a Sourcebook for Liberatory Teaching.* Portsmouth, NH: Boynton Cook.

GILYARD, K. (1991). *Voices of the Self: A study of Language Competence.* Detroit: Wayne State University Press.

KAESTLE, C., DAMON-MOORE, H., STEDMAN, L., TINSLEY, K., and TROLLINGER Jr., W. (1991) *Literacy in the United States.* New Haven: Yale University Press

KOZOL, J. (1991). *Savage Inequalities.* New York: Harper Collins.

———. (1995). *Amazing Grace.* New York: Harper Collins.

LADSON-BILLINGS, G. (1994). *The Dreamkeepers: Successful Teachers of African American Children.* San Francisco, CA: Jossey-Bass.

LEE, E. "Taking Multicultural, Anti-Racist Education Seriously." pp. 19–22. In Bigelow, B., Christensen, L., Karp, S., Miner, B. and Peterson, B. (Ed.). (1994). *Rethinking Our Classrooms: Teaching for Equity and Justice.* Milwaukee: Rethinking Schools.

MOLL, L. C. and GONZALES, N. (1994). *Lessons from Research with Language-Minority Children.* Journal of Reading Behavior, *26(4),* 439–455

NIETO, S. (1996). *Affirming Diversity: The Sociopolitical Context of Multicultural Education.* (2d ed.). White Plains, NY: Longman.

PALEY, V. (1979). *White Teacher.* Cambridge, MA: Harvard University Press.

SCHMIDT, G. (2000). Conference Proceedings, Detroit, MI, Whole Schooling Consortium Conference, June 2000.

SHANNON, P. (1989). *Broken Promises: Reading Instruction in Twentieth Century America.* New York: Bergin & Garvey.

SHOR, I. (1987a). *Educating the Educators: A Freirean Approach to the Crisis in Teacher Education.* In I. Shor (Ed.), Freire for the Classroom: a Sourcebook for Liberatory Teaching, (pp. 7-32). Portsmouth, NH: Boynton Cook.

———. (Ed.). (1987b). *Freire for the Classroom: a Sourcebook for Liberatory Teaching.* Portsmouth, NH: Boynton Cook.

STOCK, P. (1995). *The Dialogic Curriculum: Teaching and Learning in a Multicultural Society.* Portsmouth, NH: Heinemann.

STREET, B. V. (1995). *Social Literacies: Critical Approaches to Literacy in Development, Ethnography and Education.* New York: Longman.

TAYLOR, D., and DORSEY-GAINES, C. (1988). *Growing Up Literate: Learning from Inner-City Families.* Portsmouth, NH: Heineman.

TAYLOR, D., CONKLIN, D., and MARASCO, J. (Ed.). (1997). Teaching and Advocacy. York, ME: Stenhouse.

TENORIO, R. "Race and Respect Among Young Children." pp. 24–28. In Bigelow, B., Christensen, L., Karp, S., Miner, B. and Peterson, B. (Ed.). (1994). *Rethinking Our Classrooms: Teaching for Equity and Justice.* Milwaukee: Rethinking Schools.

2

Listen to the Rhythm: Crossing Multicultural Boundaries

Deborah Horan

A non–Spanish speaker turns the pages of the Spanish big book; one Spanish-speaking student reads the pages aloud to the attentive class while another acts out each page. Proud of initiative and performance, the trio asks if they can share their "book play" with a first-grade class. "And can we make costumes?" The threesome voluntarily returns to class during lunch recess to create paper props and costumes. They bring other second-grade classmates with them—lunch-line recruits who want to join the fun.

Three English-speaking students work collaboratively "finding the music" in a jungle story one student authored and then cooperatively illustrated. They also use lunch recess to practice their rap with rhythm sticks. They record one attempt on a small handheld tape player, listen to their jungle rap, and excitedly discuss how to make it sound better. They tape and self-critique several 'takes.' They replace the rhythm sticks with a kid drumming a table. Now. Their audience can hear the words better. Between singing and laughter, Jamal rolls on the floor, holding his belly and laughing, "I never knew school could be so fun! This is the best day I've ever had!"

As a first-year teacher, I was overwhelmed as I walked directly from student teaching into a bilingual second-grade classroom at a different school, the students' *third* teacher of the academic year. My first days in class appeared an untraversable galaxy away from the community I envisioned. Three months later, upon reflection, I was amazed to discover the positive impact music had not only on literacy but also on classroom dynamics. The class had transformed into a community of learners who demonstrated a love of literature. A community where students worked collaboratively and asked permission to share rap or blues versions of their own stories set to and accompanied by handclapping or arm-swinging rhythmic representations of language.

Focusing My Vision

The second-grade students I met the first weeks in January manifested emotions in what I perceived as highly charged verbal and physical expressions. Strong negative emotions, flying around the room at varying intensities, concerned me for affective reasons and challenged the community of learners. I was shocked. And I was overwhelmed.

The school's statistics hadn't prepared me for the reality of this setting. This Denver community, once predominantly African American, had changing demographics (see Figure 1). The ethnic diversity led to linguistic diversity and thus a new transitional bilingual education program. I entered the second-grade bilingual class in January of that academic year. Forty-four percent of the class had been identified by the school district as limited English proficient (LEP).

Twenty-eight percent of the class received Title I assistance and four percent special education. Miscue analysis in January revealed nine "nonreaders"—not to say these students *could not* read but that these students *would not* read for a variety of reasons. Writing was a stressful act for all but a few students, driving many to chair-pushing, pencil-breaking frustration. And that was not all.

As a novice teacher, I needed to address the varied tasks that I saw experienced professionals conducting daily with apparent ease, such as:

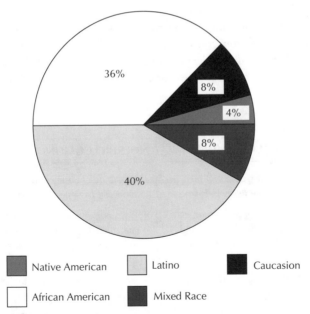

▦ Native American	▨ Latino	■ Caucasion
□ African American	▪ Mixed Race	

FIGURE 1 *Ethnic diversity: Latino students include Mexican-Americans and children from Mexico, Chile, and El Salvador*

1. working with students in forging a positive learning environment

2. planning instruction in all content areas, including art and music—no specialists provide such instruction

As a bilingual teacher I needed to orchestrate additional tasks:

3. providing language-appropriate literacy instruction based upon Spanish and English development

4. developing second-language acquisition for my native Spanish-speakers

Overwhelmed, I felt like the Leaning Tower of Pisa with each responsibility and challenge a new floor adding weight to my already tipping tower.

A New Beginning: Creating a Community of Learners

During my teacher education program, I was exposed to democratic ideals concerning the role of public schools in educating citizens so I focused my attention on learner rights and responsibilities in a second-grade classroom. What surprised me was the catalytic role music integration would have in launching our class to realize this vision.

To establish democratic norms and expectations I had to demonstrate my philosophy to the children. I posted a chart (Figure 2) and referred to it often in my first weeks with these children.

Together, the students and I generated a chart of rights and responsibilities (Figure 3) that we could live with. Figure 3 shows only the English version.

OUR CLASSROOM COMMUNITY	NUESTRO COMUNIDAD ESCOLAR
• I expect that our classroom will be a community of people ready to learn.	• Espero que nuestro salón sea una comunidad de personas listas para aprender.
• Each person is a reader and writer, mathematician and scientist, historian and ambassador, computer expert and musician, and	• Cada persona es un/a: lector y escritor, matemático y científico, historiador y embajador, experto del computador y músico, y
• EACH ONE is important and worthy of everyone else's respect.	• CADA UNO es importante y digno del respecto de los demás.

FIGURE 2   Norms and Expectations

LEARNER RIGHTS	LEARNER RESPONSIBILITIES
1. Right to learn.	1a. Be respectful of others' right to learn.
2. Right to share your ideas, views, property, and feelings.	b. Be prepared to learn.
3. Right to a supportive learning environment.	2. Be respectful of others' ideas, views, property, and feelings.
4. Right to an honest attitude.	3. Help create a supportive learning environment.
5. Right to ask to have your needs met.	4. Consider the effect of your attitude.
	5. Get your own needs met.

FIGURE 3   *Learner Rights and Responsibilities*

Journeying from There to Here and Beyond: The Discovery Process

I felt prepared teach reading and writing, math and science.

I had not anticipated art or music as core subjects. Art was joy for me to incorporate into interdisciplinary units. Music, however, created an almost heart-stopping hurdle. I systematically investigated research and district policy that would empower me and my students. I knew I was accountable to Colorado State Music Standards (Figure 4). I knew that music is a means of enriching literacy. I decided to focus on an action research question. How can integrating music into a

---

COLORADO MODEL CONTENT STANDARDS: MUSIC

1. Students will sing or play on instruments a varied repertoire of music, alone and with others.

2. Students will read and write musical notation.

3. Students will improvise/create music.

4. Students will listen to, analyze, evaluate, and describe music.

5. Students will understand various cultures through the study of music and music history.

FIGURE 4   *Colorado Music Standards: 1995*

MODEL CONTENT STANDARDS: READING AND WRITING

1. Students read and understand a variety of materials.

2. Students write and speak for a variety of purposes and audiences.

3. Students write and speak using formal grammar, usage, sentence structure, punctuation, capitalization, and spelling.

4. Students apply thinking skills to their reading, speaking, listening, and viewing.

5. Students read to locate, select, and make use of relevant information from a variety of media, reference and technological sources.

6. Students read and recognize literature as a record of human experience.

7. Students use appropriate technologies to extend comprehension and communication skills in reading, writing, speaking, listening, and viewing.

FIGURE 5   *Denver Public Schools Reading and Writing Standards: 1996*

bilingual elementary classroom impact classroom dynamics and literacy learning?

From my perspective, considering the model for balanced literacy used by the district, it appeared that music in some form or another could be incorporated into each of the three literacy categories: the writing process, the reading process, and oral language development. I also considered Denver Public Schools' Reading and Writing Content Standards (Figure 5) as a further means of focusing my integration of music into literacy.

What Can Happen When Students Are Encouraged to Find the Music in Words and Languages?

As I began my action research project, my desire was not just to introduce elementary songs for sing-alongs. My greater desire stems from my own background as a writer and multiple language learner. I wanted to share my captivation for the sounds and rhythms that characterize English, Spanish, and other languages. I wanted students to see music as a communication tool, a conveyor of history. I perceive literacy as vibrant meaning-making, a colorful spectrum, purposefully blending oral communication, the reading process, and the writing process. Consequently, I hoped that music would enhance this vibrant meaning-making for students.

To accomplish such ends, I explored a variety of activities, beginning with such simple activities as playing classical music while students wrote during daily writers' workshop. The effects of such activities were noted through gathering qualitative data: collecting baseline writing samples and reading miscue analysis, conducting a reading survey, observing student behavior, audio- and videotaping student performances of stories, collecting writing samples on an ongoing basis, discussing the new choices young authors and readers make during reading and writing, noting anecdotal records, and gathering opinions of other educators concerning changes in student behavior and classroom environment. I synthesize the three months of activities and qualitative data in a few representative anecdotal highlights.

Opening the Butterfly Jar

I began by introducing a weekly poem for students to slap-clap echo daily. At first, I chose poems that I hoped would influence students in realizing their potential as learners. Our first poem, "The Butterfly Jar" by Jeff Moss (Figure 6), remained the students' favorite throughout the year.

One day during writers' workshop, as I was conferencing with individual students, I glanced around the room and noticed one contemplative student who had not yet put words on paper. As I caught his eye, he smiled, pretended to be unscrewing an imaginary jar lid on the top of his head. "What are you doing, Rodney?" I asked. "Opening my butterfly jar," he replied. Rodney became the first to write and publish a simple story, "Living in the Jungle," which became the launching pad for students to explore the music in words.

THE BUTTERFLY JAR

We had a jar with a butterfly.
We opened the lid and it flew to the sky.
And there are things inside my head
Waiting to be thought or said.
Dreams and jokes and wonderings are
Locked inside, like a butterfly jar.
But then, when you are here with me,
I can open the lid and set them free.

FIGURE 6   *"The Butterfly Jar"*

Rodney and his two co-illustrators read their book during our first author's chair.

> Once upon a time, I was living in the jungle.
> The jungle was wild and crazy.
> Snakes slithering through the grass.
> Zebras running like lightning.
> Monkeys swinging from tree to tree.
> Alligators swimming across the creek.
> An alligator tried to eat me. I cut his teeth off.
> We went to eat lunch.
> The monkeys followed me.
> The zebras started running after each other.
> The snakes were still eating breakfast.
> And then we went home.

Among the questions I modeled asking of authors were "Did you notice there's music in your story?" "Did you do that on purpose?" "Do you have any plans to make your story into a song?" Rodney's eyes widened as he reread his story aloud, realizing with each page that he had written words that had music hidden in them.

"Can we make it into a song?" his threesome eagerly asked. An hour later, the trio voluntarily returned during lunch recess in the scenario described previously. One of the trio, Jamal, a more reluctant writer who joined this publishing group as an illustrator, wrote about this experience in his daily journal:

> Once me and Rodney and Joshua was rap stars. We are the best rap stars in the whole world. We was awesome. We loved being rap stars.

Three months later, Jamal's Title I math teacher would comment about a significant change she had seen in the students who attended her class: "When they are given free time, they choose books to read." These kinds of qualitative, observational data encouraged me as a new teacher in realizing the role music integration was having on students' literacy learning.

Jamal and his two buddies served as catalysts sparking an exciting process of transforming students' written stories into oral presentations involving music, tabletop (instead of drum) beats, rap or blues tunes, and even drama. Students began recording and critiquing their stories on a tape player. Some of the more resistant and struggling readers began asking permission to "find the music" in class library books, then taping their rhythmic renditions of Dr. Seuss and other favorite authors.

Innovations: Playing with the Rhythm of Language

Book innovations became an exciting and practical activity for both the emergent readers and those learning English as a second language. One of our first class innovations involved Eric Carle's *Today is Monday* (1993), which talks of feeding the world's hungry children. After singing our way through Eric Carle's version, students chose their favorite foods to share with hungry children.

Enlivening Social Studies through Songs

Through read-alouds and songs students began exploring and discussing various ethnic groups and cultures. During Black History Month, I focused on reading historical fiction based on songs such as *Follow the Drinking Gourd* (Winter 1988), which portrays the underground railroad. Simultaneously, students independently began writing on their own about similar issues. They expressed attentiveness to our readings and discussions when self-selecting topics for writers' workshop. One student demonstrated her awareness of slavery struggles. She wrote:

> Once upon a time there were slaves and they worked hard.
> Then there was lady who showed them the way to escape and be free forever.
> And she also helped hurt people and army men eat.
> And she helped other slaves to be free.
> Then she hid behind some bushes and prayed.
> And she lived happily ever after.

Another student's journal entry revealed his recognition of a social leader:

> Once there was a man who tried to stop people from fighting and the bad things from happening. His name was Martin Luther King Jr. He died. When he died, everyone was sad. But bad things are still happening. Everybody in the world wants him to come back.

As students began drawing on their classroom reading and music experiences, more diverse journal entries began filling students daily writing journals. "What should I write about?" became a more infrequent question as students drew upon their growing knowledge of history. Although it is possible that students may have demonstrated similar behaviors if social studies activities had not been integrated with music, I believe that music enhanced this process. I recall how one student would sing softly to himself "Follow the Drinking Gourd" as he wrote in his journal.

Enhancing Science with Music

To enhance science, songs and poems relating to units on animals and habitats provided students with vocabulary for creating fiction in their journals. During read-alouds on deserts and the ethnic communities who live in deserts, we listened to desert sounds and Native American music. When studying plants, we also watched laser disc clips of growing plants responding to varying light sources and accompanied by music. Later, we acted out the growing plants along with the music video. As increasingly diverse topics began surfacing in students' writing journals, I began to see the influence of music in students' literacy development. One student began creating fictional characters based upon animals and habitats we were studying in science.

> Once there was a frog. He loved to sing to his friends. But his friends were always busy. This frog had a boss so he was a little bit busy too. His boss said, "Catch eighteen flies, sweep the floor, find some things that I eat." Then the frog quit his job. Then he saw all his friends and sang all the songs he wanted.

Enhancing Experiential Learning

Another means of enhancing instruction was creating an anticipatory set for field trips using picture books based on songs. Prior to visiting Denver's stock show I read *The Zebra Riding Cowboy* (Medearis and Bruscam, 1992) a story that features an African American cowboy. One student shared the excitement prompted by this read-aloud in his journal:

> "We are going to the stock show. We are going to see horses and bulls. It is going to be fun. I can not wait until we go. It is on 2-5-1996. We are going to see a horse and a bull. It is fun. I can not wait."

After our field trip, his enthusiasm continued to reveal itself in his writing journal through such entries as the following.

> "At the stock show we saw an ostrich. It was big. It can run 60 miles an hour. If you was riding on an ostrich, you will fall off. I like ostriches. They are funny too. But do not talk too much because they will ignore you."

Building an Empathetic Community of Learners

As students began demonstrating their growing awareness of literacy as meaning-making, I also began noting more "community behaviors." Students initiated cooperative work groups across formerly self-imposed boundaries. I received increasing requests from small groups and individuals to come in during lunch to finish stories they were writing or reading. As I spent my lunch hours with students instead of in the teachers' lounge, another teacher commented, "They have really become a classroom of readers and writers." I wondered if students were ready for increasing challenges involving music and literature that would help us become a *community* of readers and writers.

We began watching and discussing videos connected with literature that portray stories. I purposefully chose stories with universal themes challenging how people view and treat others different than themselves, such as *Rigoletto* (Judd and Swofford, 1993). This musical video portrays a town where an innocent man is erroneously judged and killed because of how he looks. The results? Some students began transferring this empathy into their writing, enriching their writing with more universal struggles that revealed their increasing awareness of literature as a conveyor of people's real struggles. Students began to write about ethnic differences and acceptance.

The Boy Who Lived in Africa

Once upon a time there was a black boy who needed a friend.

He met a white boy. The black boy said, "Do you want to be my friend?" The white boy said, "My mother said black people is bad."

The black boy asked the white boy, "Do you do math?"

"No."

"I will tell you how to do math."

And the next day they were going to school and they were in the same class.

And when it was math time, the white boy did not know it. The black boy helped him with his math.

And they became friends.

What had appeared as an originally disharmonious classroom was evolving into a community of learners who felt safe to express their attitudes. Not only were students drawing on an increasing reservoir of ideas in self-selecting reading and writing materials, they were also honoring their classmates during author's chair.

In three months, I had seen a significant decline in student frustration and literary atrophy. In sharp contrast, I dealt with such challenges as students wanting to finish stories during lunch, pleading for time to perform books that they turned into musical presentations, sneaking books out of their desks to read when it wasn't reading time, and asking to take books home. Among these students were the nine struggling students who, in January, expressed only unwillingness to read or write. One of these nine students now fills her journal with positive thoughts about school:

> School, school is a golden rule.
> School is a fun thing to do.
> School is a pretty thing for everyone.
> Our school is the best.
> Our school is big.
> We got a lot of windows.
> We are the smartest kids in town.
> Reading is fun.
> Read every day.
> Reading is fun for you.

A final reoccurring comment comes from Jamal: "I need to talk to the principal and ask her why we don't have school on Saturday and Sunday 'cause learning is so fun."

Boundaries and Definitions: Breaking Free from Theoretical Frameworks

When I began this action research project I took into consideration current theories on multiple and cultural intelligences and readings style (Armstrong 1994; Carbo 1997; Hatch 1997). These terms are current educational attempts to expand educators' views of how students learn and manifest intelligence. However, I believe that in the process of expanding educational boundaries, such terms can also inadvertently create new boundaries that can be both individually and culturally limiting.

At a seminar on integrating music into classrooms, one of the speakers commented that African American students are naturally musical and manifest a lot of physical movement. Consequently, curriculum for African American students should incorporate song and movement. As a faithful new professional, I returned to class the next day and added more song and movement to the class for the sake of my African American students. We learned a song about nouns; students wrote their own song about verbs, used rhythm sticks to find the rhythm in English, and participated in a verb-noun pantomime game in which they acted out a verb when it was named while freezing when a noun was named. The results: African American students benefitted from these activities. So did *all* the other students. Classroom dynamics changed as students were allowed more freedom to move and physically correlate concepts of nouns and verbs. To state that African American children need song and movement implies that all African American students fit this stereotype and, conversely, that non-African American students differ in need. In my classroom, I noticed that the majority of students found learning more interesting as I implemented activities in response to educational information originally meant for only one ethnic group or one type of intellegence.

Context: A Diverse School Community

Challenged with a highly diverse multicultural classroom, I discovered that my second-grade students learned more when learning was fun, engaging, varied, challenging, and diverse just like the greater world in which we live. Current theories on multiple intelligences, cultural intelligences, and reading styles serve as constructs that yield a more interesting curriculum. My action research project allowed me to explore music as a further means of meeting the needs of these students via interdisciplinary units focused around literacy.

I discovered that integrating music into an elementary classroom builds upon students' intrinsic interests while crossing what some might perceive to be multicultural boundaries. Students are more engaged in learning not necessarily because their "intelligence" or "style" is being appealed to but because the curriculum is more engaging and democratic. In my action research project, I found enthusiasm for reading and writing skyrockets as students begin their adventure to find and capture the music in language. Furthermore, classroom discipline is positively impacted. Students manifest behaviors of a community of learners, including a love of literature and concern for one another. Not only did students learn through this experience, but I learned through and with them.

As my musical young storytellers would say as they exit the stage, "Peace. We out of here!"

References

ARMSTRONG, T. (1994). "Multiple Intelligences: Seven Ways to Approach Curriculum." *The Best of Educational Leadership*, 28–30.

CARBO, M. (March 1997) "Reading Style Times Twenty." *Educational Leadership, 54(6)*, 38–42.

CARLE, E. (1993). *Today is Monday*. New York: Scholastic.

Colorado Department of Education (1995). *Colorado Model Content Standards*. Denver, CO: Colorado Department of Education.

Denver Public Schools *Standards for Success: A foundation for Denver's Future*. (1996). Denver, CO.

HATCH, T. (March 1997). "Getting Specific About Multiple Intelligences." *Educational Leadership, 54(6)*, 26–29.

JACOBI-KARNA, K. (November 1995). "Music and Children's Books." *The Reading Teacher, 49(3)*, 265–269.

JUDD, D. A., and SWOFFORD, S. (Producers) (1993). *Rigoletto* [film]. Murray, UT: Feature Films for Families.

KOLB, G. (September 1996). "Reading with a Beat: Developing Literacy through Music and Song." *The Reading Teacher, 50(1)*, 76–77.

MEDEARIS, S. S., and BRUSCAM, M. C. (1992). *The Zebra Riding Cowboy*. New York: Holt.

ROUSELL, M. (May 1996). "Helping Kids Believe in Themselves." *Educational Leadership, 53(8)*, 86–87.

SLAY, J. V. and PENDERGAST, S. A. (May 1993). "Infusing the Arts Across the Curriculum: A South Carolina School Lifts Students' Self-esteem through Arts Study." *The School Administrator*, 32–35.

SMITH, J. L. and HERRING, J. D. (1996). "Literature Alive: Connecting to Story through the Arts." *Reading Horizons, 37(2)*, 102–115.

STERNBERG, R. J. (December 1995). "Investing in Creativity: Many Happy Returns." *Educational Leadership, 53(4)*, 80–84.

WINTER, J. (1988). *Follow the Drinking Gourd*. New York: Trumpet.

3 Discovering the First–Grade Curriculum in The Empty Pot

Wendy Goodman

I'm sitting in my sharing chair. Thirty-one eager faces just returned from lunch look up at me. The children know that it is time to take the final vote. The three top candidates sit on the Big Book easel next to me. I speak a bit about the first two books, then I hold up *The Empty Pot* (Demi 1990). "This is a story that takes place in a very faraway place called . . . " The kids fill in "China."

> Look at the beautiful flowers. I was thinking that, if we made an opera of this story we could make beautiful flowers. We could learn about planting seeds while we were working on this opera. I was thinking that I have some clothes from China that I could bring and show you, and we might even make our own clothes that look like the kind of clothing some people in China wear. . . . We could read other stories from China. We could even invite Chinese students from the university to show us a dance. Would you like to do that? [1]

When the vote was over, I panicked. I had influenced the vote, promising the kids that if they chose *The Empty Pot* we could study China. Now I had to follow through on my promise. Sitting in my sharing chair, it had sounded easy. Now, over an empty plan book, the task seemed enormous. Yet, I would not budge on the challenge I set for myself. I wanted to make sure that the students developed a sense of China geographically, politically, culturally, and historically. I

---

1 *Note:* This article presents only part of a story. The full story is highly complex involving 31 bilingual first-graders, teacher, student teacher, paraprofessionals, families, and artist in a semester-long experience in the creation of an opera. The opera process (Purrington and Rinehart 1990) itself has been chronicled in the dissertation of Dr. Pamela J. Rossi (University of Arizona, 1997). Her libretto version of the process, "Having an Experience in Five Acts: Multiple Literacies Through Young Children's Opera" appears in *Language Arts,* September 1997 (NCTE, 74:5).

needed to make sure that I did not support or inadvertently develop stereotypes. I found myself saying, to anyone who would listen, "I don't just want to drink tea and taste rice and use chopsticks. How can I access China with these young kids?" A concurrent refrain resounding through my head—as is common of all first-grade teachers—compounded my worry: "How will the students' emergent literacy blossom through this experience?"

Frances Sanchez returns from walking the kids to the bus with bilingual teacher assistant, Linda Marquez. My sarcastic nature takes over: "All we have to do now is learn all about China, work through the first-grade curriculum, make sure all the kids learn to read and write, do it all in English and Spanish, and have an opera ready to perform in three months. Oh, we also need lesson plans for tomorrow!" Our work cut out for us, we brainstorm many ideas; concepts related to China, the relationship of those concepts to different curricular areas.

We discuss the children in our well-balanced class! Thirty-one children in a small "portable" classroom with no running water. Sixteen girls. Fifteen boys. Fifteen dominant English speakers. Fifteen dominant Spanish speakers. One extremely proficient in both languages. Most Catholic. One a Jehovah's Witness. One African American; five Mexican immigrants. Fifteen Chicano students, some with Spanish heritage, some with Native American heritage (Yaqui or Tohono O'odham), some with both. It would be inappropriate to use the local term *Anglo* to describe the rest of the students in the class: one boy's mother is a French-speaking Canadian immigrant. By the end of the semester, we confirmed that not one of the 'nonminority' students in the class has an "Anglo" (or Saxon) heritage.

We think about different ways of organizing instruction. We look at our own strengths, interests, and preferences. Theme development time in the afternoons includes Linda and Rose, another teacher assistant, in the study.[2] We decide on learning centers for the theme development. Students, in small groups, will do a different center each day over a series of days. We want the centers to focus on learning about China. We also want them to support different learning styles and see that as kids work at each center, they experience math, science, social studies, art, music, reading, and writing, as they learn about China. We also agree that a focused literacy development time, "Language Arts Block," remains appropriate (Table 1).

---

2 In my school district bilingual education classes have two hours of teacher assistant time. Primary classes with more than 29 students get additional assistant time. Linda was the bilingual teaching assistant. Rose was there to help handle the large class size. Frances Sanchez was a student teacher.

TABLE 1 *Daily Schedule*[a]

8:00 am	Group time: Calendar, Attendance, Morning News
8:30	Language Arts Block:
	journal writing, guided writing; guided reading, independent reading; reading and writing exploration; first and second language development
10:00	Physical Education
10:30	Group time: singing or listening to music
11:00	Lunch
11:40	Group time: *Concept of the Day*
12:00 noon	China Centers
12:45	Explorations
1:30	Group time: Daily Closure
2:00	Dismissal

a. During the Language Arts Block, books related to the theme were available but did not form the core of the program.

The final organizational decision is student grouping. In a bilingual classroom, it is important to provide literacy instruction in the primary language, equitable access to content in both languages, and second language instruction. During language arts time, with literacy development as the goal, I group kids homogeneously by primary language and reading/writing strengths. It is also important to work in the primary language when introducing new concepts. However, mixed language groups are necessary, too. We decide to have single language groups for the first two rounds of centers, mixed for the second two, and so on. All the center groups were heterogeneously grouped by literacy abilities.

We question the appropriateness of introducing first-grade students to an additional written language. We want the kids to see written Chinese characters and we face concerns that an additional set of symbols might confuse children with emerging literacy skills. My philosophy of bilingual education rejects the notion that learning two languages at one time causes interference. We decide to take a risk try introducing some Chinese. (In retrospect, this was one of the best decisions we made).

We began by numbering the centers using Chinese characters. (I wrote phonetic English pronunciation under each numeral so I could remember how to pronounce it.) It did not take long before all the kids were able to count to ten orally in three languages and in writing using two different systems of numerals!

We divide the various tasks. Frances develops the mini-theme on flowers. I develop a learning packet about China, and Linda brushes up on Spanish vocabulary for Chinese artifacts. We seek out English and Spanish stories about China and from China, and nonfiction texts. I borrow children's books and artifacts that have come from Hong Kong, Taiwan, and the People's Republic. Frances, searching my files, rediscovers my decade-old Artist-in-Residence packet on China. I wander the aisles of a local import store, smelling spices, watching fish, contemplating calligraphy materials, and noting the price of tea from China.

Concept of the Day

Each afternoon, I opened theme time with *Concept of the Day*—ideas best presented with the class as a whole. The first Concept of the Day focused on geography, generally quite an abstract concept for six- and seven-year-olds. I began with the known.[3]

> *Me:* Where do we live?
> *Kids:* Tucson; Arizona.
> *Me:* Can you name some other places?
> *Kids:* Nogales; Phoenix; Hermosillo.
> *Me:* Tucson is the city we live in. What is our state?
> *Pamela:* United States.
> *Me:* That's our country.
> *Ivan:* Arizona.
> *Me:* Yes, that's our state. We live in the city of Tucson, the state of Arizona, and the country of United States. Who knows another country?
> *Jackeline:* China.
> *Javier:* Mexico.
> *Me:* Yes, those are other countries. How many of you have been to Mexico? (Many hands go up.) How many of you have been in Nogales, Sonora? (More hands go up.) Nogales is a city like Tucson. Part of it is in Arizona, in the United States. Part of it is the state of Sonora in the country of Mexico.
> *Javier:* Jalisco is a state in Mexico, too. The Charros sing about it.
> *Me:* Yes. There are many songs about many states. How many of you have gone in a car ride to Phoenix? (All hands go up.) Was that a long ride?

---

3 To clarify the focus of this article on the children's conceptual development, the multilingual nature of instruction that takes place in this classroom is not clearly illustrated in this writing. Conversations that, within the classroom, would have taken place very naturally utilizing both English and Spanish are written in English to provide a better sense of readability.

Kids: Yes.

Clint: Not as long as Disneyland.

Me: How many of you have gone in a car ride to Disneyland? (Most hands go up.) OK. Now, let's think about China. China is far away from Tucson. There are really two China's, we'll talk about that more later. Today let's see if we can understand how far away China is. Milan, stand up. (I place Milan in the south east corner of the classroom facing the kids.) You are Tucson. Now, Marissa, you stand up here (I place her about three inches from Milan.) You're Phoenix.

Beto: They're too close.

Me: They look close but we need them that close. Here, Beto, you be Disneyland. (I place Beto about one foot away from Marissa.) How long does it take me to drive from Milan/Tucson to Marissa/Phoenix?

Kris: Two hours.

Me: Yes, that's like from after lunch until time to go home. Now, how long does it take to drive from Milan/Tucson to Beto/Disneyland?

Stacy: All night.

Me: Yes! Now I need China. Tyler, you be China. Go stand all the way over there. (Tyler goes to the northwest corner of the classroom.)

Clint: Hey, Tyler's getting his feet wet. You can't walk to China. There's an ocean!

Kris: But if you could drive it would be awfully far.

I introduced various artifacts through Concept of the Day and the children created a "China Museum." The China Museum, with its "just look" area and "please touch" area, was on a bookcase in the center of our crowded room. After school daily, first parents, then siblings, even other students, were guided through the museum by our impromptu first-grade docents.

During Concept of the Day I introduced Fisher's *The Great Wall of China* (1995). I read parts to them. We talked through the rest. The following morning Joshua urgently shared his news, "My grandpa says that the China Wall is the only thing made by people that can be seen from the space shuttle!"

China Centers

Over the course of the theme, from late August through late November, we went through many rounds of centers. The children grew and learned. They became a community of readers, writers, thinkers, and singers. I knew that would happen. What I did not anticipate was how much the children would learn about themselves by learning about others. It is impossible here to describe all the learning events that took place. I will describe the first round of centers, some of the side themes, and some of the highlights.[4]

Centers: 1 China Study (Wendy)
           2 Build a Great Wall
           3 Flower Study (Frances)
           4 Listen to *The Empty Pot*
           5 Use Chopsticks
           6 Explore Books, Taste Tea (Linda)

China Study with Wendy

For older students, I've put together study guides to help the students learn how to do research. I decided to try this with the first-graders. I put together a packet of pages (OK, go ahead and call them worksheets.) for the students and me to do together. Each packet had:

- two pages with the outlines of Chinese flags

- a page where students could fill in information about Pandas

- pages where kids could learn to write Chinese numerals

- a page with a few facts about the Great Wall and space for the kids to write their own notes

For a number of reasons I put English and Spanish on each page. I try to be consistent about it—Spanish on the left, English on the right. I want the students to begin to recognize the visual differences between the two languages. Later, when the kids share the packets with their parents at home the presence of both languages provides an invitation to bilingualism for those families who want to explore it.

At center time, I give each child in the group an outline map of the world. We pinpoint the United States and color it yellow. We color Tucson brown. "Brown for the desert," some children say. I get out the atlas. We find the United States and then I ask the kids to find China. Each group found two Chinas: China, Republic of Taiwan

---

4 Note to the reader: I trust that you get the idea that each activity was imbedded in the curriculum and that curricular requirements were being met in authentic learning situations. I tried to go into detail about curricular tie-ins but they made the chapter too lengthy.

and the People's Republic of China. I'm prepared to introduce this "difficult" concept.

> *Me:* A long time ago there was one China. All this area. Some of the people had different ideas from other people and now there are two Chinas.
> *Ivan:* (thoughtfully) Like two Americas.
> *Czarina:* Yes, like here, we used to all be Mexico and now some are Arizona.
> *Me:* (in my head) This is a fluke.

Each group came up with a similar analogy. I remember never to assume that "little kids don't know stuff." Each group chose a color for each China and shaded it in on the map. "Take these home to your parents tonight. Ask them if they know there are two Chinas. Talk with them about what you've learned."

We look at our U.S. flag and discussed its attributes. We open the packets and look at the black-and-white outlines of two Chinese flags.

> *Me:* Is it OK to have a U.S. flag with just any color?
> *Kids:* No, it must be red, white, and blue.
> *Me:* All flags are like that. They have special meanings and special designs.
> *Rosana:* Like red, white, and green is Mexico.
> *Me:* What colors do we need for these the flags?

Some children immediately read the names of the colors prewritten in each region. In groups that can not, I suggest looking on the paper of the crayons for matching words.

The China Study with me lasts for two rounds of centers. During the second round, I read to the kids from a book called *Panda* (Bonners 1978). When I'm done, we read each line on the Panda page together and discuss possible answers (Figure 1). Each child writes his or her own answers. If they ask to spell a word, we find it together in the book.

Build a Great Wall

The Lego center has three rules:

1. The whole group builds only one wall (cooperative learning).

2. The wall must stand on its own (problem solving).

3. The whole wall must be stable (engineering).

Pandas live ______________________________

Pandas eat ______________________________

Panda babies ______________________________

I learned that Pandas:

____

____

FIGURE 1 *Panda Page in China Study*

Drawings and photos of the Great Wall accompany building materials. As kids build, Rose meanders over. When building is going well, she promps thoughtful discussion: "What if each Lego 'brick' was as big as the ones used in the Great Wall?" If the wall is unstable, she draws attention to the pictures in the book. "I wonder why they put the bricks like this . . .?" And, if a group's just not working together, she gently prods, "There is only one Great Wall, how can you accomplish that?"

Flower Study with Frances

Our story, *The Empty Pot*, comes from a Chinese cultural view of flowers. In preparation, Frances has gathered fine art watercolor prints of flowers. The prints are on a bulletin board near a table. A wholesale florist, thrilled with the idea of kids learning more about flowers, lets Frances stop by before school twice a week for a few not-quite-fresh flowers. The "few" turned out to be two 5-gallon buckets of a variety of flowers. Our room smelled great! At the center, each child chose a flower.

As scientists, the kids dissect and look at the parts with the "naked eye" and with handheld microscopes. They describe colors, explore nuance of shades of colors, and find where the seeds grow. Some they get sticky with pollen. When the scientific interest begins to wane, Frances relates what the kids have seen to what the artists portray in the prints. She gets out watercolor paints and manilla paper cut into 6 × 6 inch squares. She models use of the paints (including cleanup).

Using a second flower as a subject, each child paints a watercolor. As they finish, Frances pins their masterpieces up beside the art prints. We plan the flower study for one round of centers. The children kept it going—two more rounds of centers, the third with black paper. After that watercolors became a regular option during "exploration" time.

Listen to The Empty Pot

I translate the story into Spanish and record it on an audiotape. I tape the original version in English, as well. I used a small gong for the turn-the-page signals. I make this center an illustrator study with other books by Demi to explore when the tape is done. The favorite: *Dragon Kites and Dragon Flies: A Collection of Chinese Nursery Rhymes.*

Using Chopsticks

The kids met chopsticks as a Concept of the Day. Frances read *How My Parents Learned to Eat* (Friedman, Say, and Friedman 1987) to the class. I like its perspective when describing forks and chopsticks even though it is not a Chinese tale.[5] We distributed a pair of chopsticks (disposables purchased at a local import shop) to each student. I demonstrated how to use them. Students practiced for a while. We collected the chopsticks, wrote their names on each pair and the sleeve it came in, and made them available with the center materials.

I designed a game to facilitate agility with chopsticks.

Materials:	Procedure:
6 colors of plastic math cubes, 12 each of each color	1. I mix all the cubes together in the large bowl.
6 colored paper plates, 1 for each cube color	2. Students select a plate
1 large bowl	3. Using chopsticks, they "serve" themselves only cubes that match their plate.
	4. The first student to get all his or her cubes wins.

The kids love the game. There is a lot of peer coaching during center time. Many students choose to revisit it during *explorations.*

---

5 I have learned since then that the portrayal of the young Japanese girl is not very accurate. If I were to do this unit again, I might look for a different text.

Explore Books and Taste Tea with Linda

To teach the significance of tea to Chinese culture our idea is to use nonfiction books with an adult as a resource to read captions and text. A tasting experience is appropriate here, too. This center does both. We choose books with photographs for this center: Chinese cookbooks, travel books, and so on. One beautifully illustrated book has a nice section about tea. We have a few different teas in transparent containers so the kids can see the difference.

Linda and the kids chat about tea as they walk to and from the main building to fill the tea kettle with water. As the kettle heats on the hot plate, the kids explore different teas with visual, olfactory, and tactile senses. Each child has a cup and jasmine tea bag. The tea steeps and cools, the children sip, Linda reads to them about tea. When the tea is gone, one book at a time they discover China together.

Complex Learning

While some of the centers—the blocks and the listening—are typical of first grade other are not. We questioned whether we were asking too much of the kids. Were the centers too challenging? Did they exceed first-grade attention span? We went into the centers with the notion to revise as needed. In retrospect, I have concluded that the way in which we approached it made all the difference. The kids wanted to learn about China. We admitted to them that we knew very little and that we could all learn together. It was in this atmosphere of mutual discovery that these six- and seven-year-olds showed us their capacity for perseverance with highly complex learning.

Over the subsequent weeks we designed a number of centers. Each set provided new and different challenges. As we proceeded, the kids' enthusiasm carried over into their homes. Soon we had enough parent volunteers to have an adult at every center every day. In fifteen years of teaching I'd never achieved that before. And then, since the adults were available, we were able to have even more complex activities at the centers.

Additional Centers

Why the Rat Comes First: The Story of the Chinese Zodiac (Yen 1991) is a book that Frances discovered first in Spanish. It is one tale of the origin of the Chinese zodiac. After her reading the kids used paper plates to make calendars of their own. In the process, they realized they were born in either the year of the snake or the year of the dragon. That spawned a side study of dragons. We found many stories about dragons, both in English and Spanish, that were good read-alouds, and we even found a number that were perfect for shared and guided reading.

Masks are an important part of Chinese culture. We made dragon masks at a center spanning two days. Our dragon mask pattern takes precise cutting, scoring, folding, and gluing. At the same time it allows for personalization and creativity. Due to the complexity of the project, parents pretraced the pieces on special strength paper for the kids to support their success. They did some cutting for students who became frustrated. The final products, measuring about 24 inches by 16 inches by 6 inches deep, were hung around the room and later hung as a backdrop for our opera.

Dragon puppets and pull toys (ideas captured from old craft books), created at two different centers, were simple enough that the directions were set out for the kids to follow on their own. The pull toys were very popular.

One day, Pam tattled, "Jeremy sold his pull toy to his brother." When Jeremy brought in 50 cents to donate to our "costume fund" I asked the kids how they felt about what Jeremy had done. They liked the idea. Soon kids were making pull toys during explorations time and selling them to supplement our costume fund-raiser (selling fortune cookies in the cafeteria after lunch). They even decided to make three lengths for three different prices.

The listening center was part of every rotation. The second round we listened to *The Story About Ping* (Flack 1933). The kids found it humorous that the duck in that story had the same name as the hero of *The Empty Pot*. Later on, our Chinese guests explained that Ping is a very common name. We also listened to *Rikki Tikki Tembo* (Mosel 1989), the folktale about why Chinese children have short names.

Guest Teachers

Three Chinese visitors had a profound impact on all of us. I had followed though on my promise and arranged for a graduate student to come visit our class. She brought two others with her, all teachers in their homelands. One was from Taiwan. The other two came from the People's Republic, one from Shanghai and the other from Peking.[6] Our Taiwanese visitor was surprised that the kids had knowledge of two China's! Each of the three visitors brought something special to share.

Our guest from Peking went first. He had brought a Cantonese children's book, a patterned language folktale. He showed them the

---

6 *Note:* I do not provide the guests names because I don't know how to write them in English.

cover and told a bit about the characters. He opened to the first page of the book, held it out for the kids to see, and began to *tell* the story. Three pages into it:

> *Rafael:* That book's not in English
> *Clint:* Why aren't you *reading* the book?
> *Guest:* Well, this book is in Chinese. See, here are the Chinese characters. I thought I'd tell you the story in English so you can understand it.
> *Rafael:* But, I want to hear it in Chinese.
> *Milan:* Me, too.
> Other voices chimed in until there was a chant: "Chinese. Chinese. Chinese."
> *Guest:* OK. I guess you're smarter than I thought!

He read the rest of the story in Chinese. By the end of the book, the kids were reciting the repetitive lines and naming the characters in the story. From the pictures, their prior experience with folktales, and the context of the situation, a discussion following the reading revealed that they had all constructed a fairly accurate understanding of the story. Rafael wormed his way to the front of the group, put his finger on a Chinese character, and said, "This means 'old man.'" He was right.

It was a perfect opening for our next guest as he took the kids into his confidence.

> I have brought four sacred objects from ancient China. A long time ago, in ancient Shanghai where I come from only the most important people could read and write. To become rich you had to be able to read and write. Today in China, all people read and write but then, poor people were not allowed to have any of these four sacred objects.

One by one he revealed the objects; paper, brush, ink, and inkpot. He showed the children calligraphy written by his son at age seven and asked if they would like to learn some brush strokes. They went to their tables and got out pencils and paper. He showed them how to write 中. He showed them characters for school and boy and girl. He wrote his name. The children asked if he could write their names in Chinese for them.

He replied,

> English and Spanish are written with sounds and letters. Chinese symbols have meanings. But there is a way to write your names using the characters that mean a word that sounds similar.

Marisol showed him the page on Chinese numerals from her China packet. That prompted the class to count in Chinese for the guests who, in return, helped refine the pronunciation. The kids spent the rest of the morning practicing their names and other Chinese writing. At lunchtime, I had to insist that the kids take a break.

After lunch, our third guest taught us a Taiwanese song and dance of friendship. We tape-recorded the song so we would remember it. We danced and danced. When we were all danced out, we came back together as a group. The three guests sat in front on chairs. We all sat on the rug. I set the tone,

> *Me:* "What questions do you have that you would like to ask our guests before they leave?"
> *Javier:* Do they have horses in China?
> *Guest:* Yes. But we don't have cowboys like you do.
> *Beto:* Do you eat with chopsticks or forks?
> *Guest:* We use a fork when we have to but chopsticks are easier.
> *Karina:* How long did it take you to learn to use chopsticks?
> *Guest:* How long did it take you to learn to use a fork?
> *Pamela:* How long did it take you to get to Tucson from China on an airplane?
> *Guest:* Two days!
> *Tony:* Why does my cousin say Chinese have slanted eyes?
> *Guest:* Because he never met me.

As a result of their visit magic happened. We set up a center with brushes and black paint. I just couldn't get myself to allow the kids to use real ink. I discovered a wonderful paperback book, *Long is a Dragon* (Goldstein 1992). It is the size of a coloring book, and the wrapping is deceptive. In a few pages with concise phrases the book contains the history of writing! It also teaches many Chinese characters. I read this book to the class and then put it at a Chinese Writing center.

The kids became very interested in Chinese music. They listened to our Taiwanese song tape and a tape of Chinese children's songs (from the public library) at the listening center. The nature of the musical compositions in our opera changed; their songs took on a distinctive oriental tone.

An intense focus on the details of written language grew, and not just Chinese. All the children began to form letters more carefully in daily writing. A few students began reading everything in sight. Students who had only begun to construct meaning from print suddenly found familiar words in new contexts and took risks with harder texts. And the two students who had just begun to attend to print made an amazing discovery.

Marisol and Marissa were looking at the books in Chinese. They had picked up one that was, in fact, a first-grade basal from Taiwan! I saw them taking turns getting other children to come and see the book they had.

Amber came to get me.

Amber: Look, it's the story of "The Chick and the Duckling."[7] In Chinese. Look here, We figure this must be "chick" and this must be "duckling."
Me: Why do you think that?
Amber: Well, see here, these are the talking marks. So this must mean 'me, too' and after that it has to say, "says the chick." See, it says it here and here and here, each time the chick talks!

I took Marissa and Marisol, both beaming, and we photocopied and collated thirty-one copies. That afternoon, we used that story as our Concept of the Day. Amber shared her discovery. We talked about her reading strategy. We poured over the pages and hypothesized what other characters could mean. We talked about picture cues and context cues and how our knowledge of the story helped us. And to think that I had been worried that an in-depth study of China would interfere with teaching the kids to read or that introduction of another writing system would prove confusing!

As the weeks progressed, our learning became more and more intertwined. The children's writing became more readable; their reading, more independent. We'd become a learning community. Students would approach me in small groups with ideas for centers or with questions of things they wanted to learn.

Tyler, Arron, and Beto found a book in our collection that had kite designs.

Arron: We found this. Look, here are the steps for making a kite. It is a diamond-shaped kite. The directions are easy.
Beto: Yeah, even the kids who can't read could follow these directions. See the numbers.

---

7 I had opened the school year in first grade with an illustrator study of José Aruego. A favorite of this group was *The Chick and the Duckling* by Mirra Ginsberg (1988).

Me: Do you think this would be a good center for the whole class?

Tyler: Yeah, it wouldn't take much supplies and you know how we've all been wondering about how kites work. Kites come from China.

Me: In order to create a center, I'll need a list of materials.

Arron: Paper and glue and. . .

Me: Can you boys write a list? Look in the book and see what it says and then make a list that tells me how much I need so that all the students could make one.

Beto: And they need to have copies of the directions

Me: One copy for the center or one copy for each student?

Beto: Each student. 'Cause then they can teach their parents about it.

Arron: And this page, too. It has information about kites and China. We could read it at the center and then take it home and teach our moms.

Tyler: What about the Spanish kids? This book is in English.

Beto: Is there one like this in Spanish?

Me: I haven't been able to find any good kite books like this in Spanish. What should we do?

Beto: I know, we could read this together after lunch in English. Then we could talk about it like we do so everyone understands. We could make a chart of the words like kite and string in Spanish so even Tyler will learn them.

Tyler: Yeah, and at the center, if we want, we could copy the Spanish words down.

Me: Sounds like a plan!

The three boys go off together. Arron gets paper. Beto sharpens a pencil. Tyler gets Clint, who all three agree is a "much better writer" to serve as scribe.

Next door to my favorite import store is a Chinese restaurant that serves a lunch buffet. The owner was very accommodating. "Come at ten-thirty before we open. We will show the kids the kitchen. Don't you want the kids to eat lunch here? I usually charge two dollars a child for lunch. I tell you what, I'll charge two dollars for everybody so lots of parents can come." And come they did. Not one child was absent that day. We had thirty-one first graders, five siblings, and twenty-eight adults!

When we arrived, the owner had set the banquet area for us. Each place setting had a pair of chopsticks and two placemats of the Chinese zodiac, one to use and one rolled up to take as a souvenir. All around the room, I could hear, "Look mom, there's me, the year of the dragon!" "Look, dad, take the chopsticks apart like this, then you hold one like this and. . . ."

We toured the kitchen in small groups. As each group finished the tour, they visited the buffet and got their lunches. The kids sat down with their food and immediately began using their chopsticks. A waiter came out with forks. Some of the parents had asked for them.

As kids finished eating lunch, parents escorted small groups to the import store to see the sights and smell the aromas. The import store has produce and canned goods as well as clothing, furniture, and decorations. One group came back with a package of *salitos*. *Salitos* (more properly in Spanish, *saladitos*) are heavily salted prunes, a popular treat in our community. The children were looking at the Chinese writing as the parent read the English to them, "Imported from China." This event prompted a bit of independent research by my students who discovered that all the *salitos* they eat come from China, even when they buy them in Mexico!

Another group returned to me very excited. They had found out that the store sold "shoes that look just like the ones the kids wear in the book." "Maybe," Milan said, "if we sell enough cookies and pull toys, we'll have enough money to buy a pair of shoes for each of us, too." Czarina and her grandmother had been in that group, as well. The next day, Czarina arrived with a check from her grandparents' butcher shop. It was a donation sufficient to purchase a pair of Chinese slippers for each child.

In the past, I'd made field trips as either initial or concluding activities. Now I know the value of taking the trip in the middle of a unit. The children have enough background to support serious learning and there is time afterward to learn even more. It was after the restaurant trip that the parents joined our community.

In addition to the slippers, we raised enough money to make a costume—a pair of pants, a top, and a belt—for each student. I wanted to finish the costumes by October 31 in time for our schools' storybook character parade. I was overwhelmed with volunteers. Rose made copies of the patterns in various sizes. Parents pinned and cut broadcloth in ten bright colors. We set up three sewing machines in the classroom and parents worked all day every day for two weeks making costumes. I made some, too.

On October 31, the children dressed up in their costumes and put on their "magic singing shoes" (as we had begun to call our Chinese slippers). Only Joseph was absent; his parents kept him home on

Halloween so his religious beliefs would not be compromised. Our class joined the character parade singing the first song from our opera:

> My name is Ping.
> I live in China.
> I like to plant.
> Fruit trees, flowers and seeds.
> Fruit trees, fruit trees.
> Flowers, flowers.
> Seeds, seeds.

There is so much more to tell about this experience. One day I decided since the classroom had no water, for all thirty-one students to make papier mâché flowerpots outdoors at the same time! (Yikes!) There was the side theme on rice where once a week we tasted rice dishes of different cultures: white rice, brown rice, Spanish rice, fried rice, Filipino jasmine rice, arroz con leche, sweet rice, and Horchata. I could list facts the children learned. Facts like when the Great Wall was begun, when it was finished, and how long it is; or the number of Giant Pandas left in the world and the dangers they face; or the difference between an emperor and a president; or why red is an important color. Not every child learned each fact, even though all learned some and some learned many. I could also make a list of the truths the kids discovered and discussed during this unit, beginning with the moral of the story of *The Empty Pot:* "Be honest and try your best." Or other universals: "Kids all over the world wear jeans and T-shirts today." "You never know what people are like until you meet them." "Writing was invented by people." There's just too much to write.

In the course of learning about China, we learned about ourselves. Each of us grew in areas important to ourselves and important to others. Children became readers, writers, and thinkers who ask tough questions and look for serious answers. Our study of China did not detract from the first-grade curriculum nor did it interfere with student learning. It was through the study that all aspects of the curriculum were developed in authentic ways. And it was through the study that the class of thirty-one individual children and four adults became a united learning community.

I had not set out to teach a "multicultural" lesson to my students but I did learn one myself. I found that in learning about others, children make discoveries about themselves. As they make discoveries about themselves, they become empowered as learners. As empowered learners, children are more open to new concepts and ideas that make it easier for them to learn about others.

References

BONNERS, S. (1978). *Panda*. New York: Scholastic.

DEMI. (1986). *Dragon Kites and Dragonflies: A Collection of Chinese Nursery Rhymes*. San Diego: Harcourt Brace Javonovich.

———. (1990). *The Empty Pot*. New York: Henry Holt & Company, Inc.

FISHER, L. E. (1995). *The Great Wall of China*. New York: Aladdin Books.

FLACK, M. (1933). *The Story About Ping*. New York: Viking Puffin.

FRIEDMAN, I. R., SAY, A., and FRIEDMAN, A. R. (1987). *How My Parents Learned to Eat*. New York: Houghton Mifflin Company.

GINSBURG, M. (1988). *The Chick and the Duckling*. New York: Aladdin Paperbacks.

GOLDSTEIN, P. (1992). *Long is a Dragon: Chinese Writing for Children*. Berkeley: Pacific View Press.

MOSEL, A. (1989). *Rikki Tikki Tembo*. New York: Henry Holt & Company, Inc.

PURRINGTON, S., RINEHART, C., and WILCOX, W. (1998). *Music! Words! Opera!* Saint Louis: MMB Music, Inc.

YEN, C. (1991). *Why Rat Comes First: The Story of the Chinese Zodiac*. San Francisco: Chilrens Book Press.

4 Questions of Power and the Power of Questions

John Pryor

W hen I first visited the school, a senior teacher described the neighborhood as "shitsville." It was difficult to disagree with him. The rubbish-strewn street was lined with burnt-out cars, and there were telltale signs of people living behind the boarded-up windows. Nonetheless his words were disquieting—descriptions of inner-city environments all too easily spread by association to the people who inhabit them. As teachers we can choose to recognize the difficulties faced by inner-city students and teachers and move beyond negative stereotypes.

The classroom interaction presented here shows how aspects of the multicultural context with specific attention to issues of power can contribute to a richness of experience and quality of learning. Issues of power are often treated in a very abstract way. My intention is to avoid overabstraction by grounding the discussion in the context of actual classroom events.

Practicing teachers often find that the typical method of portraying the classroom in print—a description based on researcher's field notes backed up by occasional snippets of classroom dialogue—lacks the feel of the classroom and is a little too tidy. It tends to mask the complexity of the events and has a tendency to hide a most important feature of the pedagogical process, the struggle of teacher and learners to construct understanding from each other's mobile and fragmented inputs. This suppressed level of activity and difficulty for the teacher needs to be acknowledged, as does the fact that, although the text seeks to allow the participants to speak for themselves, it is my own construction. The transcript is simplified, for the camera and microphone only pick up one version of events and the transcription process involves choosing to notice or disregard different features. Moreover, to keep the text to a readable size further editing has removed whole sequences (marked by ". . . [ ] . . .") including interruptions from classmates who are not engaged in this activity. The transcript is a resource for the rest of the chapter, which readers may prefer to return to rather than read closely the first time.

It is helpful to preface the initial reading with key ideas that underpin my analysis. The concept of power as developed by Seth Kreisberg rejects the notion that the exercise of power needs to be characterized by domination:

> Dominant discourses of power restrict power to relationships of domination, to *power over*, and . . . this has confined us to a conceptual straightjacket in which the only way to effective action is through the imposition of one's will on others. This view of power . . . is a limited one, sustained by the hegemony of domination in our culture and filtered through ideologies and material relations of domination. (Kreisberg 1992, p. 192)

He describes an alternative, *power with,* derived originally from the 1920's writings of Mary Parker Follett (1924). *Power over* occurs in a context where power is seen as scarce, where the fact that one party has more means that another has less. *Power with,* on the other hand, is produced by (and in turn produces) conditions of abundance, where the power of one person or group empowers another. It is characterized by dialogue, where the voices of different participants are heard, decision-making is shared, and assertiveness and openness are in balance. Within schools there is unlikely ever to be a symmetrical power relationship between students and teachers. Teachers have greater responsibilities and "authority of expertise" recognized by both groups. Nonetheless, awareness enables teachers to mitigate some of the less desirable effects of this imbalance and to work toward the ideal. So in this chapter I show a classroom where synergy between teacher and students enables *power with* to be generated. I am concerned with exploring the structures and processes that enable it to be produced. The transcript enables these ideas to be questioned and critiqued.

It also has this function with respect to parts of another conceptual framework, that contained in Banks' (1993) five dimensions of multicultural education, identified as follows:

- *Content Integration*—the extent to which teachers use examples, data, and information from a variety of cultures and groups (p. 5)

- *Knowledge Construction*—teachers help students to understand how knowledge is created and how it is influenced by the racial, ethnic, and social-class positions of individuals and groups (p. 6)

- *Prejudice Reduction*—children's racial attitudes and strategies that can be used to help students develop more democratic attitudes and values (p. 6)

- *Equity*—pedagogy approaches, theories, and interventions that are designed to help students who are members of low-status population groups to increase their academic achievement (p. 6)

- *Empowering School Culture*—Restructuring the culture and organization of the school so that students from diverse racial, ethnic, and social-class groups will experience educational equality and cultural empowerment (p. 7)

These categories are not mutually exclusive but interrelate in complex ways. They are useful both in terms of providing a way of understanding curriculum and pedagogy, and as indications of further areas where practitioners may concentrate their effort. They draw attention to the idea that the development of multicultural practice is neither straightforward nor static and provide a means of characterizing what has often been called in the United Kingdom the "saris, samosas, and steel bands" approach. Banks' typology provides a basis for the generation of more complex, critical, 'antiracist' methodology (e.g., Gaine 1988). By seeking to articulate different dimensions it is possible to avoid the pitfalls of multiculturalism, which can too often become "a code word . . . that has been fulsomely invoked in order to divert attention from the imperial legacy of racism and social injustice . . . and the ways in which new racist formations are being produced" (MacLaren 1994, p. 196). The example at hand provides a possible way of identifying the processes whereby the teacher and students collaborate to produce power in the classroom.

The Setting

The transcript comes from a large data set collected during the first of two research projects investigating classroom assessment practices in England.[1] We looked in particular at student motivation and the way in which issues of power were played out (Torrance and Pryor 1998).

1 *Teacher Assessment at Key Stage 1: Accomplishing Assessment in the Classroom,* funded by the U.K. Economic and Social Research Council (grant no. R000 234668) and *Investigating and Developing Formative Assessment* (grant no. R00023860). The first involved basic research by the university faculty, the second collaborative action research by a team of university and school teacher researchers.

Gaynor,[2] an experienced but still fairly young white teacher, teaching a Year One class (five- to six-year-olds) was one of some forty-five teachers from a variety settings who collaborated with the Teacher Assessment at Key Stage (TASK) project. In her inner-city school, in a neighborhood with high economic and social tension and a shifting population, several languages are spoken. Most of the children are bilingual, with Portuguese, Chinese, and several African languages being the most common. Some students are recent arrivals from areas of conflict. Most of the children in the transcript attended the school's nursery unit (preschool) and reception class (kindergarten). Gaynor has deliberately put the seven children she considers the most articulate speakers of English together for this activity. Five of them contribute to discussion in the transcript. Rebecca was born in London. Her mother comes from the Caribbean. Both Saria and Fatia were born in Nigeria, though they do not share a mother tongue. The linguistic background of Etienne is French; his family comes from Mauritius. Thandi's parents come from Southern Africa. I did not succeed in obtaining more detailed information about Thandi. Except for Rebecca, whose household was English-speaking, all the children said that more than one language was habitually used at home.

The group is engaged in a project on finding out about Jamaica, part of the geography (social studies) curriculum. One reason Gaynor has chosen to focus on Jamaica is that a support teacher who was born there recently went back to visit her relatives. She has offered to be interviewed. The group is preparing questions. The children are gathered around a flipchart on which Gaynor has already written some of their questions.

The Transcript[3]

1	Rebecca	(*do they) have schools in Jamaica
2	T	well—what do you think
3	Cs	> yes <
4	C	> schools in <

---

2 All the names used in this chapter have been changed.

3 Some of the text of the transcript, with slightly different editing and for different purposes, was used in the book *Investigating Formative Assessment: Teaching, Learning and Assessment in the Classroom* by Harry Torrance and John Pryor, published in 1998 by Open University Press, (Philadelphia).

Normal prose punctuation is not used except that capital letters are retained for proper nouns and the first person singular. Times of day are placed in bold on a separate line as each minute elapses.

(*)	inaudible (probably one word)
(**)	inaudible phrase
(***)	longer inaudible passage (e.g., sentence)
(*Tuesday)	inaudible word, "Tuesday" suggested by transcriber
—	short pause
disapp\	incomplete word
<u>these</u>	word emphasized
Bold	word pronounced with lengthened vowel and diphthong sounds
COME HERE	words said very loudly compared to other utterances of this speaker
=	rapid change of speakers turn (used at end the utterance of one speaker and beginning of next speaker's utterance
> It's mine <	simultaneous speech (use spare lines to make it clear)
Italics	nontextual material (stage directions)
the/cat/sat	word for word enunciation with flat intonation (e.g., emergent reader)
T	teacher
C	unidentified child
Cs	unidentified children
… [ ] …	edited for space

FIGURE 1 ■ *Transcription Conventions*

5	T	do you remember—did you see any schools in the books that <u>you</u> looked through
6	Cs	yes
7	T	right—is there any question <u>now</u> that—you that they know have schools in Jamaica but can you
8		ask a question about the schools in Jamaica
9	Fatia	I know
10	C	do they—do they
11	C	what does it look like in schools in Jamaica
12	T	OK—can you be more a little bit more specific—can you ask >something <=
13	C	> miss < =
14	Etienne	= > what does < that mean =
15	T	= think of something—about—I mean—think of something that we do at school—and then think—
16		well—do they do that in Jamaica

17	Etienne	did do they like do write\ writing when when you've finished at the holidays when the holidays
18		are finished—like you like like you—you tell us to do writing
19	T	right so I tell you to write about what you did at the weekend—yeah—but maybe what you
20	Fatia	= Miss, I've got a
21	T	OK
22	Fatia	have they got—have they got—
23		...[ ]...
24	Fatia	have they got trolleys
25	T	have they got trolleys
26	Fatia	bug\—buggies
27	T	buggies- what would you do with a buggy
28	Cs	(laughter)
29	Thandi	push the babies[4]
30	T	oh for babies
31	Fatia	yeah
32	T	oh we'll ask that

33 *T goes to write on flipchart.*

34	Etienne	miss—
35	T	why do you ask that question Fatia
36	Thandi	she wants to know how =
37	T	= yeah I know she wants to know but why did you ask it—what made you think of that—what
38		made you think about—what made you think that—they might have buggies—to move the babies
39		around in—why did you think that—no—no idea—OK

40 *Fatia shakes head. T goes to write on flipchart.*

41	T	what you—right—let's go back to the one about schools—try—well we know that they have
42		schools in Jamaica—but they might not > be the same <
43	Thandi	> what sort of < I know =
44	T	= Thandi sit down here please I can't talk to you when you're over there =

---

4 Buggy is the usual term used in the United Kingdom to denote what would be called a stroller in North America.

45	Etienne	do they have playgrounds in the schools
46	T	have a think—
47	C	no =
48	Thandi	= they might have
49	Saria	they might
50	T	right—think about what sort of quest\—we know that they have schools in Jamaica but what sort
51		of > questions—you could ask <
52	... [ ] ...	

53 *T points to Thandi.*

54	Thandi	what do they have in their school
55	T	well—what do you mean—what kind of—what are you thinking about 'cause they could just—Mrs
56		Magenta could just give you a long long list of the things they have in their school and you
57		would just fall asleep it would be so long—I mean she could be talking about—nails or -> pins
58		or pencils—crayons <
59	Thandi	> I know one <—what—what kind of—what kind of playgrounds—what kind of playgrounds do
60		they have
61	T	what kind of =
62	Thandi	what kind of playgrounds do they have—do they have no poles or >do they have<
63	Etienne	>I know something<
64	Thandi	do they have no slides or do > they (**) <
65	T	right—you just tell me the first part of your question—what kind what kind of
66	Thandi	playground do they have
67	T	what kind of <u>playgrounds</u> do they have in Jamaican schools

68 *T writes.*

69	Fatia	what's that (*)—every time you write that (*)—
70	T	Fatia—just wait

71 *Fatia points at writing.*

72	... [ ] ...	
73	Fatia	miss you've just made a mistake—look =

74 *Fatia points to flipchart.*

75	T	= it doesn't matter—it's

76 *T alters writing on flipchart.*

77	T	right Etienne sit down
78	... [ ] ...	
79	Thandi	do they have have English (*books) in Jamaica or their or their own writing
80	T	oh—that's a good one—that's a really good question ... [ ]...Thandi—do you mean like books
81		that have come from England
82	Thandi	yeah—do they have English books or their own writing
83	T	or their own — =
84	Thandi	= language
85	T	what language do you think Jamaicans speak
86	Fatia	I know 'cause I've been
87	T	do you know

88 *T points to Rebecca.*

89	Rebecca	(*) 'cause I've been there—and my mum —my mum
90	T	did you go there

91 *Rebecca nods head.*

92	Rebecca	we're going back there when my grandma and (*my) granddad's got money
93	Fatia	I know
94	T	right—OK—well let's write Thandi's question down so—do / they

95 *T starts to write.*

96	Thandi	have English writing or—
97	T	is this in schools or generally

98 *Thandi nods her head.*

99	T	in schools—or just everybody in Jamaica

100 *Thandi nods her head.*

101	Thandi	in Jamaica
102	T	for everyone— all right ... [ ]... right—so—you were talking about a Jamaican language—do they—

103		so—you were also saying do they s\ write and read in English or do they read in Jamaican
104		language
105	Thandi	they read in Jamaican language
106	T	is there a question you can ask about that—'cause you don't know do you—do you know—whether
107		they write in English—or speak in English—or they speak in Jam\ in a Jamaican language
108	Thandi	they speak in Jamaican
109	T	well can you ask a question

110 *T leans forward and touches Fatia on the knee.*

111	T	sit down
112	Thandi	(*) when they speak English and the next (*) they speak English again and then they (*) to speak
113		(**)
114	T	so can you turn that—we need to find that out—we need to clarify that because we're not sure
115		whether they speak English or whether they speak another language—in Jamaica ... [ ] ... how
116		can we turn that into a question— how can we find that out from Mrs Magenta ... [ ] ...
117	Rebecca	> what **language** <- what <u>language</u> do people speak in Jamaica
118	T	right well good—what language do people speak in Jamaica

119 *T writes question on flipchart.*

120	T	OK—well—going to ask Fatia now ... [ ] ... right—OK—I missed out Fatia's question so—what
121		was it
122	Saria	> do they have churches <
123	Fatia	>(***) <
124	T	tell me what it was
125	Thandi	do they have churches in

126 *T wags hand at Thandi.*

127	T	shh—
128	Fatia	do they have churches in Jamaica
129	T	right—OK ... [ ] ... what if Mrs—um Magenta just says yes

130 Thandi	what if she says everything is (*)
131 T	well she she might not but—what if—to that to that question—do they have churches in Jamaica
132	what if she just says yes—is there anything you ah might want to ask anything else you might
133	want to ask—right if she says yes they have churches in Jamaica—is there anything else you
134	could ask about churches in Jamaica
135 Saria	I know (**)
136 Etienne	Do they > eat sandwiches < for lunch—I mean not lunch but—
137 T	no—no—I'm I'm thinking about the question—that that Fatia has just asked
138 Thandi	does people go to the church in Jamaica
139 T	yeah—anything else- can you think of anything—if we said to Mrs Magenta—do they have
140	church\ churches in Jamaica and she said—yes—
141 Saria	(**)
142 T	well what else—well is that enough—does that tell you enough about it
143 Cs	yes—no—yes
144 Rebecca	it's—um—what—kind—of—chairs
145 T	what
146 Rebecca	chairs
147 T	what kind of churches do they have—right—'cause there
148	are lots of different—like in England there are lots of different types of churches—aren't there
149 C	yeah
150 T	yeah—what different types of churches can you think of in England
151 Rebecca	in Jamaica I saw—

| 152 | *T begins to write again.* |

| 153 Rebecca | I saw a different church |
| 154 Thandi | on—I- yesterday I went to Jamaica and guess what we saw—we saw a = |

| 155 | *Etienne turns round and points at Thandi.* |

| 156 Etienne | which church do you go to |
| 157 | ... [ ] ... |

158	Fatia	I go to Nigerian church
159	Cs	I know (**)

Constructing Knowledge

The choice of Jamaica as a subject for study is appropriate for several reasons. It falls within the field of multicultural education because its subject matter, life in Jamaica, relates to a culture other than the mainstream one of the country in which it is taking place—Banks' (1993) first dimension, content integration. Many of the children at the school, most notably Rebecca, have family connections with the Caribbean islands and Jamaica. Significant achievement by black people in Jamaica has been well documented, potentially enhancing students' self-confidence and helping them to develop what Ogbu (1994) calls "effort optimism," the sense that people like them can succeed. Moreover, at the time when this event took place, the local area was covered with placards advertising a film about the adventures of a Jamaican team at the Winter Olympics, so interest in Jamaica was high. The availability of Mrs. Magenta was also important, though a teacher without her would be able to arrange a similar source of information.

However, as Banks (1993, p. 37) points out, "several serious problems result when multicultural education is conceptualized only, or primarily as content integration." In my own experience, I've seen poor multicultural education characterized by teachers choosing to teach exotic locations in a decontextualized way. The gaze directed at the people studied is essentially voyeuristic. The standards used to judge what is seen are alien to the situation reinforcing prejudices of those who are not associated with the culture in question and demeaning those who are. This kind of work is often tokenistic and associated with very limited cultural knowledge in the teacher.

Gaynor's status as an "outsider" makes her relationship to knowledge about Jamaica problematic. It might be possible, but not easy, for her to present Jamaican life adopting a Jamaica perspective. The use of her colleague partially solves this problem. The interpretation is contextualized by someone whose personal experience is informed by knowledge of past struggles against slavery, colonialism, and oppression. However, Mrs. Magenta is not in a position to take over the teaching entirely and so Gaynor is still left with resolving her orientation to knowledge. She approaches this through the inquiry approach she adopts. Knowing that, she positions herself alongside the students as someone who does not know, but is keen to find out.

So, from the transcript, we do not know whether Gaynor is knowledgeable about Jamaica. The issue of her knowledge is side-stepped by the pedagogy, where she is an inquirer rather than an authority. She avoids answering questions, even relatively straight-forward ones such as in line 1. Even when she probably does have the relevant knowledge (e.g., talking about language), she says, "we need to clarify" (line 111); in the context this succeeds in placing her with the children, without the patronizing overtones often apparent in teachers' use of "we." The outcome of the lesson will be collabora-tively constructed by three parties: the informant (Mrs. Magenta), the teacher (Gaynor), and the children. Banks' category of knowledge construction seems particularly appropriate. The term itself invokes ideas of the social constitution of knowledge and seems to describe well the way that Gaynor concentrates on facilitating the children's inquiry. If the critical dimension does not emerge explicitly at this level, it is not for lack of effort. Gaynor tries hard to make the chil-dren aware of the thinking behind their questioning. She tries in the way she questions Fatia about the buggies (lines 25–29) and then later when she asks them to think about English churches, a strategy obvi-ously aimed at avoiding controlling—power over—the children

Researchers critical of child-centered progressive education con-clude that this kind of approach often has negative effects. Teachers withholding knowledge, dressed up in the asking of pseudo-open questions, far from handing over power to the students merely mask their control (Walkerdine 1988). Although they do not specify what children are to say, they retain the right to judge what is acceptable as knowledge. The structure of classroom talk in such situations means that every utterance of the children is explicitly or implicitly evaluated (Mehan 1979). These practices have also been shown to make the pur-pose of classroom talk unclear (Edwards and Mercer 1987), and the lack of explicitness about classroom structures is particularly disabling for children with less access to mainstream culture (Elsworth 1989).

These criticisms are not valid in interactions like the transcription shown here. It is only on the level of procedural knowledge (know-how) that Gaynor is taking an active part and being very assertive. Rather than withholding knowledge in order to maneuver children into giving the correct answer, she is using her knowledge of what might be a fruitful question to scaffold the children's questioning. So although not answering questions about Jamaica, she is very persis-tent, both in the school question and the language question, in get-ting the children to formulate their inquiry in a manner which is likely to be productive (e.g., her response to Thandi's question about what they have in school).

Equally significant is the fact that the children themselves are active in the construction of knowledge. The inquiry format where they get to formulate questions enables them, at least in principle, to construct knowledge about Jamaica in the light of their own experience. The type of questions that the children ask reflects not just a childish perspective, but a culturally situated one. For example, when discussing churches, Rebecca suggests inquiring about chairs. It emerged from talking to the children afterwards that seating arrangements in churches were to them a significant feature: the English church with which the school is associated[5] has formal pews and the worship is also formal and restrained, whereas many of the black churches, attended by many of the children and their families, like Fatia's "Nigerian" one, have informal seating and more extroverted and participatory worship. Asking about chairs in Jamaican churches would be a way of seeking to place them with respect to the different knowledge the children had.

That Gaynor did not make the most of this opportunity highlights the problematic nature of classroom interaction. She appears not to have heard what Rebecca says and, whether by accident or intent, turns the question into a more general one about churches. It might therefore be argued that the social critical element of "knowledge construction" is missing. Ideally Gaynor would not only have accepted the question as it stood, but used it as a means of highlighting the way in which group and individual experience and cultural identity play a part in the construction of knowledge, an idea that is ultimately much more important for the children to grasp than any particular facts about Jamaica. This may seem to be too much to ask with such young children. However, on another occasion Gaynor does make a serious attempt to move the conversation in this kind of direction. This is with the question about buggies, where she seeks to explore the thinking behind Fatia's suggestion. When asked about this later she said:

> There's some of their background and their experiences like Fatia asking a question about the—the buggy, I mean I think that might come from the fact that she's just had a—her mum's had a baby brother and the fact that she's Nigerian and—you know—some Nigerians carry their babies round in different ways.

---

5 A daily act of worship is a legal requirement in publicly funded English state schools. Many of them (including this one) are jointly funded by the Church and the state.

In this case Gaynor recognized that Fatia was attempting compare the two cultures of her experience, and to place Jamaica with respect to them. Had Fatia responded to Gaynor's question and confirmed Gaynor's hunch, the point that people's own experience and culture influence what they notice could have been made. As it is, the unanswered question leaves this implicit. Gaynor showed her awareness of the issue, but in the context of making meaning it was hard to realize the potential of the situation. To judge this as failure would be harsh: Rebecca may have been able to ask her question of Mrs Magenta; Fatia may have realized that she was making use of her cultural knowledge. In both cases, although Gaynor was not able to make an ideal intervention, her pedagogic approach, whereby the children were engaged in inquiry, left open the possibility of partial success.

The Importance of Inquiry

Inquiry works on several levels. It is most overt in the sense that questions are being formulated to pose to another person. It can also be seen in the way that the words produced by teacher and pupils are treated as text to be interrogated. In Gaynor this process is quite self-conscious. She often finds it difficult to understand what the children are saying. The chairs/churches confusion is an example where her interrogation appears to be cut short and she seems to miss the sense. However, a counter example where she continues the inquiry is when the word 'playgrounds' is suggested. Gaynor does not recognize this word until Thandi mentions slides. What is striking is the collaborative action to construct common understanding by teacher and pupils. This can be seen, for example, in the groping toward the formulation of this particular question, but it is also apparent more generally where the normal turn-taking of classroom discourse breaks down and children interject and interpret each other's statements (e.g., when Thandi says, "she wants to know how" in line 36).

This approach to interaction can be linked to Banks' dimension of equity pedagogy. The teacher attempts to focus the talk yet leaves it sufficiently open to bring in the differing perspectives of the pupils. Not easily accomplished, this makes great demands on teachers' capacity to act as chairperson. Freewheeling turn-taking can easily become a confusing cacophony. Inevitably the times when the teacher's interventions enable collaborative meaning making will be balanced by those where their chairing role appears to result in arbitrary and controlling moves (e.g., the question of Fatia's in line 69—"what's that—every time you write that"—which is never responded to). The creation of space in which all the children can contribute is a fundamental way in which a teacher can create power with children. At the same time, for children to be able to initiate ideas in meaningful ways requires a context where they feel empowered. So, although we see examples of Gaynor closing down the discussion and exerting power over the children, there are also times when children are confident enough to initiate. Thus Fatia is reluctant to say why she had asked the question about the baby buggy (line 35), presumably because, when a teacher asks you why you have done something, there is an implication that you are doing wrong. Yet the same child is later able to correct Gaynor's writing (line 73). Another good example is where Etienne is able to ask Gaynor to explain the meaning of the term "specific" (line 15). These different incidents, exemplifying both a teacher's controlling *power over* children and emancipating *power with* children, seem to suggest that both can be present within the same context. Thus an equity pedagogy is not unproblematically brought into existence, but needs to be striven for constantly, and continually reconstituted in dialogue.

Assertive Risk Taking

Etienne's question points to another tricky issue; the importance of high teacher expectations (Rosenthal and Jacobsen 1968). Throughout the transcript it is apparent that Gaynor's expectations are high. She doesn't just require the children to formulate a coherent question, but one that is productive—sufficiently specific yet open enough to encourage Mrs. Magenta to give a full answer. Gaynor pursues that aim fairly single-mindedly and one needs to remind oneself that the children she is working with are only five or six years old. There are dangers in pitching a lesson too high and giving too little help to the students. Such a strategy is risky. (Newman *et al.* 1989) Success depends on student engagement and all parties striving for understanding, Important to this are power relations where students are able to interrupt teachers to ask for help. This seems to be an example of what Kreisberg means when he talks of empowerment as "both the knowledge that one can make a difference and the actual ability to act" (1992, p. 108).

Power with requires risk taking. We see here how the openness of Gaynor toward these children means that she has to work very hard at a procedural as well as an intellectual level. Her relationship to the children is therefore not cozy or romantic. Although some of the dialogue, particularly that relating to children in the rest of the class, has been edited out, it is still apparent from the transcript that she needs to intercede to maintain some order. When the children's movement threatens to distract attention, she intervenes by telling Thandi and Etienne to sit down (lines 44 and 77). In this classroom there is no room for a teacher who is not prepared to be assertive. The language in which some of this assertion is couched may appear abrupt and coercive, but it has to be viewed with reference to the collaborative ethos of the discourse and the way in which the teacher takes responsibility, both intellectual and moral, for what is going on. When asked what she considered motivated their engagement in the task she said:

> Well, I think part of their motivation is that—that I've asked them—to think up questions—and they're using the information that they've already found out—to—'cause they know that that's what I want—in a kind of subconscious way to please me, they're thinking, well, I know this about Jamaica but I can still ask to turn it into a question and I think that's part of it really.

This recalls the point made by Cynthia Ballenger (1992) in her article about working with children from a Haitian background: she found that previous tried-and-tested methods with children from what she calls the "mainstream culture" of the United States were ineffective. A child informed her that the reason that children in her class should do as she asked was "because you like us." This led Ballenger to see that her previous language of control, motivating children to behave according to guidelines by invoking material consequences through a system of cause and effect, was in fact culturally specific and inappropriate for the children she was teaching. What was more successful was an appeal to its effect on relationships.

Making the Rules Explicit

I've seen the importance to the children we worked with of clarity about criteria, not just those used to define the accomplishment of the task (what to do), but those used to assess the quality of performance (how to do it well). Good classroom assessment is centered around dialogues where criteria are clarified, particularly for those with the greatest cultural distance from the teacher and the dominant discourses of the school (Torrance and Pryor 2000). Furthermore, because these criteria are communicated and bound up in teachers' interaction with students, those children who can make sense of the rules of each interaction are most likely to succeed (Pryor and Torrance 1999). This finding chimes in well with much other work, par-

These were the final questions that the group successfully used in the interview and that later resulted in an interesting presentation to the rest of the class about Jamaica.

1. What type of food do you eat in Jamaica?
2. What do you drink?
3. What kinds of clothes do people wear in Jamaica?
4. What are the trees like in Jamaica?
5. What is the weather like?
6. What do the houses look like?
7. What kind of shops do they have in Jamaica?
8. Do they have parks in Jamaica?
9. Do they have libraries in Jamaica?
10. Do they have shutters or curtains in their houses?
11. What kind of playgrounds do they have in Jamaican schools?
12. Do they have buggies for babies?
13. Do people have pets?
14. Do they have English books or Jamaican books?
15. What language do people speak in Jamaica?
16. What type of churches do they have?
17. Do they have police in Jamaica?

FIGURE 2   *Final Questions*

ticularly in the field of multicultural and antiracist education. For example, Delpit (1995, p. 583) has noted that "if you are not already a participant in the culture of power, being told explicitly the rules of that culture makes acquiring power easier."

In this sense the dialogue in the transcript is assessment rich: the group has not just been told the criteria for a good question, but are exploring them and through the interaction are bringing them to life. We have seen already how the Gaynor's assertive pedagogy is active in this and seeks, often with only partial success, to surmount the problems caused by mutual misunderstanding. Through prompts and commentary, she keeps returning the children to the criteria. Occasionally communication still breaks down. Each cultural group is left asking, "Why don't those people say what they mean?" as well as, "What's wrong with them, why don't they understand?" (Delpit 1995, p. 584)

Despite this the dialogue seems successful not only in creating suitable questions but also in establishing ways of judging their quality. I would suggest that the key to this is the curricular context. The rules of a good question are being generated not in some academically remote way, but from what might be termed a "real context"—an interview that will actually take place. The children may well be active in searching for clues about what is in the teacher's mind but they are also able to access the criteria by referring to what they will later do—interview Mrs Magenta. Thus good questions will demonstrably be those that provide them with the most knowledge about Jamaica. In other words, this is an authentic task with a real purpose; therefore the evaluation is built into it, and it is not purely reliant on teacher judgement.

Conclusions

I am not claiming that what is portrayed is perfect. In the transcript, a fragment of a lesson, a few minutes amongst the thousands that a teacher will spend with a class, indeed my intention has been to make it problematic. Moreover, no teaching and learning is likely ever to be perfect for every child. However, participating in this lesson as an observer I was struck by many features about it that seemed interesting and admirable. In particular it disrupted my own preconceptions about teaching and learning in early-years classrooms and about multi-cultural education in the setting of an inner-city school. My analysis has been an attempt to theorize the contrast between what took place in the transcript and what I might have expected in the light of my experience elsewhere.

The key feature is that the object of the activity is to generate questions rather than to produce answers. The teacher is clear about what she considers to be a good question, but the lesson is essentially dialogic and the agenda of the different participants is able to emerge. The questions are not all of the sort that an adult might ask (e.g., the one about buggies). The inferences the children will then make about Jamaica are liable to have meaning for them and are genuinely constructivist: they seek to accommodate their previous disparate experience and this experience is being acknowledged and validated. Sometimes the teacher is aware of this, as in the case of the buggies, but sometimes she is not, as in the case of the chairs.

The linguistic form of generating questions is important, but it would be pointless to advocate it for all lessons. It is just one manifestation of an inquiry approach, where the teacher enters into dialogue with the children where she attempts to make clear both what she knows and what they know as the lesson works towards the direction of discovering what both parties do not know. A lot of her knowledge is procedural, how to go about finding out, and cultural, what counts as good work. In order to make the dialogue work she needs to be assertive, but also to respect and be interested in the children's difference. She also needs to take the risk of having high expectations of students' potential achievement. All this hinges on the children's engagement with a task, which is real to them and whose authentic context indicates its own criteria for success.

The example, however, remains problematic. The teacher sometimes misunderstands the students and they in turn misunderstand her. Some children are more readily able to access power than others and show different degrees of confidence. Their confidence ebbs and flows even within the small section quoted. Nevertheless the transcript shows an example of power relations, which, although still asymmetric, has characteristics of *power with*. This will always be difficult. It depends not only on the teacher making more equitable relations available, but on children being able to recognize opportunities to share in power. This chapter has attempted to illustrate ways within an authentic context a teacher and students struggle to construct a pedagogy that respects their different interests and perspectives. Despite its problematic nature, the transcript shows a moment when teacher and students work together on "shaping and reshaping alliances for constructing circumstances in which students of difference can thrive" (Elsworth 1989, p. 324) and begin to speak in what Debra Goodman (Chapter 1) calls "a language of possibility."

References

BALLENGER, C. (1992). "Because You Like Us: the Language of Control" *Harvard Educational Review (62,2)* 199–208.

BANKS, J. (1993). "Multicultural Education: Historical Development, Dimensions, and Practice." *Review of Research in Education (19)* 3–49.

DELPIT, L. (1985). *Other People's Children: Cultural Conflict in the Classroom.* New York: New Press.

EDWARDS, D., and MERCER, N. (1987). *Common Knowledge: The Development of Understanding in the Classroom.* London: Methuen.

ELSWORTH, E. (1989). "Why Doesn't This Feel Empowering? Working through the repressive myths of Critical Pedagogy." *Harvard Educational Review (59)3,* 297–324.

GAINE, C. (1988). *No Problem Here.* London: Hutchinson.

KREISBERG, S. (1992). *Transforming Power: Domination, Empowerment, and Education.* New York: State University of New York Press.

MacLaren, P. (1994). "Multiculturalism and the Postmodern Critique: Toward a Pedagogy of Resistance and Transformation" in H. Giroux and P. MacLaren (eds.), *Between Borders: Pedagogy and Politics of Cultural Studies.* London: Routledge.

Mehan, H. (1979). *Learning Lessons: Social Organization in the Classroom.* Cambridge, MA: Harvard University Press.

Newman, D., Griffin, P., and Cole, M. (1989). *The Construction Zone: Working for Cognitive Change in School.* Cambridge: Cambridge University Press.

Ogbu, J. (1994). "Racial Stratification and Education in the United States: Why Inequality Persists," *Teachers' College Record (96)* 264–71 and 283–98.

Pryor, J. and Torrance, H. (1999). "Developing a Framework for Classroom Assessment," Paper presented to the Annual Meeting of the *American Educational Research Association,* April 1999, Montreal, Canada.

Rosenthal, R., and Jacobsen, L. (1968). *Pygmalion in the Classroom: Teacher Expectation and Pupils' Intellectual Development.* New York: Islington.

Torrance, H., and Pryor, J. (1998). *Investigating Formative Assessment: Teaching, Learning and Assessment in the Classroom.* Philadelphia: Open University Press.

———. (2000). Paper presented to the Annual Meeting of the *American Educational Research Association.* New Orleans, April 2000.

Walkerdine, V. (1988). *The Mastery of Reason: Cognitive Development and the Production of Rationality.* London: Routledge.

5

Turning Over the Wheel:
Discovering the Strength in Diversity

Cindee Karns

T he water in our favorite Alaskan river was shallow, but not nearly as shallow as before the rain. I dropped the anchor into the bow, pushed the boat into the current, and slipped in before I got my shoes wet. The sun gleamed on the ripples as the motor dropped into forward gear. Curt, my husband, read the river well, just as he had for most of his life. The kids, oblivious to the skill it takes to travel the Salcha without getting stuck, settled into the bow to count cabins and take bets on how long it would take to get there. I carefully unsnapped the canvas cover from above my copilot seat, so that I could stand up to spot moose, enjoy the scenery, or help find floating debris in the water.

The rhythm of a wild river is often a back-and-forth rhythm, traversing from cut bank to cut bank to where the bulk of the water runs. The rhythm ends abruptly, however, when the river tries cutting a new channel, taking out trees, sandbars, cabins, or anything else that stands in its way.

As copilot, I often find myself reading the river and making those critical decisions in my head—how soon to turn before we hit a sweeper, where the deep water will be around the next bend. I'm always pleased with my river-reading skills when my decisions are the same as Curt's. Even though I've only been practicing for a few short summers, it really is very easy to do. I'm a pretty good pilot.

So, Curt says, "OK, Cindee. It's your turn. You need to practice driving in case something happens to me. Here you go." He stands up.

"I already practice while you're driving," I say. "I know how to drive. Don't worry."

"You should still get the feel of the boat. Here."

I take the wheel.

Suddenly, I'm not sure. Here comes the first turn. The water is running way to the outside. I'm going to have to go very close to shore then cut hard to the left. Yikes. "Curt, I'm not sure I can do this."

"You're right on target. Head to the shore and then cut hard to the left."

My stomach knots up. Whooh! I did it. Oh no, here comes another one. "Where do I go?"

"There's the channel. You've got it. Watch those sweepers on the left and then veer right. See? . . . Turn! . . . Yes, no problem."

"No, problem," I mutter. Ugh.

Now for the next one. On no, it's the rock wall! I see the V where it's funneling in. If I can keep the motor in the deep, and keep the bow in the shallow part . . . Curt's not saying anything . . . Here, we go . . . I did it. "No problem!" I say more confidently.

The rhythm of the school year feels normal and easy to my eighth graders as they enter my classroom. They feel confident and assured that they definitely know what they are doing in school, until I hand over the wheel. They're usually reluctant just like I am in the boat. This year was no different.

We return from summer vacation to teach in a conservative, small, rural suburb in Alaska, which is mostly caucasian. Reluctantly, we carry our coffee mugs into the lounge for the first staff meeting of the year. The principal passes out the school board's goals for the year. The top item: to create tolerance and diversity in every classroom in the district; to target our school for immediate action promoting tolerance and acceptance. I wasn't surprised that our school came out at the bottom of our district's racial tolerance survey. Andrea, a seventh-grade teacher, leaned over and whispered, "I checked the surveys over after the kids did them and most of them wrote down that they didn't have any minority teachers. Do we have to spell it out for them?" Her teaching partner is Hispanic. The students didn't recognize very obvious diversity. And a lot of them were moving up to my team in the eigth grade. That was a red flag to me.

From my years of experience as a classroom teacher and as a parent, I know that kids thrive at figuring out the impossible. I wondered if I could get my eighth graders to identify diversity, figure out how to use it to their advantage, and then celebrate it. Could they discover the importance of diversity for themselves? A lot of structure and scaffolding would have to be in place for that to happen. I decided right then that diversity would be my classroom's year-long theme.

At the onset of every school year, I start with expectations. They all cheer when I tell them they are not allowed to fail my class and that they get to redo it until they get it right. What they don't realize is how hard that really is. I ask: "How many of you think that some kids are smart and some kids are not?" Most of them raise their hands. "If I asked you right now, could you tell me who the smart kids and the dumb kids are?" They overwhelmingly agree that they could. Then I ask, "Do you agree that everyone learns differently?" They agree. I continue, "Do you think everyone could be smart?" They nod. I explain. "Some of you learn best by listening, some of you learn best by watching someone else, some of you can't learn unless you do it yourself, and others need to read it. This year we are going to try to teach you according to your intelligences and about the intelligence of others, so we want you to evaluate yourself."

Last summer at a special education conference in Anchorage I heard a teacher describe the Gardner's Multiple Intelligences (Gardner 1983) in an easy way. I copied it and made posters of each intelligence to hang on the wall for the year: Number Smart, People Smart, Word Smart, Self Smart, Body Smart, Music Smart, and Picture Smart. The students were amazed at the results and how accurately they were described. Some of them picked two or sometimes three styles. I had them make a poster that explained their intelligence so that others—including their peers and their parents—could understand. They posted those around the classroom. Then came the clincher question: "Can you accept that all of us are smart, but can't always express it in the way schools want us to?" They agreed.

OK, I Had Them in the Boat

They soon figured out that the rhythm of this school year would be different from all the rest. After just a few weeks Candice wrote:

> This year I have learned that everyone is different in their own way. For example some people are number smart, music smart, word smart, body smart, people smart, picture smart and self smart. Everything means you are good at different stuff. I'm self-smart.

Maybe it came to the students so easily because middle schoolers categorize other students all the time. Whatever the reason, *they were with me and they were interested enough to sit in the copilot seat, start watching, and pay attention to the trip.*

During the entire school year we worked on diversity. Our first project was done individually: to present a diary of a member of their first-generation American family coming to America. Everyone was enthusiastic about his or her own intelligence. I wanted to generate that same enthusiasm about their individual ethnic backgrounds.

As we were working on those diaries, I started giving mini-lessons at the beginning of each class. I introduced the age-old debate: Is

America a melting pot where immigrants arrive, leave their culture behind, and become American? Or is it a salad bowl where people become American citizens, but hold on to their language and culture? They were confused. They really wanted me to tell them the right answer. They obviously were not used to having their own opinion and supporting it. They wanted the right answer. They were not just uncomfortable with their uniqueness, they were uncomfortable with their own opinions. It took several days. After much discussion, they reluctantly formed opinions and supported them.

I Finally Got Them to Take the Wheel

Formulating opinions is very different from the worksheets and end-of-chapter questions of their former social studies classes. I asked them to write their opinions and give reasons for them. Jason wrote:

> Some people believe in a "melting pot" where we come together and leave our individuality and some believe we are like a salad bowl where we come together but keep all our individuality. I don't believe in either. I think we should keep our individuality but speak the same language and learn the same language. I think we should leave some of our individuality behind."

Like Jason, several students felt safe enough to discount both theories and go with their own beliefs. Other students like Shawna were willing to give reasons for both theories.

> I think that the U.S. tries to be like the melting pot theory. Like everyone dresses alike, talks the same. But in reality we are more like a salad bowl. Everyone is different, religions are different and we speak different. I think it is better to be like a salad bowl you get a taste of everything.

All seventy-five students were able to voice opinions and back them up. *Okay, we were on our way. They handled the first corner with lots of coaching. However, the fast water was still up ahead.*

Our next project was to form our own congress and pass a bill, which the president (me) would sign to solve "the problem of immigration" once and for all. We looked at previous immigration laws and then started our own discussion of the current problem by reading articles from the internet. Mexicans illegally crossing the border into America, boat people trying to get here, companies hiring illegal immigrants because they were cheap, illegal immigrants trying to have their babies in America to get American citizenship, and so on. Discussions were hot!

Their goal was to send a bill that they all agreed on to the president in two weeks and everyone in the class would get an A. They could all sponsor separate bills or they could sponsor bills together, but whichever bill they passed, they would have to compromise with each other and the other body and only send one bill to the president. My job was really more of "the press" than anything else. I walked around observing. Whenever they asked me something, I would ask, "What would they do in the real congress? I have their e-mail addresses if you'd like to e-mail them." No one did. They wanted to get back to the problem.

During this unit we learned about solving group problems. The constitution provided the specific rules of play. Each morning when they entered, I gave mini-lessons: ways to compromise; to disagree with the idea—not the person; to take others' learning styles into consideration when explaining things; the problems with majority rule; and a good problem-solving process: describe the problem, brainstorm solutions, choose one and see if it works. It was interesting to watch. They carried their arguments into the lunch room when someone proposed having Americans injected with blue-tinted blood, easily identifiable in a detector. They yelled at each other when the Senate brought back a proposal to invade Mexico and take over their government and schools. I smiled and sent encouraging nonverbal cues to the Speaker of the House. That was a hard job.

When kids got too angry or excited, disrupting the process, it was my job to pull them out of the group and explain techniques other than yelling to get their point across. I pulled John out one day. He was interrupting everyone and yelling his opinion. It took over a minute for him to calm down. "They are all idiots and they are slandering me. This is so stupid." While we were out in the hall, the house voted him out of the group, as outlined in the constitution. The next day John came back to class and asked the speaker for permission to talk to the house. He apologized and asked that he please be reinstated. They voted and he was back in. By the end of this unit, the kids knew they had the power to make decisions as a group, they could compromise, they could vote and support the decision.

All the while I worked to demonstrate how students with different intelligences choose to learn. For the Body Smart learners we made the classroom into a slave ship and sailed to America. Students laid spoon style (head to toe) on the floor and were made to dance for exercise above decks. The Word Smart kids read about it, the Music and Body Smart kids learned by dancing on the upper deck for exercise.

We continued debating issues throughout American history—the Dawes Act (Should Native Americans be allowed to keep their land?), the Industrial Revolution, and the new Third World slaves who are making our clothes and chocolate cheaply in other countries. By March I felt fairly confident that these students knew how to voice their opinions, listen to others, and disagree with the idea, not the person.

Suddenly I came around the bend and there was a fork in the river—a big sand bar in the middle. I flashed back to several years before in my mother-in-law's air boat, when we came around a corner just like this one and found a log jam blocking the river. She had turned the boat around in a hurry and the wave from the motor hit the log jam and came over the back end of the boat—sinking us.

I started worrying. I knew they could identify diversity, voice opinions, and make decisions. But could they put it all together in one big project? What if this was too much to ask of students? What if I hadn't prepared them enough? What if they didn't care?

Sinking is not a good feeling. Neither is seeing your belongings float away downstream.

The boat kept moving and I had to choose the fork. I went right. I watched as I continued upriver. I looked over and saw lots of water on the left side and ahead less and less water. I had made my choice. There was a big sandbar between the forks, so there was no turning back. If I slowed down, we would surely be stuck. Ahead the water funneled through a small gap of 3 to 4 inches of water. I gritted my teeth and tried to turn the bow into the shallow to keep the jet in the water as we turned. Rocks scratching across metal is not my favorite sound in the world, but we made it. We were back into the deep water. We pulled over to a sand bar. The kids jumped out with the anchor. Curt pulled on his hip boots, grabbed a screw driver, and pried the rocks through the grate of the jet motor. Oh well, mistakes have to be made. I asked him why he didn't say anything. He just smiled.

I Had to Give Up Control of the Wheel

It's important to learn from mistakes. I had to allow students to make them. We'd cruised up the river pretty far this year. They'd watched from the copilot seat, and they'd driven in the slow water, so now they were ready. Before we embarked on this final cruise, I wanted to make sure that they understood. Again I asked for a fast write so that I could make sure everyone was ready. Theresa wrote, "It [diversity] teaches us to deal with differences and it helps us see other people's point of view." Sharelle said, "Everyone is different and it's OK to be different. Everyone learns in different or special ways too. You don't have to be like anyone else, just stay yourself, different from others." All the students could explain its importance, but they were about to experience it! Since they could explain it, I felt confident they could use it.

Life Jackets

I decided that choosing their groups was like insisting everyone wear life jackets—a nonnegotiable item. From previous attempts at group selection, I knew that if I allowed the kids to self-select their groups, they would find groups with their friends, leaving some groups with no leaders. Group work requires members who are leaders and nurturers, organizers, and so on (Cohen 1994). I selected groups of four or five where each group member had a different learning style. They embarked on their five-week journey investigating one of the decades of the 20th century. To make sure the parents knew exactly what was happening, I wrote and sent a newsletter on teamwork (Figure 1 pp. 84–86).

Like Curt directing me in the boat, I advised them as they headed toward the first set of rapids. I recommended that they review their intelligences and assign jobs accordingly. Not every group followed my advice. I hoped that they would correct their mistakes as they went. While they were finding their information in the library and on the computers, groups worked very well together. They knew how to break up the work and get it done.

When it came time for groups to begin putting these projects together, the trip got very interesting. My job was the observer. I started taking copious notes and photos of kids at work. I needed to see if they could use what they had learned all year and apply it to their group.

Each Group Took a Different Speed and a Different Channel Up the River

That was hard for me. In fact, I wasn't sure we were all on the same river. One group drove an air boat and stayed in the shallows the whole time while others were in rafts, continually dodging the other boats. Some groups took the wheel with confidence. Others drifted. Sally's group all worked on their exhibits at home and brought them in as they were done and spent class time sitting in the reading area talking about what still needed to be done.

HISTORY DECADES PROJECT: TEAMWORK AS A LIFE SKILL

Teamwork is a concept usually only taught in a team sport like basketball. The skills we learn by being a part of the team are the ones we need to do our jobs well in the world in which we live. Since not everyone is cut out for sport competitions, all students should learn those skills in the classroom: the ability to depend on each other to succeed, to pass the ball to teammates and to trust them to do the right thing, to set up plays together to score, to cheer each other on, to comfort each other when they blow it, to be able to come back and continue playing after they make a mistake, to control their tempers so they aren't pulled out of the game and penalized, and to listen to the coach and do whatever he or she says even if they disagree.

In almost every job we need to be able to work as team members. The big companies are saying that the people they are hiring right out of school are really lacking in those teamwork skills. Our educational system needs to produce good team members. That is what we've been working toward all year.

TEAMWORK AND LEARNING

I will be evaluating students as team members using this model while we learn history during the fourth quarter. There will be six teams in each class and each team will be responsible for learning everything about a 20th-century decade in order to teach the rest of us. Within each team every person has a job. Just like in basketball, where there are guards, centers, and forwards, in history there will be an Ultimate Master, a Task Master, an Information Master and a Presentation Master. Each student will be in charge of a large portion of the work.

ULTIMATE MASTER:

This is the group member who:

- finds information and takes notes
- makes sure the group meets the deadlines
- hands out and collects papers
- talks with the teacher to get clarifications
- brings teacher directions back to the group
- helps each group member with their individual jobs

INFORMATION/CORRECTNESS MASTER:

This is the group member who:

- finds information and takes notes
- checks everyone's notes before they are turned in
- makes sure each note page has the bibliography info. at the top
- checks each paper for accurate information
- finds reliable/correct sources (at least 20 sources—5 different kinds)
- reports incorrectness to the UM

FIGURE 1   *The Newsletter, p. 1*

TASK MASTER:

This is the group member who

- finds information and takes notes
- explains to the group every day what they have to finish
- keeps every member on track and enthusiastic
- role-models great work habits
- tells frustrations to the UM

PRESENTATION MASTER:

This is the group member who

- finds information and takes notes
- helps the group decide which stations to do
- writes the parts for each group member
- is in charge of practices
- makes sure the presentation is 30–40 min.
- reserves school equipment needed and collects it BEFORE class

TEAMWORK TAKES PRACTICE

Although we've been working on this all year, it is still difficult to work as a team. For students who have never played on a sports team, it's hard to understand how it works. For students who have, it's really difficult not to just take over. Everybody needs a chance to learn to work as a team.

A GOOD COACH

My job as the teacher/coach is to help teams succeed. The teams will be set up according to the students' learning styles. The ideal team would be made up of: a Word or Self Smart learner, a Body Smart learner, a People Smart learner and a Picture or Music Smart learner, so that they can rely on each other's talents. (Those are Learning Styles based on Howard Gardner's Multiple Intelligences. Ask your student more about them.) I will be observing each team member as a coach does. I will be able to give pointers to teams who are having trouble or just need more practice than other teams. Occasionally I might have to pull kids out of the game and make them sit on the sidelines for a while, until they can learn to play as a team. Likewise, when the team keeps making fouls and goofing around, I'll have to call a time out for them for a while. I may also hold teams in at lunch to work on their team strategy. Hopefully, by the end of this project, all students will understand how important teamwork is.

TOGETHER WE CAN!

Sometimes students and parents are concerned about the quality of their team members. If there is one "unskilled" team member, the other members can assist him/her, so that they improve. To my knowledge, there has never been a team member that became worse after playing with an "unskilled" player. It just doesn't work that way. On the other hand, if a team chooses to ignore a willing "unskilled" player and work around him/her, that player starts feeling bad and ultimately works against the team to make sure it doesn't succeed. It isn't fun being on a losing team.

FIGURE 1   *The Newsletter, p. 2*

SCORING

During this project, each team will receive a team score for their final presentation based on a rubric designed by the class. Each team member will also get an individual score for his/her own work on the team based on my observations as a coach as well as the student's self assessment.

TEAMS NEED FANS!

What we need from you, their fans, is to cheer them on, to encourage them to work hard at being good team players, and to do their best. Then, success will be inevitable! I feel strongly about this approach to learning, because I feel like I'm educating not only students, I'm educating citizens of the future.

THE NITTY-GRITTY DETAILS:

Each group will be inviting the class to an exhibition highlighting a decade of the 20th century. This interactive museum is highly recommended as one in which people can experience history—not a boring one in which kids beg their parents to leave. There should be things to do, touch, listen to, and so on. The proprietors in this museum usually dress according to the time period.

1910s—including World War I (April 27th)
1920s—The roaring 20s (April 28th)
1930s—including the Depression (April 29th)
1940s—including WWII (April 30th)
1950s—including the Cold War (May Day)
1960–80s—Years of Protest and Change (May 4th)

FIGURE 1   *The Newsletter, p. 3*

Sara's group reminded me of a raft trip down the Nenana River—a class-five white-water river. The captain of that crew was yelling, "Bail! Bail!" But the crew wasn't listening. They were sinking fast. Sara wasn't using the decision-making methods we had learned. In her self-reflection afterwards she wrote:

> It is difficult learning to work in a group with others that are different from you. It's important, though, because when you get out into the real world you might not be able to work with people just like you. It teaches tolerance and acceptance of new people and new ideas. Sometimes you have to just give up and do your own thing, instead of trying to get people to work and pay attention. You also get to learn things about people that you never knew before, such as that (another student) is a lazy layabout who doesn't think before he does something stupid. I think that I learned to keep my temper better, because I got no where near as mad as I would have liked. I think I learned some important people skills doing this project.

Sara wasn't the only one who learned about working together. The "lazy layabout" wrote in his evaluation: "Working on teams prepare us for later hardships in life." Their group did manage to get most of the important facts of their decade out to the rest of the class, but it wasn't very smooth.

Often groups tried to suck me into taking control. Early in the project one group was having troubles. On April 10th I wrote in my journal: "Aaron just isn't cooperating and listening to the other group members. He seems to enjoy working with Phillip, but works against the group when someone else tells him what to do." The group asked to have a group meeting in the hallway and wanted me to come. I agreed but vowed only to take notes. They addressed the problem well, but they couldn't think of any solutions. I felt like they wanted me to decide, but I wouldn't. I suggested they think about it overnight and come back with possible solutions. They agreed. The next day they decided to vote that group member out. They did it without me.

The one group that really impressed me was Kristy's group. There were only three people in the group instead of the regular four, but they had one member who rarely turned in any work, never participated in classroom discussions, and just wasn't interested much in school. Sharelle and Kristy knew he was a Body Smart learner and started planning on that. In the library the girls would find the pictures they needed and send him to make the photocopies. They assigned him only one section of the presentation on sports and the Olympics—a subject he was very interested in. Afterwards Sam wrote in his self-evaluation,

> All of my group member had different creativity levels Christy made a lot of cool stuff like cars, and trains of wood. Sharelle did a ton of the seting up and planing and work me I got information, and cut all the stuff out for the presentation I think that this was a good and fun set up and it was quite fun to make.

Although Sam might not have learned as much content as the other two, he participated, took orders—a great life skill—and felt positive about his part in this project. Kristy learned a lot, too.

> I learned how to be a leader to others and to except the challenge of helping others. This is important because I learned more about diversity and how to work cooperatively in groups. It was hard at first but then I exepted the fact every one learns in there own ways and work at there own pace.

That was the key to the success of the group. They had learned about diversity and could apply it.

When I put the groups together, I placed at least one leader type in each group. However, in one group that leader wouldn't lead. They were floundering. Apathy had set in. I was determined not to step in. It was very hard for me. I paced through the room and the hallway where all these exhibits were being built. Clipboard in hand, I walked out of the room—if they were paying attention, they would have known I was fuming. I wrote: "This group is crashing and burning." I knew the parents would be upset with poor grades, so that night I decided I had better ask them some questions to see if they had the same perceptions. "Tiffany, what are you doing right now?" "I'm getting a drink." "How's it coming?" "Fine." "Are you going to be done?" "I guess." I moved on to Jason. He didn't give me much more information. I decided they must have it under control somehow.

Suddenly the presentation was at hand. At 7:40 A.M. on Friday, April 24th, before Monday's presentation, Jason's mom came in with Jason in tow. She said she felt that Jason, as the Ultimate Master of this group, didn't have things under control for their presentation. I turned to Jason and said, "Is it under control?" "No." His mom looked at me and said, "What can we do at this late date?" I looked at Jason and said, "I don't know. Jason, what do you still need to do?" "I'm not sure." His mom asked, "Could we get the kids together at my house and work on it?" I turned to Jason and said, "Do you have phone numbers of your group members?" "No." His mom asked Jason, "Could you get them?" He said he would. Since it was now almost time for class, I excused myself and assured both of them it would be alright.

At 7:55 another mom from the same group came to me in a rush without her son and asked to talk with me in the hall. "Cindee, I have no idea if Simon has got his presentation ready for Monday." At this point I said, "Just a minute, I'll get you the phone number of the other mom in that group who's as concerned as you are." She looked relieved and headed out the door just as the tardy bell rang. I was pretty sure they'd get the group together over the weekend, but I had no clue to what was going to happen.

When I got home on Saturday afternoon, I had a message on my answering machine, "Oh, Cindee, we need to talk to you. Please call us as soon as you can." I wasn't happy. In fact I ignored the call all together. She called again on Sunday. "They seemed very confused about this whole project, Cindee. They don't know what they are doing." Calmly I asked if they had their directions there and all their notes. "Yes, but they didn't know how to put it all together." I responded with a simple, "Oh." She went on, "So, we got their poster board, we got the music, they wrote out their speeches, we timed it all out, and it's perfect." I really didn't know what to say. I was attempting to give students control in the classroom and they had missed the whole point. She continued, "I hope you don't mind, we went out and got stuff for root beer floats and french fries. Can the parents serve it?" I was pretty much speechless. I felt frustrated that the parents never saw the big picture. The parents of this group couldn't stand to watch them flounder, so they stepped in and took over the wheel. After thinking about it, I realized the newsletter I sent to parents never talked about the importance of letting the kids be in total control. I'd have to change that for next year.

We made it to shore—not exactly as I had planned, but we were there. The exhibits plastered all the walls of the first floor hallways. Other students and parents came to look at everything: the bomb shelter from the 1950s, the 1930 race track, the models, and the 1920s photo booth among other things. I asked students to respond on a Decades Test about the significance of the trip. Everyone had really insightful things to say, but Bobbi summed it up best:

> It's very important to be able to interact with people who are different from you. Working on teams while in school can help prepare us for the larger world and people who are far different from what we imagined. The people in school are different, but they are linked by the fact that they live in the same place as you, they go to the same school, they're your age, and you know a lot of the same people. When you're grown up (and have possibly moved away) and have a job, you'll meet all kinds of people from different countries who knew different people and went to different schools. Working on these teams will help us to realize how different people can be, how to get along with them, and how to use the talents they and you have so your group can succeed.

Bobbi was able to take what she learned, use it in the group, and then explain why that might be important in her life beyond school. All the other students agreed that this process will help them in their future jobs.

If you go far enough on the Salcha River, you come to the big log jam. The only way to get through is to approach very slowly and with extreme caution. There is a fallen tree across the narrow gap. To make sure there aren't collisions, some boaters turn off their motors and just listen before jumping the log. When my students leave my class and run into log jams, I hope they will at least remember to proceed with extreme caution.

References

ATWELL, N. (1987). *In the Middle.* Portsmouth, NH: Heinemann.

BROOKS, J., and BROOKS, M. (1993). *The Case For Constructivist Classrooms.* Alexandria: VA: ASCD.

CAMPBELL, L. (1997). "How Teachers Interpret MI Theory." *Educational Leadership 55(1)* 14–19.

COHEN, E. (1994). *Designing Groupwork: Strategies for Positive Classroom Management.* Portsmouth, NH: Heinemann.

Fairbanks Daily News Miner. May 13, 1998, p. 1.

GARDNER, H. (1983). *Frames of Mind: The Theory of Multiple Intelligences.* New York: Basic Books.

GIBBS, J. (1995). *Tribes: A New Way of Learning and Being Together.* Sausalito, CA: Center Source Systems.

KOVALIK, S. (1994). *ITI: The Model.* Kent, WA: Books for Educators.

SCHOLTES, P. R. *et al.* (1988). *The Team Handbook.* Madison, WI: Joiner Associates.

SHORT, C., and BURKE, C. (1991). *Creating Curriculum: Teachers and Students as a Community of Learners.* Portsmouth, NH: Heinemann.

6

Mediating Different Worlds: Bicultural Students at School

Ana Inés Heras and Eileen Craviotto

The construction of a bicultural identity is a process both delicate and always in transformation. Often children play a specific role in this process, that of the mediation of different, frequently conflicting, worlds. In one short passage, fourth-grader Miguel makes visible his cultural, national, and linguistic identity. He chose to write in Spanish.

> Cuernavaca es mi pueblo donde nací.
> Vine a los Estados Unidos a encontrar mi nuevo estado.
> Vine muy feliz y sé que me iré sin fin.
> *I was born in the town of Cuernavaca. I came to the United States to find my new state. I came here very happy and yet I know I will leave this place [forever].*

Miguel is a bilingual student at McLaughlin Elementary (a pseudonym) in a midsize Southern California city. McLaughlin Elementary sits on top of a hill that looks north to Pacific ocean and south to the city. The school building, a spacious and well-kept Spanish colonial structure, hosts approximately 580 students, 30 teachers, 30 teacher aides, two secretaries, one nurse, and one principal.

Closed for several years, the school was reopened in 1986, with a principal who was selected to create a school program to respond to the specific needs of the community attending the school (85 percent Mexicano descent and native-Spanish-speaking or bilingual in English and Spanish). The school mission is to provide a homelike learning environment for all children attending the school; to consider that families and teachers alike are the children's educators; and to educate all children without making a distinction because of their socioeconomic or linguistic backgrounds. The principal promoted a participatory decision-making model for faculty and families on issues that affected the school community.

Beginning in 1991, a team of teachers designed a bilingual program to provide education in two languages for all children. At the earliest grades a natural approach is used. Literacy is introduced in the first language, and the second language is used in context to promote language development in a relaxed atmosphere. The expectations for native English and native Spanish speakers are different. Students whose first language is Spanish are formally introduced to English in the second grade, and they are expected to function in English-only literacy instruction by the end of the fourth grade. Students whose first language is English are exposed to the Spanish beginning in kindergarten. Systematic Spanish instruction for them takes place in grades four and five.

It was in this context that we first began our collaboration. In 1992 Ana was a Ph.D. candidate and Eileen was a bilingual teacher. Although we were introduced to each other as part of a larger team conducting classroom research, our focus became directed at exploring students' language use in the classroom context. Soon, we were able to document the specific ways in which language and culture are intimately related, the ways in which opportunities for first- and second-language development through the direct use of students' cultural resources can be provided in the classroom context.

In 1995, Ana started teaching and doing research working in the Chicano Studies Department at the University of California, Santa Barbara. We continued our partnership so that we could support one another in critical dialogue about pedagogy and classroom practice; we also wanted to promote collaboration across the university and the fourth grade to support meaningful academic and social connections for our students.

Ladson-Billings (1995, 1998) has guided our work. She has written about the importance of using a model of culturally relevant pedagogy that affirms students' cultural and linguistic identity and promotes student achievement and a critical understanding of the world. There are three aspects to Ladson-Billings' approach.

1. a focus on academic achievement

2. a focus on the students' cultural competence

3. a focus on developing sociopolitical consciousness

As Ladson-Billings puts it: "It is not enough to individually be an academic achiever and be culturally competent, you also have to have a greater sense of community and be in a position to critique your own education" to understand how social forces shape the experiences of others differently (Ladson-Billings 1998, p. 62). As we continued our partnership for a number of academic years we developed a university–fourth-grade instructional collaboration. Concretely, over the years 1992 to 1998, we developed several activities where our students interacted with each other to explore issues addressed in their curricula, shared their learning experiences, and used different forms of literacy to do so (oral, aural, written, visual, and so on.).

In 1995, we applied for and received a Community as a Classroom Grant from our County Education Office. We proposed that we would develop a curricular experience focusing on literacy and social studies through the use of oral history. Thus, oral history could foster students' connections with their home-cultural resources through using knowledge in their families. We emphasized the use of oral communication with both fourth graders and undergraduate university students as a way to understand and reflect upon their positions in their families, their communities, and the school.

We educated the undergraduates in issues of oral history, classroom ethnography, and fourth-grade curricular design. We purchased twenty-five tape recorders and audiotapes as tools for both the fourth graders and the university students. We designed several activities to accomplish our goal. The activities included:

1. Weekly visits by the undergraduate students to the fourth grade classroom (an average of five students per week visited the classroom for a whole academic year)

2. Three annual visits by the fourth graders to the UCSB campus (one to include families for an undergraduate presentation on educational organizations that support underrepresented students)

3. Attendance by the undergraduate students at Eileen's Family Math Nights every eight weeks

4. More recently we have begun to match the themes addressed by both the fourth-grade social studies curriculum and the curriculum for Chicano Studies in the classes I teach.

For example, in the winter of 1998, we asked our students to explore similar issues on a parallel schedule for one quarter, those related to prejudice, discrimination, and access to educational opportunities for different social and ethnic groups in the United States.

Over the years we have discovered that an important part of bringing the students' cultural and linguistic resources into the classroom lies in the micro-interactions between classroom participants, the everyday dialogues between the students and teachers, and between students and students (Cummins 1995, Heras 1995). We have observed that through dialogue and discussion, students developed several skills:

- the ability to reflect on their personal experience as it relates to that of others, or to the issue under study
- the ability to dialogue and push critical questioning and curiosity to the limit
- the ability to pose their thoughts orally and use the languages of several disciplines to do so
- the capacity to use multiple forms of literacy (aural, oral, written, and visual) to engage in dialogue.

In the fourth-grade classroom, there are multiple opportunities for micro-interactions. Dialogue takes place in several different formats: whole-class space (all students and the teacher dialoguing about issues under study); peer space in small groups; and pairs. The classroom is set up as an open space where visitors come regularly. Mixed groups or pairs of undergraduates and fourth graders are common.

Eileen works to foster a sense of inquiry through the use of multiple texts in their classroom; through seeing family knowledge as relevant text; and through the investigation of literary resources in Spanish and English. Students in her class have several opportunities to investigate their cultural and familial backgrounds in the context of the work done at school.

For example, in the fall quarter of 1995, several activities fostered students' inquiry on their backgrounds:

Interviewing family members on what respect means to them	September 1995
Reflecting on family geographical origins by identifying where their families come from on a map	September 1995
Interviewing family members on the origin of their names	October 1995
Interviewing family members on traditions around the Day of the Dead and Halloween	October 1995
Reflecting on best and worst school experiences	November 1995
Reflecting on people or places they missed	September through December 1995

The interviews and reflections were collected through oral and written means; when a piece of oral history was collected the fourth graders were asked to bring it to class to use it as part of their learning experience in language arts and social studies.

Miguel wrote about his identity as a recent immigrant Mexicano child in a letter to his teacher at the beginning of the year in a piece entitled "Mi Primer Viaje" (My First Trip)[1]:

> La primera vez que vine a los Estados Unidos fue para [b]enir a los quin[s]e años de mi prima y después de eso fui a México y después me [b]ine a vivir aquí.
>
> *The first time we came to the United States was when we came to celebrate my cousin's fifteenth birthday and then we went back to México and then we came back again to live here.*

Miguel's writing in class often revealed memories of his life in the other side of the border. (Translated from Spanish) "When we used to live in Mexico, we used to play with water balloons after school, every Friday." Miguel provided other cultural pieces of information through his writing as well. He wrote down a rhyme he remembered from his hometown.

> 'pa[c]é por tu ventana
> me tiraste con un limon
> la cascara cayo al suelo
> y el jugito en mi corazon.
> *I was walking down your street and you threw a lemon at me; the peel (skin) of the lemon dropped on the floor and the juice poured into my heart.*

One day, in response to a piece of literature they were reading and discussing, Eileen asked the students to reflect on a place or person the children had missed, Miguel wrote in Spanish that he missed "his Mexico and his dog named Pipucho."

Miguel's choice of content and of Spanish as his main language of expression demonstrate the fact that he saw himself as a Mexican immigrant child, who was happy to be here and in search of what he called his "new state." Miguel also identified himself as a bicultural and bilingual child, as attested by his conversations, his writing, and observations of his interactions. At the end of the fall quarter, Miguel's class

---

1 [ ] around letters or words indicates nonconventional spelling.

visited the university campus and shared their writing with Ana's undergraduate students. Each undergraduate was paired up with a fourth grader. The undergraduates taped one-hour interviews with the younger students. They followed up with a written account of their perspective on the fourth-graders' learning experiences. In his interview with Malín Ramírez, Miguel made explicit how he saw the connections between immigration, prejudice, and the hypocrisy associated with the motto "America, the land of freedom." Through oral sources (interviews with family members) and textual resources (newspaper clips), he learned about facts and he provided his views on the facts he collected through his research. Speaking in English, Miguel told Malín that "[Governor Pete] Wilson was the worst gringo of all because he wanted to get rid of all the Mexicans." Miguel further elaborated on his topic in his written text. His message said that "Wilson wanted Blacks and Mexicanos out of the country and that, therefore, this place could not be considered the land of freedom."

Malín took the initiative to visit Miguel at school twice during the fall quarter. In a paper entitled "Empowering the Youth of Aztlán: An Analysis of the Educational Experience of Miguel," Malín reflected on the issues posed by Miguel. Guided by previous course work in Chicano studies, Malín identified Miguel's struggle with his bicultural and bilingual identity and the influences of larger societal issues on his everyday experiences. Miguel did not use the terms bilingual, bicultural identity, or larger societal issues. Malín presented these issues as "cultural identity; bilingual/bicultural education; strong sense of self when immigrating to the United States." She used vocabulary and concepts learned in the Chicano Studies class Ana was teaching that quarter. In her final paper for the class, Malín describes Miguel's experience as one in which his strong sense of self had helped him navigate the state of border-crossing and borderland. Malín was impressed by the fact that Miguel, at such an early age, was able to reflect on these issues; she also stated that these issues had been a part of her own experience while growing up.

As part of our collaboration, Ana visited Eileen's classroom at least once a week. During these visits she assumed the dual role of researcher and educator, documenting the work the bilingual fourth-grade classroom, on the one hand, and teaching and learning with and from the children, their families, and their teacher, on the other hand. We collaborated on the Family Math Nights and used the parent workshops as opportunities to get to hear the families' perspectives on different issues. Additionally, Ana conducted interviews with a small group of students every two weeks, during lunch time, to understand the schooling experience from their perspective. Ana utilized field notes to supplement the tape-recorded interviews and to record her own reflections:

Miguel shows that his understanding of prejudice and immigration is informed by his membership in the Mexicano community. He is aware that part of the reason his family immigrated, according to his dad, was because his family was looking forward to having access to a different kind of education, and to becoming bilingual in English and Spanish. He perceives this process as a complex issue.

Ana's reflections are supported through interviews with Miguel. In one interview, Miguel describes an incident at the border when U.S. border patrol agents chased and hit Mexican immigrants.

> *Miguel:* You know that person that was in the car and they beat him
> *Ana:* Aha
> *Miguel:* So I put how can they say this place is liberty they should take off that Statue of Liberty
> *Ana:* Mhm
> *Miguel:* Mhm
> *Ana:* Because why
> *Miguel:* Because they are not treating us like liberty

Miguel elaborates on this topic in a written piece that he entitled "Cómo Agarran el Pan del Día" (How Immigrants Get Their Daily Bread).

> We, immigrants do whatever we can in order to work so we can get food. We work in the sewing [industry] and we are also selling [things] on the street. We do not do any harm to other people and yet when we are on the streets, selling things, the police comes and they get what we have earned, even if that is our money to buy food.

As part of the curricular opportunities provided by Eileen, late each school year she asks students to choose topics of self-interest in order to conduct mini–research projects. Many students are interested in several topics, but choose to research only one. What was distinctive about Miguel, as compared to other students in his class, was that he was interested in several topics and he pursued research in all of them.

Originally, Miguel had chosen to study UFOs, Nazis, and immigration. During the inquiry process, Miguel decided not to explore UFOs but to concentrate on immigration, Nazism, and the formation and history of the KKK. Miguel explained his choice to further explore the issue of immigration "because half of my family is composed of immigrants." Miguel continually wrote notes and reflected on his research topics.

One day Eileen asked her students to reflect on an issue that was problematic for the society at large, and on possible contributions they could make to help solve this problem. Miguel had been watching the news on incidents taking place at the border-crossing. It had been reported in the news that week that immigration officers had chased a truck of Mexican immigrants and had beaten a woman after the chase. Miguel wrote in both Spanish and English.

> Nuestro problema más grande es la guerra. Yo creo que podría ser parte de la solución si yo le dijera a la policía que no peguen a la gente, que nada más los arrestaran. Our biggest problem is the war. I think I can help be a part of the solution by telling the police not to hit people—just arrest people.

It is interesting that Miguel chooses the word *war* in English. *Guerra* in the Spanish can mean war. Yet it is commonly used to refer to "daily struggle" in the Mexicano/Chicano community. Miguel's use of *guerra* portrays his understanding of the daily struggles faced by immigrants, and the obstacles encountered when facing police violence. Continual reflection is even evident in Miguel's written brainstorm of questions about the KKK:

> who to interview: Ana, WWW [the World Wide Web], and Ms. D. [another teacher]
>
> ¿Qué significa la cruz quemada? [What does the burning cross symbolize?]
>
> ¿Porqué usan el uniforme blanco? [Why do they use a white uniform?]
>
> ¿Cómo empezó el grupo KKK? [How did the KKK get started?]
>
> ¿Tendrán contacto con los Nazis? [Did they have contact with the Nazis?]
>
> ¿En qué partes hay KKK? [Where is the KKK found?]

¿Ha sentido racismo? [Does racism make sense?]

¿Ha sentido prejuicio? [Does prejudice make sense?]

In April, Miguel wrote a letter to Ana.

Querida Ana,
    Ana me gustaría que vinieras a jugar con nosotros y que si me podrías ayudar en mi reporte de inmigración.
    Dear Ana, Ana I would like you to come and play with us and also I would like to ask you if you can help with my report on immigration.

Ana responded with a note, also in Spanish, that she had also enjoyed talking with him and hearing about what he is learning in class, and about the book they were reading in class. She stated that she'd visit his classroom soon to help him out with his immigration report and that she would look up some material for him at the library. On Ana's next visit she worked with Miguel. Ana reflects in her field notes:

Miguel and I sat down to talk about Miguel's report. I had taken home Miguel's report and read it over the weekend. I came into the class to help Miguel and other children organize the information they were collecting for their reports. Miguel and I sat down mostly to organize the information; I had already talked with him about the content of his report. I had discussed with him the fact that he showed a very special awareness on this topic. Miguel had asked me to provide him with a notebook where he could write a book on the experience of being an immigrant, and I had done so (I bought a spiral notebook like the ones I used to write down my notes while visiting his classroom).
    During our interview, Miguel read out loud the pieces he had written on immigration, showed me the interview notes he had taken while talking with his aunt about her immigration experience, and worked with me on organizing the way the final product (a poster on immigration) would look like. We discussed his ideas and drafted a possible plan to continue and finish his project.

To help them carry out and complete their research projects, Eileen's students were once again paired up with Ana's students. The undergraduates helped the fourth graders do research at the university library on their self-selected topic. Students visited campus during the month of May. Following the visit, the fourth graders sent letters to their university buddies. This time, Miguel's undergraduate buddy was Heather Ligtenberg. Miguel wrote his letter to Heather in both English and Spanish, knowing that Heather's first language is English and that she wanted to learn more Spanish:

> Dear Heather,
> Thank you for everything you did for me. And for helping me with my report. Also, thank you because you spent $5 for my copies. We hope you have the opportunity to see the video of [immigracion]. If you can rent it, we would like to see it. Thank you for everything. After we ate we went to the Beach. Miguel [a drawing of a computer is on the page]

Heather answered:

> Dear Miguel,
> Thank you so much for the thoughtful thank you letter. You were a pleasure to help in the library. You are a very intelligent student, and you know a lot about immigration and Governor Wilson. I hope we found enough information about immigration to help you with your research paper. I believe your research topic is a good topic and you will learn a lot from it. After I left the library I went to my Spanish class. I'm sorry I have not written your letter in Spanish but I am not yet good enough in Spanish to write you a letter in it. Thank you again and have a wonderful summer.
> Sincerely, Heather Ligtenberg

In this letter exchange, it is interesting to notice that Miguel did indeed exercise his bilingual skills as a way to ensure communication with his buddy, and as a way to assert his bilingual identity. However, Heather chose to write only in English, and to comment that her Spanish was not good enough to write back in that language. When we asked the undergraduates to reflect on their learning experience with the fourth graders, Heather said that she was impressed by Miguel's knowledge of the subject and that she was also curious to know whether Miguel had formed his opinions on Governor Wilson at school or at home.

Miguel formed his opinions on the subject of immigration and discrimination of immigrants both at school and at home and as a member of the larger immigrant Mexicano community. Miguel, supported by his teacher, collected information from several sources in the context of this school assignment. When he researched the financial aspects associated with immigration, Eileen helped him locate one of his classmate's mothers as a resource. Miguel also interviewed his family members, took notes (in his small spiral notebook) on all his interviews, and used these pieces of information to write his report.

The project enabled him to reflect on his family's perspective on issues related to their rights, such as education and liberty. It is possible that for Miguel, these issues were central to his experience, and were not seen as schoolwork, but as information he was interested in gathering. It was important that school provided him with the opportunity. Children like Miguel become aware of the circumstances surrounding their lives at a young age; they also become culture brokers for their families in the processes of making sense of who they are, what their rights are, and how to "make it" on this side of the border. Miguel's awareness of policies, politics, and practices against working-class immigration is an example of the importance that these issues have on immigrant children's everyday lives.

Through our analysis of six years of fourth-grade classroom data collected, we have found six key characteristics of curriculum and classroom practices:

1. Families are seen as resources for knowledge generation.

2. Multicultural literature is used as a resource for understanding different perspectives.

3. Students are regarded as active knowledge generators.

4. Classroom dialogue is a fundamental aspect of classroom discourse.

5. The classroom is an inviting space for exploration, learning, and dialogue.

6. Languages are used as resources for communicating and learning—not just Spanish and English but also the languages associated with academic disciplines, such as the discourse practices associated with social studies, maths, language arts, science, and arts education.

An emergent theme identified throughout our collaboration was that of children as cultural mediators. Thus it is important to consider the formation of bicultural identity as a process where both conflict and harmony co-occur, and are in constant interaction. In acting as mediators, children from borderland families serve as links between their communities of origin—ethnic communities, families, peer groups—and larger social contexts or institutions in the "host" society. Miguel is an example of a student who has started to integrate different aspects into his identity, those associated with his active membership to the Mexicano, working–class, immigrant community, and those associated with his access to becoming bilingual and bicultural in his "new state." Miguel's awareness of his status as an immigrant and as a member of the working–class Mexicano community points to the obligation we have, as educators, to make every effort possible to understand children's everyday lives.

Reference

LADSON-BILLINGS, G. (1994). *The Dream Keepers: Successful Teachers of African American Children*. San Francisco, CA: Jossey-Bass.

7 Literacy Liberation with Trade Books in Social Studies

Thomas A. Caron

I n children's earliest years, the development of competence in accessing the literate world really represents the freedom to take control of one's own life. Children developing literacy proficiency are engaging in a process of learning about themselves and their worlds through what is read. During later elementary years, as more emphasis is placed on "reading to learn," literacy itself absorbs the deeper aroma of learning in subject areas from elementary to middle school. The taste and turn of each phrase are enhanced with purpose and association as content learning provides meaning for what is read much as salsa adds flavor to meat. Yet the process of reading to learn is still as much one of learning to read as it is gaining knowledge.

Most reading researchers agree that learning through reading must involve learning to "use" reading in various and changing ways, trimming and training the mind's eye to "see through" words and phrases and sentences, informing a mind actively constructing knowledge (Gambrell *et al.* 1999). The reading process—that is, "making sense of print" (Goodman 1996)—is identical from the earliest emergent phases of reading through the adult years (Smith 1978).

As children progress through elementary school, the greater demands on "content" learning go hand in hand with strategies for "reading to learn" as well as "learning to read." Many students, faced with the need to understand material in print, have not yet learned to read for information and have trouble applying successful reading strategies for content learning. Faced with often densely or poorly written textbooks, many of our students tune out reading for information and risk not learning the critical thinking and vocabulary strategies that will be so important to them in the future.

Some educators, under the daily pressures of curriculum and testing, are tempted to package knowledge and concepts so that children can remember "facts" as needed and have a chance to score well on state and district reading tests. In such a package, vocabulary development is reduced to rote memorization of the spellings and definitions of finite lists of words.

Yet in our world just years from now these very children will need to navigate independently in a growing and changing world of information exchange with a quick and critical eye, not regurgitate facts and often outdated opinions. Environments rich with literature and challenge, filled with insights and questions, flush with contrasts and comparisons are what these children need in preparation. Critical thinking and learning thrive where there is a wealth of literature and talk, emotional and cognitive response. Vitality and engagement in a milieu rich with literature and thought are what is needed to provide the necessary basics for children learning the strategic thinking needed in the futures they will live, not the pasts that we imagine for them.

Authentic, sustained engagement with children's literature entices children into active literacy. We are obligated in schools to provide this context for engaged and meaningful learning. This change may affect the rest of our students' lives. Yet the value and benefit is still challenged by some. The challenge is as strong now as it has been at any time in modern education.

Why do interest, motivation, yes, even pleasure in reading, leave some experienced teachers thinking no "real" work is going on, no important learning occurring? And, on the flip side of that coin, when children show us that some methods simply won't "work" for them, how can we adhere to those same approaches and methods, ignoring the need for change?

Even the so-called "Reading Excellence Act" (h.r. 2614), passed by the 105th Congress, provides narrow and supposedly definitive answers in a field where acrimonious debate continues to rage about the actual questions. Our representatives in government, in their haste to do good, have rushed past reading theory toward supposedly clear, authoritative answers with a simplicity more suited to single-digit arithmetic than thoughtful planning. Though the issues that divide research and theory in literacy learning may never be resolved, they clearly demonstrate the complexity of the field. Our elected leaders now spurn debates and reason in favor of simplistic solutions. The "information highway" within which we live is really an ocean from which legislators, lobbyists, and extremists find useful islands to develop, intent as prostitutes to "turn a trick," and equally as thorough.

Even in the face of peer challenges and legislated limitations, even under pressure to raise test scores at any cost, many brave educators continue to meet the needs of their students. Such educators maintain personal theories of literacy learning.

They are familiar with an abundance of reports and suggestions for using literature in social studies published in reading as well as social studies journals (Roser *et al.*1997). The high student interest encouraged by this approach is cited in many articles and books.[1]

This chapter describes the journey of one such teacher and the second, third, and fourth graders in a cross-grade, West Virginia classroom who engage in significant learning in literacy and social studies using trade books.

West Virginia Studies Using Literature

The teacher was a participant in a West Virginia project designed to explore the benefits of using children's responses to literature in literacy-rich environments for children studying social studies. We chose to explore the impact of using meaningful activities with relevant books instead of traditional textbooks to support student learning in social studies and literacy.

Following a thorough search, the teacher selected three relevant books: *The Golden Horseshoe*, a story of time travel through West Virginia history, by Frances Gunter; *Shiloh*, a "boy and his dog" story set in contemporary West Virginia, by Phyllis Naylor; and *When I Was Young in the Mountains*, a simple story of an Appalachian childhood, by Cynthia Rylant.

The Golden Horseshoe was chosen as a read-aloud. It is a story about children, visiting family in West Virginia, who are magically transported through time to various historical moments in the state's history, including the Mound Builders (Native American history), Blennerhassett Island (where former Vice President Aaron Burr plotted to create a western "separate country"), Harper's Ferry (where John Brown captured the arsenal, a crime for which he was later tried and hung), the Hatfield-McCoy feud, and the Mine Wars

---

1 (Holmes and Ammon 1985; McClure and Zitlow 1991). Methods, materials, units, and techniques are outlined and described in other sources (Perez-Stable and Cordier 1994; Kovalik 1993; Norton 1990; Rasinski and Padak 1990). Zarnowski (1990) describes in some detail a combined reading/writing approach to literacy learning using biographies. Zarnowski and Gallagher (Eds. 1993) describe books and their various uses in social studies teaching.

(which led to labor unions). The reader learns facts related to these historic moments through the time travels of the children in the story, rather than through the more formal and abstract structure of a textbook.

The Golden Horseshoe

Twice each day, once in the morning and once in the afternoon, part of *The Golden Horseshoe,* was read aloud to the class. Discussions that followed the readings often included style and imagery, how Gunter wrote descriptions that stimulated readers to "picture" the scene in their heads. To increase understanding about these elements, students were asked to draw the scenes of a coal camp and a company store based on the author's descriptive writing, and to discuss what these must have been like in the past. Further examination of the relationship between descriptive text and imagery came when students wrote their own descriptive paragraphs about something familiar to them. They then shared these paragraphs with another student and the second student drew an illustration of what was described. The students then wrote a story during writers' workshop using the picture as a stimulus. These back-and forth-experiences with writing and imagery allowed students to become familiar with the relationships between the author's craft of descriptive writing and a reader's generation of images in the mind's eye.

Other discussions included words unknown to some or all the students. The teacher usually brought up words, reread the sentence(s), and opened up discussion about the surrounding context. This process serves a twofold purpose. It enables the students to discover word meanings for themselves, supports deeper learning, and models effective nonfiction reading strategies. No one doubts the importance of vocabulary knowledge and development in supporting readers' growing understandings of literacy as well as social studies concepts. The richer the language used, the deeper can be comprehension and understanding in reading (Hanson and Pearson 1983).

Hands-on experiences enriched the learning experience for all the children. During this time the class took a field trip to Cass, a historical mountain railroad. They also watched movies related to the concepts in the books, including *Hatfields and McCoys, Matewan,* and *Blue and Gray.*

Following the special activities, the teacher introduced a Venn diagram to compare a coal camp and a logging camp. Student discussion followed about why timber was more important than coal to our county even though coal mining is a major industry in West Virginia. Students wrote journal entries following their discussions.

Readers' and Writers' Workshop Block

The older group of students, nine and ten year olds, in the cross grade classroom, read *Shiloh*. In addition to learning the social studies concepts, the teacher's goal for these students was to encourage development of critical thinking. The teacher utilized a variety of reader response techniques—some known to the children from prior studies, others newly introduced. Techniques included literature discussion, ReQuest, Directed Reading Thinking Activities (DRTA), DRA, Predict/Confirm/Change, self-dialogue in journal, and rewrite as a play. Prior to reading, students made mini-books, called "Our *Shiloh* Journal," with their own cover designs. They each wrote a prediction on the first page.

As a structure for the literature study, the teacher chose a list of vocabulary words prior to reading. Most words were known by the group. However, no student knew the complete list prior to reading. The teacher wanted the word study to remain in context. As the kids encountered the words in their reading, they noted the page number where each appeared. Following each chapter, students' discussion about each chapter began by noting where each word was found and the meaning of each based on the context clues. Vocabulary words were kept in a card holder in the back of the *Shiloh* journal.

The younger group, the seven and eight year olds, read *When I Was Young in the Mountains* as a source of historical information and as an example of how a biographical book can be a source of information. Prior to reading, they too made a journal with an illustrated cover. Students were also given a list of words to focus on as they read. These words were discussed as they appeared in the text, providing a meaningful context in which students learned and studied the uses of important vocabulary in the story. After their discussions, word cards were made and placed in the back of their journals. This "word bank" collection of new words learned was available for students to use as a vocabulary resource in their writing

As another prereading activity, the teacher copied illustrations from the book and gave each student a picture to describe orally. Students were also asked to relate their picture to the title. Then students were asked to position themselves around the table so that they were in the order they thought the pictures occurred in the story. As the story was read to them, students moved as needed, involving them in listening to understand events in the story sufficiently to recognize and place each picture in order.

At the next session students were given pages of text from the book. Asked to read their page aloud each student had opportunity to practice fluency as they read the familiar text. Once again, students were asked to position themselves around the table in the order of the story. Students listened as the story was read again and changed positions as needed. After that, they discussed why they'd selected the order they had, an opportunity for students to share their understanding of events in the story.

In the next session students were asked to rewrite the book in their own contexts. After class discussion of the story, which portrays and uses artifacts and circumstances of "life in the mountains" of West Virginia, students rewrote the book one page at a time. Students dictated their part of the book to the teacher and then illustrated their pages. This combination of illustrations and story enabled students to develop an understanding of the relationship between story and imagery. Without knowing it, these youngsters were learning to read like writers, and to write like readers!

During the rewriting process children came to understand more clearly how events in the story are tied to historical reality. They developed this understanding further as they wrote stories reflecting their own lives and experience. For example, in reading about food that was eaten and cooked in West Virginia country homes when Rylant was a young girl, students began to explore what foods would be discussed if the story had been written today. As alternatives such as "chicken nuggets" and "big hamburgers" are generated, it is evident that not only are the foods selected different, they also represent a different culture. Foods change and also the cultures in which they are cooked and eaten are changing. There is a vast cultural distance between sitting down to a home-cooked meal and fast food. Yet these are cultural differences that may not truly "hit home" until children begin to ask "What are my favorite things to eat?" as part of a literature response activity. The cultural learning from this seemingly simple experience is far reaching indeed.

Another activity that led to surprising learning was a seemingly simple comparison of the movie with a book. Students compared *Shiloh* in book and movie form. In relation to the Native American elements of West Virginia history, some students read *The Indian in the Cupboard*. They compared it to the popular movie of Lynn Reid Bank's book. The students noticed that the book is set in England while the movie of the book is actually set in the United States. This affects the vocabulary as well as specific experiences and leads to natural differences. In addition to the cultural differences children explored, such as skateboarding in the movie, which does not happen in the book, there are the differences probably due to movie versus book "culture" that children immediately pick up on. A dominant theme in student discussions of the book was Banks' in-depth exploration of "personal responsibility" and "historical integrity." These themes are virtually absent from the movie themes. Children noted that the movie highlights violence and ignores cultural integrity to follow its theme. What is even more amazing is the ease with which the kids go beyond merely comparing the two media and discuss the cultural differences seen in the comparison of book to movie.

Evaluation of Progress and Performance

Several forms of assessment were used throughout this work using literature: anecdotal records, portfolios, running records, observations, conferences, and student written products. Clearly throughout this project students had opportunities to demonstrate their learning in both social studies and literacy in a variety of ways.

The school does not assign grades, or tests. Classes are multigrade and students' progress is based on where they are when school starts and where they are at specific times throughout the year. Instead of report cards with grades, students take home a checklist and narrative that focuses on six domains: social studies, scientific thinking, mathematical thinking, language arts, and physical development. A system called "Work Sampling" is used to track performance. Progress is very much based on authentic assessment of all kinds including frequent teacher-student conferences. This teacher's consistently excellent rapport with all her students enables and is enabled by the ongoing assessment process.

While the school community places greater value on the authentic assessment, the state still has its testing requirement: the Stanford 9. A review of the standardized test scores demonstrates the literacy development for students in the project school. The results of the end of the year Stanford 9 multistate testing are significant. The school's scores resulted in 56 percent in the top two quartiles.[2] The third-grade class

---

2 Since this is a cross-grade grouping, the grade "levels" refer to the "assigned" grade for each child.

scored the highest in the county (54 percent). The fourth-grade class was five points below the third grade (49 percent). This school is one of only two county schools fully accredited based on test scores.

Conclusions

Test results and, more important, teacher assessments, clearly show the literacy growth through students' progress. Analysis of literature response products created by these children demonstrates growth in their knowledge and understanding of West Virginia and social studies concepts and objectives for learning. The teacher participating in this project consistently affirms that the performance of these children meets the state requirements for learning in social studies as well as literacy through using these methods. At the same time these learning experiences provide children with an opportunity for in-depth learning and critical thinking about the topics that relate to their experience in life and culture. In addition, these children demonstrate a high degree of self-motivation for reading and learning that will support their continued growth through school and life.

Experimental

Books in use in the work include such texts as:

ANDRE, R., S. COHEN, and W. WINTZ (1995) *Bullets & Steel: The Fight for the Great Kanawha Valley 1861–1865*. Charleston, WV: Pictorial Histories Publishing Company, Inc.

KEATS, E. J. (1973) *John Henry*. New York: Knopf.

LESTER, J. (1993) *John Henry* (including an introduction on "historicity") New York: Dial Books for Young Readers.

LOEWEN, J. (1995). *Lies my teacher told me: Everything Your American History Textbook Got Wrong*. New York, NY: New Press.

MUSICK, R. (1965). *The Telltale Lilac Bush and Other West Virginia Ghost Tales*. Lexington, KY: University Press of Kentucky

RICE, O. (1985) *A History of West Virginia*. Lexington, KY: University Press of Kentucky.

WILLIAMS, J. A. (1993). *West Virginia: A History For Beginners*. Charleston: Appalachian Editions

and books by West Virginia writers, Burnside, Harshman, Ryan, Rylant, and Smucker.

References

EEDS, M., and WELLS, D. (1991). Talking, Thinking, and Co-operative Learning: Lessons Learned from Listening to Children Talk about Books. *Social Education* 55, 134-7.

FOUNTAS, I. C. and PINNELL, G. S. (1997). *Guided Reading: Good First Teaching for All Children.* Portsmouth, NH: Heinemann

GAMBRELL, L., MORROW, L. M., NEUMAN, S., and PRESSLEY, M. (1999). *Best Practices in Literacy Intstruction.* NY: Guilford Press.

GOODMAN, K. (1996). *On Reading: A Common-Sense Look at The Nature of Language and the Science of Reading.* Portsmouth, NH: Heinemann.

HANSEN, J., and PEARSON, P. D. (1983). An instructional study: Improving the inferential comprehension of fourth grade good and poor readers. *Journal of Educational Psychology,* 75, 821–829.

HOLMES, B. C., and AMMON, R. I. (1985). "Teaching Content with Trade Books: A Strategy." *Childhood Education 61,* 366–70.

KOVALIK, S. (1993). *ITI: The Model: Integrated Thematic Instruction.* Oak Creek, AZ: Books for Educators.

MCCLURE, A., and ZITLOW, C. (1991). "Not Just the Facts. *Language Arts 68,* 27–33.

MCGOWAN, T. M., ERICKSON, L., and NEUFELD, J. (1996). "With Reason and Rhetoric: Building the Case for the Literature–Social Studies Connection." *Social Education 60(4),* 203–7.

MCGOWAN, T. M., and SUTTON, A. M. (1988). "Exploring a Persistent Association: Trade Books and Social Studies Teaching." *Journal of Social Studies Research* 12(1), 8–16.

NORTON, D. E. (1990). "Teaching Multicultural Literature in the Reading Curriculum." *The Reading Teacher, 44(1),* 28–40.

PEREZ-STABLE, M., and CORDIER, M. (1994). *Understanding American History through Children's Literature: Instructional Units and Activities K-8.* Phoenix, AZ: Oryz Press.

RASINSKI, T., and PADAK, N. (1990). "Multicultural Learning through Children's Literature." *Language Arts 67,* 576–80.

ROSER, N. *et al.* (1997) "What I Wanna Know Is: Why Did Sam Huston's Mom Name Him After a City?" NRC Yearbook.

RUDDELL, M. R., and RUDDELL, R. (1997), *Teaching Content Reading and Writing* (2nd Ed.). New York: John Wiley and Sons.

SMITH, F. (1978). *Understanding Reading: A Psycholinguistic Analysis of Reading and Learning to Read.* Hillsdale, NJ: Lawrence Erlbaum.

WALKER, B. J. (1988), in *The Diagnostic Teaching of Reading, Techniques for Instruction and Assessment.* Upper Saddle River, NJ: Prentice Hall

ZARNOWSKI, M. (1990). *"Learning about Biographies: A Reading-Writing Approach for Children."* Urbana IL: NCTE

ZARNOWSKI, M., and GALLAGHER, A. (Eds.) (1993). *Children's Literature and Social Studies: Selecting and Using Notable Books in the Classroom.* Dubuque, IA: Kendall/Hunt.

8

"We've Never Read Any Book About Laos":

Culturally Relevant Books in Literature Study Circles

Katharine Davies Samway

O ne day, I was a member of a literature study circle involving five Laotian boys and their teacher, Gail Whang. We had just embarked on an open-ended discussion about *Children of the River* (Crew 1989), the story of a Cambodian teenager who flees her homeland during the war, endures unbearable hardships, and eventually relocates to Oregon. In Oregon, she encounters racial prejudice on the part of both European Americans and her Cambodian family members, cultural dissonance, and love with the star of the high school football team. One of the boys, Eata, opened the conversation with some recommendations as to who should read the book, referring to both immigrants/refugees, and sponsors:

> I would recommend it to people who just came from (to) America like for only two year. No, I mean like a sponsor. Read it to see how they really feel.

The other students did not respond to Eata's comment, so after a short conversation in which students talked about incidents in the book that had caught their attention, Gail returned to Eata's initial comments in order to better understand his point[1]:

> *Gail:* What did you mean at the beginning when you said you'd recommend this book to sponsors?
> *Eata:* Because some sponsor really wouldn't know how to feel.
> *Gail:* Um. So you thought this book really lets you know how somebody who just came to this country feels.

---

1 Discussions such as these are hard to put into print. In print the dialogue loses the talking over each other that is natural in conversations.

In his reading journal, Eata had also reflected on the potential usefulness of the book to newcomers to the United States, including himself:

> A book that help my life was Children of the River. If you just came to America and know how to read, this book might help you think what it's like in coming to America when your from another country. Your life might not be the same as in Children of the River, but it will help you understand a little more about America and what it might be like when your from another country.

Although the book was about a Cambodian refugee, it had offered Eata the opportunity to access his family's experiences as a refugee.

Students in Gail's class frequently commented on the value of *Children of the River*, particularly for those who were themselves immigrants or refugees, as well as those interested in knowing more about the experiences of immigrants and refugees. At another time, Sung, also a refugee, recommended *Children of the River* for both groups of people:

> [I would recommend this book] to the people that would like to learn about how people escape from there country. And to the people that had to leave there country because of war.

In these book recommendations, Eata and Sung both reveal their expertise in understanding how different a refugee or immigrant experience is from a more mainstream life experience in the United States . . . and how books can help bridge these distinct and often very different experiences.

As the literature study circle discussion continued, it became very clear to Gail and me that *Children of the River* had resonated with these Laotian boys in ways that were markedly different from their reactions to other books that they had read and enjoyed. It wasn't until later in the conversation, when San Ching spoke, that we came to understand exactly what the underlying issue was, the importance of seeing oneself, one's life experiences, and/or one's own part of the world in books, as this part of the discussion illustrates:

> *San Ching:* This is the only Asian book I've read.
> *Nopphavanh:* Mines too.
> *Chansamone:* Mine too.
> *Gail:* Really? This is the first book about Asians that you've read?

Chansamone: There's no book about Laos.

Gail: So why did that make it special?

Eata: Oh, oh, what about *Journey Home*? From last year.

San Ching: Oh, yeah.

Gail: Did you read that? That's about a Japanese-American.

Eata: Plus, what's that? *Jar.*

Chansamone: Journey to Topaz

Eata/Gail: Jar of Dreams.

Gail: Yeah. She was Japanese, too.

San Ching: First Cambodian book.

Gail: Right. This is the first book about (a) Cambodian. In fact, that's the reason I picked this because I've *never* read any book.

Eata: We've never read any book about Laos.

Gail: I think you're right. You're right. I haven't read a book. I would love to get a book about Laos.

At first, the boys' comments suggested that they hadn't read any books about Asians, which surprised Gail and me because we knew that they had all read several books about Asians and Asian-Americans—for example, *Journey Home* (Uchida), *Jar of Dreams* (Uchida), *Journey to Topaz* (Uchida), *Sadako and the Thousand Paper Cranes* (Coerr), and *In the Year of the Boar and Jackie Robinson* (Lord). Eata clarified that they *had* read books about Asians, but Chansamone and San Ching got to the heart of the issue when pointing out that they hadn't read any books about Laotians and it was the first book about Cambodians that they had read. In fact, it was the only book about Southeast Asians that they had read and, although *Children of the River* was about a Cambodian experience, these young Laotian students identified very strongly with it.

A teacher in a family literacy program, Angie Barra, overheard this conversation. At the end of the discussion, she approached the group with an armful of books about Southeast Asia. As she introduced the students to the books, it was clear that they were captivated and were anxious to borrow and read them:

Angie: This one's from Laos. But it's from the Hmong. But it *is* from Laos. It's really a neat story, if you guys want to borrow it.

San Ching: Is it in English?

Angie: It's in English. And this one is about Cambodians in the refugee camps. What happened to them.

Students ooh and aah and lean forward to look at the books.

Nopphavanh: Clay marbles.

Angie: Yeah, they have clay marbles and it's called *The Clay Marble.* It's about what happened to a little girl in a camp in Thailand.

Nopphavanh: It's long.

Angie offers to lend the books to the children.

Eata: I'm gonna read this.

Chansamone: I wanna read this.

The Class and Literature Study Circles

The literature study circle discussion just described took place in a multi-age, fifth/sixth-grade class in an inner-city, multilingual, multi-ethnic, year-round school in Oakland, California. There were many refugees and immigrants in this class of more than thirty students. English was a nonnative language for most of them.

The reading program in Gail's class was grounded in literature study circles, which was often the first experience that these upper-grade students had reading complete texts. In the past, many of them had read only the selections found in their literature-based reading textbook, and many of the selections were excerpts or abridged versions. For literature study circles, students choose what they read from a selection of four to five books, which the teacher introduces in a book talk. Upon receiving the book, groups of students meet with the teacher to decide the date by which they need to have finished the book, and approximately how many pages they must read per day in order to complete the book by the deadline. The book discussions that follow are open-ended, with the teacher participating as a co-discussant and mentor.

Daily, the students in Gail's class have more than an hour of class time to read books, in addition to homework time. At the beginning of the year, most students could not read independently for such a long time, but with practice and the motivation to finish reading in order to join their literature study circle group, students quickly developed this skill. At the beginning of the year, book selections were often shorter to support the students as they became familiar with an entirely new experience with books. Throughout the year, the selection of books almost always included some shorter, less complex texts. Although students selected which literature study circle books they read, Gail would make recommendations to struggling readers, which they tended to follow. We learned that offering books that were grounded in or about experiences that the students were familiar with were often particularly successful. In many cases, these books dealt with some kind of conflict, whether the conflict one might experience as a young person entering adolescence or the conflict that many immigrants encounter.

Several of the students were immigrants from Southeast Asia who had lived for some time in the refugee camps in Thailand. *Children of the River* evoked strong emotions among many of these students. Choulaphone corresponded about books via the computer with another Southeast Asian student, Chansamone, and in one exchange, they discussed a dilemma that many immigrants face, whether to abide by their native customs or those of their new country. Chansamone wrote to Choulaphone, "*I think Sundara should choose who she want to date or merry because she is in America now and she can disobeys her culture sometimes.*" Choulaphone agreed, and wrote, "*I think Sundara should do what ever she want to.*" Although many pre-pubescent and adolescent children experience conflicts with their parents, an additional tension is often present for immigrant and refugee students as life in their new country is frequently very different from the ways of their native land, which can lead to huge conflicts in their families.

Conflicts Grounded in Language

One of the conflicts students such as Chansamone and San Ching often face is grounded in language. Many of the students in Gail's class spoke a language other than English at home, but very few of them had participated in bilingual education, where both English and the native language are developed. Because their schooling had been almost exclusively in English, the students were frequently more fluent in English than their parents and grandparents. In fact, sometimes they seemed more fluent in English than in their home language. At times, the students felt torn between the demands of the dominant language and culture (English) and those of their home language and culture, and they sometimes commented on the conflict that these demands placed on them. For example, during another discussion of *Children of the River*, a group of students talked about how Sundara was torn between her native Cambodian culture and her adopted American culture. The students began to talk about similar situations that they had experienced:

> *María:* When I'm here, I talk English and then when I get home, I want to talk English, too, and then my mom's like, "No, you're (inaudible).
> *Sylvia:* Eres Mexicana. *You're Mexican.*

María: And she's like, "You're Mexican, you know?" and I'm like, "So?" and I'm like (chuckles). She's all like, "Well, you have to talk Spanish 'cause . . .

Angelina: You'll forget it.

María: I'm all, "Uh huh, yeah, sure."

Several students are speaking at the same time.

María: In Mexico, I have a problem with my dad because he knows English. I'll talk to him in English, and my mom's like, "There's Mexicans here."

Angelina: Yeah. That's how my dad is. My dad won't let me talk English at my house. He says, "You'll forget! You'll forget how to speak Mexican." I'm like, "Oh, OK."

Gail: He wants you to be bilingual.

Angelina: And then we go to Mexico and I'm forgetting English because I'm talking Spanish all the time.

Although the girls in this conversation are not Southeast Asian or refugees, as Sundara was, they are members of immigrant families, and shared similar experiences to those that Linda Crew attributed to Sundara. This conversation was very animated as the students explored what it felt like to be torn between two languages/cultures. Despite the large numbers of immigrant and refugee children in the United States, very few books written for this age group are grounded in the immigrant or refugee experience. Perhaps this explains in part why *Children of the River* hooked so many of the students in Gail's class.

Even when students were from the same culture and spoke the same native language, they did not always agree on the meaning of a custom or term, which frequently led to fascinating discussions in which they negotiated meaning. During the discussion of *Children of the River* involving Angelina mentioned earlier, the conversation began to focus on biracial marriages. Angelina mentioned a Mexican term, "pocha," which led to a vigorous exchange between three Latinas, Angelina, Sylvia and Rosa, and a rather confused Filipino, Jarvis who thought they were talking about a car:

Angelina: When my brother, he had a pocha for a girlfriend and

Sylvia: Oh, a Mexican–American?

Angelina: He had a pocha, yeah.

Jarvis: A Porsche?

Several students say "pocha" very emphatically.

Angelina: And then he had

Gail: Do you want to tell Jarvis what a pocha is?

Sylvia: Pocha is, like, like, I'm a pocha because my parents are Mexican and I was born here.

Rosa: No, a pocha, a pocha.

(Other students agree with Sylvia.)

Angelina: Yeah, wanna bet?

Rosa: No, you know what a pocha is? A pocha is when your mom is, um, is Mexican, and your dad is American. That's a pocha.

Angelina: No.

Sylvia: No it ain't.

Rosa: Ask Daniel. Ask Daniel. (Referring to another student in the class)

Angelina: It says in the book, it says in the book, *Lupita Mañana*.

Students argue, disagreeing on this point.

The Latina students drew on prior experience when discussing the meaning of the term *pocha*. They were familiar with its use, but could not agree on whether the term was grounded in differences in the country of birth of children and their parents or in differences in where their parents were born. After checking with a friend who teaches Chicano Studies, I discovered that *pocha* and *pocho* are used to refer to Latinos who speak English, but cannot speak Spanish well.

Book Discussions Leading to Greater Understanding

When I first visited Gail's multiage fifth/sixth-grade class, I observed a literature study circle group that was discussing *The Cay* (T. Taylor). In this book, set during World War II, the narrator is a Caucasian boy who grew up in the segregated southern United States. While living in the Caribbean, the boy becomes friends with an elderly black man, loses his sight, and is cared for by the elderly man, who dies while protecting him. The conversation initially focused on the front cover illustration and other literary features, but after about ten minutes, Laurie, an African American fifth grader, wriggled her body forward on the rug where the group was meeting and thrust her head into the open space at the center of the circle. She then spoke for the first time:

I felt bad when I read this: "I saw a huge, very old Negro sitting on the raft near me. He was ugly. His nose was flat and his face was broad; his head was a mass of wiry gray hair. For a moment, I could not figure out where I was or who he was."

Laurie guided us to the page and added, "You don't hear, 'An ugly old whitey.' This book is very racist." At first, the rest of the group was silent as they thought about what Laurie had said. Soon, though, the group launched into a long, emotional, and thoughtful discussion about the narrator's point of view and their own firsthand experiences with prejudice, both their own prejudices and those of others. As a consequence of Laurie's comments, grounded as they were in her own expertise, ethnicity, and sense of pride, the group of students (as well as Gail and me) learned more about each other, were able to teach others about our respective cultures, and were able to further develop understanding and respect for ourselves and each other.

A favorite book among Gail's students was *Roll of Thunder, Hear My Cry* (M. Taylor), which describes what life was like for poor, rural African Americans living in the south in the 1930s. In many classrooms, students learn about prejudice and discrimination toward African Americans only in January, when they study about the bus boycott, Martin Luther King, Jr., and the civil rights movement. Like most students, few students in Gail's class had much understanding of the history of African Americans. *Roll of Thunder Hear My Cry* and other books by Mildred Taylor, *Song of the Trees* and *Mississippi Bridge,* allowed students to better understand the experiences and history of African Americans living in the Southern United States before World War II. Many students commented that they had no idea what it was like to live in a segregated society. Several non-African American students commented in literature study circle discussions and in their reading logs that other family members were biased against and distrusting of African Americans. This ignorance and fear was particularly apparent amongst students from Southeast Asia, who knew little about African Americans, even though they often lived in predominantly African American neighborhoods. Mildred Taylor's books helped students to understand more about U.S. history, to explore issues that frequently troubled them (such as the racist attitudes of family members), and to articulate and deal with their own feelings of and experiences with prejudice.

The Value of Books That Reflect Students' Experiences

In contrast with Mildred Taylor's books, books set in more recent times and in urban contexts allowed students to become more aware of the life experiences of their contemporaries as well as to see similarities in their own urban experiences. Books by African American writers including Walter Dean Myers' *Scorpions*, Candy Dawson Boyd's *Circle of Gold*, and Joyce Hansen's *Yellow Bird and Me* were especially popular with Gail's students. In many cases, they had firsthand knowledge of similar experiences to those of the characters in these books. The books acted as an affirmation for the few African American students in the class; they also helped non-African American students view their African American peers and neighbors with more understanding and less hostility.

Some of the students in Gail's class had already had the life experiences of much older children, which gave them a maturity that other children may not possess. Some books that they read allowed them to integrate this knowledge of life and academic learning. For example, after one group of students had read *Scorpions*, which is set in an inner-city neighborhood and is about the pressure placed on a young boy to join a gang, they drew upon their own knowledge of gang life and explored why young people join gangs and whether they do, in fact, have many choices available to them. The group of students did not agree about what happens when a person wants to leave a gang, which led to a long discussion about dealing with peer pressure and the sociopolitical origins of gangs. Through their reading and interactions with others, students tried to make sense of something that they often considered irrational and inexplicable—whether the benefits of joining a gang are worth the risks. Travera particularly appreciated books that addressed issues she was struggling with herself. After reading *Scorpions*, she wrote in her reading log that the knowledge she gained from the book and literature study circle discussion allowed her to support family members who had not thought through a situation as well as she would have liked:

> How the books and reading discussions has helped me with problems is that when I go home and hear problems that I read in books is that I tell my family I think I know a way to solve the problem. I also tell my cousins that when you get asked to be in a gang think about it and think about all the things that happen when your in a gang because theres alot of risks to take when your in a gang.

In these situations, it was clear that the urban themes addressed in these books helped the students deal with their everyday lives.

A book that resonated particularly well amongst Latino students was *Lupita Mañana* (Beatty). In this book, a teenage sister and brother cross the Mexico/U.S. border in search of an aunt living in Los Angeles. The story describes how dangerous it can be to cross the border without documentation; the work of immigration officials; and the hopes, dreams, and sometimes inflated expectations of immigrants coming to the United States. *Lupita Mañana* was one of the few books that Angelina read that was grounded in her own family's culture. She loved this book, and while reading it, wrote twenty-four separate comments and questions about the book on idea bookmarks, many more than she wrote for any other book that she read. She asked questions: "Leaving the children, Lupita came back to the door, which she left 'ajar.' What does 'ajar' mean? p. 21." "Does Pocho mean born in the U.S.A. and your parents were born in Mexico? Where did that word come from? p. 25." She related the story to her own roots in Mexico: "On the hill side of my town in Mexico poor people some times they are so many that the town gets bigger every year! p. 18." She also stated her opinion, as when she wrote, "They called Mexicans with out papers 'aliens.' How rude." When discussing *Lupita Mañana* , Angelina shared her experiential, linguistic, and cultural knowledge with pride and animation, and non–Latino students clearly regarded her and other Latino students as experts.

Sometimes, books prompted students to share features of their own culture that others were not aware of. Samesi, a sixth-grade Tongan student whose mother had recently died, read *Stone Fox* (Gardiner). In this story a dog, Searchlight, dies heroically in a dogsled race. Samesi's comments in his literature log and the literature study circle discussion showed evidence that the book had helped Samesi come to terms with the grief he felt at the loss of his mother. In the literature study circle discussion, he shared an aspect of his own culture that was embedded in death and spirituality, as the following illustrates.

> *Richard:* I wonder if the dog really died.
> *Miguel:* It says right here that his heart burst. Of course he's dead.
> *Samesi:* Even though he passed away, I think his spirit is still alive. Searchlight knew what Little Willie and Grandfather were going through. Little Willie had faith in himself. Searchlight knew what Little Willie and Grandfather needed. That's why they won the race. . . . It's disrespectful to say "dead" in our culture. That's not a good way. We say they passed away. When my mother passed, I heard her voice calling. My dad had a dream after my mother passed. She was on a place and told him she had to go.

In just a few words, Samesi shared a great deal about himself and his home culture, much of which was unfamiliar to the rest of the students. In raising these issues, it was clear that Samesi trusted the group, and expected that they would respond to his insights with respect, understanding, and appreciation, which they did.

Importance of a Trusting Learning Environment

I do not think that the honest, informative, and often highly charged literature study circle discussions that occurred in Gail's classroom would have occurred if a safe, supportive environment had not been created. If students' comments and personal revelations had been greeted with snickers or putdowns, it is unlikely that they would have been prepared to reveal so much about themselves the next time. Gail implemented a program called Tribes (with norms) of appreciations, mutual respect, attentive listening, the right to pass, and no putdowns (Gibbs 1994). It appeared that the structure of the literature program also contributed to the development of a supportive and respectful classroom community. Students appreciated having choice over which books they would read. They looked forward to the spirited book discussions and to learning about each other. They valued books that were strong in plot, character development, and theme. They enjoyed being introduced to books that they may not have encountered otherwise. And they appreciated reading books about their own cultures, as well as books about unfamiliar cultures.

Selecting Books

When selecting books for literature study circles, I consider a range of factors, including the following:

1. How well written is the book?

   I look for books that are rich in a literary sense, the kind that grab our attention, not just on the level of action and plot, but in the way in which we are drawn into the lives of characters. These are the books that may satisfy us as readers, but still leave us filled with questions; it is often these questions that lead to rich conversations and book discussions. These may not be the books that young readers would pick up on their own, but it is an opportunity for me to extend their reading horizons.

2. How likely is it that the readers will be engaged by the book?

   Books may be well written and may engage me as a reader, but they may not have the same impact on other, younger readers. I seek out books that are likely to resonate with the students. I have learned that books exploring issues familiar and of interest to students are often particularly successful.

3. How accurate is the cultural and historical information presented in the book?

I am constantly seeking out books that reflect as diverse a range of cultures and experiences as possible. Although more authors of color are published than ever before, many books about underrepresented groups are not written by members of that culture. For example, Scott O'Dell (*Sing Down the Moon*) and Paul Goble (*The Girl Who Loved Wild Horses*) have both written extensively about Native Americans. Although I don't limit my book selections to books written by members of the culture portrayed, I do investigate as best I can the degree to which authors have thoroughly researched their books. For example, in a foreword to *Children of the River*, Linda Crew explains how she researched her book about the Cambodian refugee experience. In the prologue to *Journey to Topaz*, Yoshiko Uchida discusses the interment of Japanese Americans and reveals that she was interred as a youngster. In a picture book about the heroic acts of the Japanese ambassador to Lithuania in the Second World War, which led to the saving of thousands of lives, *Passage to Freedom: The Sugihara Story*, author Ken Mochizuki explains how he conducted his research while writing the book. Karen Cushman provides an "Author's Note" at the end of *Catherine, Called Birdy* in which she lists the resources that she found helpful while writing the book.

4. How well does the book fit with other curricular areas?

As an immigrant to the United States myself, I have learned a great deal about American history through reading historical fiction. I realize the value of well-written, informative books in subject area learning, and when selecting books for literature study circles, I take into consideration topics that are being or will be explored in, for example, social studies. The open-ended nature of the discussions remains constant. I do not turn literature study circles into occasions for drilling students on factual information.

Some Final Thoughts

As a reader, I have been introduced to new worlds and experiences through books, and have broadened my understanding of and appreciation for difference. At the same time, I feel a special connection when the book I am reading is grounded in or is related in some way to my own experiences. In my own schooling, I rarely encountered books that were set in familiar surroundings or explored issues that I encountered. I was one of the few students who became a reader despite my school experiences with books. Many other students did not become readers on their own, which is a phenomenon that is all too familiar even today. I have found that including books that reflect diverse cultures and experiences goes a long way towards supporting youngsters in becoming enthusiastic, informed, and successful readers.

I am not suggesting that children should be limited to reading about only their own culture and experiences. However, if they never or rarely see themselves or their families in books, it is inevitable that a dangerous message is conveyed: "You aren't important." Although the number of authors from underrepresented groups is growing (and much of this literature is very well written), many of the books that children and young adults are assigned to read in school are still about middle-class Caucasian characters. As responsible teachers, we need to make a conscious effort to locate books that are grounded in diverse experiences, thereby validating all students' backgrounds and cultures, while also extending their understanding of and tolerance for difference.

Children's Literature Referred to in This Chapter

Beatty, Patricia (1992). *Lupita Mañana*. New York: Beech Tree Books.

Boyd, Candy Dawson (1984). *Circle of Gold*. New York: Scholastic.

Coerr, Eleanor (1977). *Sadako and the Thousand Paper Cranes*. New York: Dell.

Cushman, Karen (1994). *Catherine, Called Birdy*. New York: Harper-Collins.

Crew, Linda (1989). *Children of the River*. New York: Dell.

Gardiner, John R. (1980). *Stone Fox*. New York: Harper.

Goble, Paul (1978). *The Girl Who Loved Wild Horses*. New York: Bradbury Press.

Hansen, Joyce (1986). *Yellow Bird and Me*. New York: Clarion Books.

Ho, Minfong (1991). *Clay Marbles*. New York: Farrar Straus and Giroux.

Lord, Bette Bao (1986). *In the Year of the Boar and Jackie Robinson*. New York: Harper.

Mochizuki, Ken (1997). *Passage to Freedom: The Sugihara Story*. New York: Lee and Low Books

Myers, Walter Dean (1988). *Scorpions*. New York: Harper.

O'Dell, Scott (1970). *Sing Down the Moon*. New York: Dell.

Taylor, Mildred (1987). *Mississippi Bridge*. New York: Bantam.

———— (1976). *Roll of Thunder, Hear My Cry*. New York: Puffin.

———— (1975). *Song of the Trees*. New York: Bantam.

Taylor, Theodore (1977). *The Cay*. New York: Avon.

Uchida, Yoshiko (1981). *Jar of Dreams*. New York: Macmillan.

———— (1978). *Journey Home*. New York: Macmillan.

———— (1985). *Journey to Topaz*. Berkeley, CA: Creative Arts.

References

BROWN, K. K., BLASI, M. J., FU, D., and ALTWERGER, B. (1996). "Forging New Roles and Relationships in Literature Studies." *The New Advocate 9(3)*, 209–225.

EDELSKY, C. (1988). "Living in the Author's World: Analyzing the Author's Craft." *The California Reader 21*, 14–17.

EEDS, M., and PETERSON, R. (1991). "Teacher as Curator: Learning to Talk about Literature." *The Reading Teacher 45(2)*, 118–126.

EEDS, M., and WELLS, D. (1989). "Grand Conversations: An Exploration of Meaning Construction in Literature Study Groups." *Research in the Teaching of English 23(1)*, 4–29.

ESPINOSA, C., and FOURNIER, J. (1995). "Making Meaning of Our Lives through Literature: Past, Present, and Future." *Primary Voices 3(2)*, 15–21.

GIBBS, J. (1994). *Tribes: A New Way of Learning and Being Together*. Windsor, CA: Center Source Systems, LLC.

KEEGAN, S., and SHRAKE, K. (1994). "Literature Study Groups: An Alternative to Ability Grouping." *The Reading Teacher 44(8)*, 542–47.

PETERSON, R., and EEDS, M. (1990). *Grand Conversations: Literature Groups in Action*. New York: Scholastic.

SAMWAY, K. DAVIES, and WHANG, G. (1996). *Literature Study Circles in a Multicultural Classroom*. York, ME: Stenhouse.

SAMWAY, K. DAVIES, WHANG, G., CADE, C., Gamil, M., Lubandina, M.A., and Phommachanh, K. (1991). "Reading the Skeleton, the Heart and the Brain of a Book: Students' Perspectives on Literature Study Circles." *The Reading Teacher 45(3)*, 196–205.

SMITH, K. (1995). "Bringing Children and Literature Together in the Elementary Classroom." *Primary Voices 3(2)*, 22–32.

————. (1990). "Entertaining a Text: A Reciprocal Process." In K. G. Short and K. M. Pierce (Eds.), *Talking about Books: Creating Literate Communities*. Portsmouth, NH: Heinemann.

YOUVELLA, C (1995). "Looking for a Dreamcatcher: Trying Literature Studies With Native American Students." *Primary Voices 3(2)*, 8–14.

9

A Different Spin on Parent Involvement:

Exploring Funds of Knowledge within a Systems Perspective

Leslie Patterson and Shelia Baldwin

To put it bluntly, the inquiry and conversations triggered by our Houston Funds of Knowledge Project brought us face to face with our ignorance, and our arrogance about the role of teachers and schools in the lives of immigrant families.

We learned that the realities of our students' families are like those of our own families—unique, dynamic, and complex. No two families are the same, although we share similar hopes and dreams for our children's futures. We came to realize that school is not—and need not be—the center of their universe. Social and economic networks are often more significant than family involvement in school activities. We had to admit that traditional communication from school to home—parent conferences, newsletters—fail to address the complex and sometimes contradictory systemwide forces at work. Our inquiry and our conversations forced us to take a new look at the big picture, complex and dynamic, including families, neighborhoods, relationships to schools, roles within larger social, economic, and political networks.

We used to think that "parent involvement" meant to invite parents to school, serve food, and explain to them how they could help us do our job. We were puzzled when it never seemed to work. After all, our beliefs about parent involvement were simple:

1. Successful students have parents who are involved in school-related activities.

2. Parents who are not involved simply do not yet understand the best ways to help their children be successful in school.

3. Our job is to teach parents how to be "involved."

Dissatisfied with our lack of success, a group of us decided to explore other solutions. For two years our group of teachers and university professors learned more about parent involvement. We came to see inquiry and conversation as powerful tools for opening boundaries and strengthening connections between the astonishing complexities of home and school. Our questions have shifted from "What's wrong with these parents?" to "What's wrong with our picture of these families' lives?"

The Houston Funds of Knowledge Project

We work in Houston, Texas—home to many new immigrants.[1] A primary problem this new wave of immigrants faces in schools is teachers who know very little about these growing populations of immigrant families. Irma Guadarrama, a colleague at the University of Houston, introduced us to a research project called the "Funds of Knowledge," developed by Luis Moll, Norma Gonzales, and their teacher researcher colleagues in Tucson, Arizona (1992, 1993). The purpose of our Houston project was to build on the work of Moll and his colleagues, particularly with newcomers to the United States.

Each of eight classroom teachers chose one student's family to visit a minimum of three times during the year. The group of researchers, consisting of the eight teachers and four university professors, met monthly October through April. Early meetings included suggestions for recording observations and completing interviews. Later ones offered opportunities for researchers to debrief about experiences. At the end of that year, participants completed written reports that we compiled into a publication (Guadarrama 1997).

Seven of the eight families involved were from Mexico. One was from Vietnam. Three of the teachers were English/Spanish bilingual; four could communicate to some extent in Spanish; and one had the assistance of elders in the church who acted as translators. Each teacher researcher wrote field notes of observations in the home, taped the conversations with parents when appropriate, and wrote reflections after each visit. The university researchers made notes of the debriefing conversations.

In their few visits, the teacher researchers came to know the families and made discoveries useful to their teaching. The teachers' final

---

1 Projections suggest that by 2050, the population will be 52.8 percent white, 24.5 percent Latino, 13.6 percent African American, 8.2 percent Asian, and 0.9 percent American Indian (*Houston Chronicle*, March 14, 1996).

reports elaborated on new understandings of their families' cultural practices and the complexities of learning a new culture. In some instances, teachers cited specific changes in their teaching, but more often, they reported general shifts in their attitudes toward students and families from diverse backgrounds. In fact, the emerging friendships between teachers and parents soon became a central focus in our conversations. These new friendships forced us to confront our previous stereotypes about immigrant families, families living in poverty, and school-family relationships.

Parent Involvement and Systems Thinking

Natural scientists tell us that living systems, from the tiniest organisms to huge ecosystems, consist of interdependent parts or components, each one functioning in relation to the others. If one part is missing or if it changes, the system itself undergoes a transformation. Scientists also tell us that, in all systems, change is inevitable and that the nature or direction of that change is essentially unpredictable.

In our Funds of Knowledge project, we have come to see that schools, classrooms, families, neighborhoods (and the potential learning communities within and across these groups of people) resemble complex self-organizing systems similar to organisms and ecosystems studied by scientists (Capra 1996, Eoyang 1997, Gell-Mann 1994). Under certain conditions, the flow of information and energy into and within the system trigger recurring behaviors and responses among participants. Recurring responses develop patterns that resonate through the system, sometimes triggering systemwide behaviors that lead to reorganization of the whole system at higher levels of complexity (Eoyang 1997).

A very simple example of a self-organizing phenomenon is when kindergarten students first walk into class:

> The teacher is sitting in the rocking chair beginning to read a story aloud. The story is so engaging that, as students come in, they begin listening and move close to the teacher. Those who want to hear the story signal to the others to be quiet and listen. In a very few minutes, everyone in the room is deeply engaged in listening to the story. The class has self-organized into a "listening system."

In this phenomenon "the whole is equal to more than the sum of its parts." This experience among learners is sometimes called a "shared epiphany" or "synergistic learning." Our goal is to help groups of learners (students, teachers, and/or parents) participate in this kind of complex adaptive system where information and energy flow freely in ways that encourage systemwide self-organization in response to new information or changing circumstances.

Self-Organizing Systems and Funds of Knowledge

We saw this self-organizing phenomenon in our Funds of Knowledge experiences. As we learned more about our families and developed closer relationships with the parents, we saw three changes.

1. We recognized that our previous work was based on unquestioned assumptions about parents and families.

2. Our new understandings made it necessary for us to change our teaching.

3. We moved beyond the classroom system, to work with and for our students in the larger community.

Interestingly, we were not conscious of these three areas of transformation until we reflected in writing and conversation about our experiences, individually and collectively.

Discovering and Challenging Old Assumptions

A theme resonating through the teacher researchers' stories was that the children are unique human beings with families who want a good life for them and recognize education as the key to that life. Our interviews with students and their families forced us to question our assumptions about why these families came to the United States.

Liz, in her second year of teaching in an urban middle school, grew up in the school community and assumed that her knowledge about the families was complete. But even Liz had to question what she knew:

. . . going into somebody's home and talking to them . . . I was just wrong. My assumptions were wrong . . . I hear teachers talking all the time in the halls and in the teacher's lounge: "Oh, these parents yu-ta-da-ya-ta-da-" . . . "they don't care for their kids," "they don't do this" . . . "they're like this." [The teachers] have no idea what they are talking about because they have not been to one single student's home or talked to

one single parent about what aspirations and ideas they have for their children. And it's a shame, you know, for so many teachers to assume that these parents don't love their children and that they want less for them, which is not the case at all. . . . Meeting a student and their family in their home, as opposed to at school . . . puts a whole different spin on how you perceive your students . . . As other human beings, as opposed to that herd that comes shuffling through your door every eighty-five minutes.

Shelia worked for years with students of diverse linguistic and cultural backgrounds. Our research forced her to reassess her assumptions about her students' capabilities:

Why did it take me so long to get to where I am now? I have worked with second-language students for years, . . . caught up with being within the law, providing courses for our students to take considering their limited English proficiency, getting enough credits, passing the state mandated test. . . . perceiving . . . that language was going to interfere with their achievement—their limited English as a deficit rather than their approaching bilingualism as an asset. Hearing teachers complain that the ESL students do not have enough English to be in their classes must have influenced me.

Shelia had assumed that immigrant families had left oppression or poverty, that they were coming to the United States for a more comfortable and prosperous life. She found that in her family, that assumption did not hold.

Mother told me the reason they came to the United States was so Carolina could learn English. I was surprised, expecting her to say more, given the sacrifice the family was making to do this. Cristobal and Carolina helped me to understand this better while we had lunch together at school. "Yes, I can go back to Mexico and get a job too easy because I know English." Carolina added after my reference to the dilemma of the illegal status of many of our students, "They come here to learn English."

It became clear that their time in the United States equips our students with the tools to succeed in life wherever their circumstances take them. Their parents have the same dreams for their children's lives that our research team has for our own children.

Jennifer was a participant in the "Teach for America" program, beginning her teaching as she worked on teacher certification. She had grown up in the Northeastern United States and had lived in South America for a period of time until before taking her job teaching second graders. She noted how much her own experiences influence her assumptions:

Delores' mother and I also spoke at length about the safety of the neighborhood, particularly her concerns about letting the children go outside to play, something I took for granted all children did.

Pat, also in her first year in public schools, had taught several years in private preschools. Like Jennifer she learned how parents' customs lead them to make what are, for Pat, very puzzling decisions. Pat's Vietnamese second graders stayed inside their apartments most afternoons and evenings: "[The mother] mentioned that she probably would let the children go out more if it was not so dangerous in their neighborhood."

The church elders, who served as translators, explained that the availability of parks in the surrounding area doesn't resolve parents' concerns: "All this running around town is just not part of the way they live their lives."

Deb had years of experience as a parent and community volunteer before her first year teaching kindergarten. She discussed the impact of the visits on her thinking:

The interview left a lasting impression on me. It was a very pleasant visit; [my student] and her family are very amiable people, and I was definitely the entertainment of the day. . . . I think that most important for me, this home visit broke the ice and I visited several children's homes. . . . I never did another formal interview, but I went to socialize. . . . My slight command of Spanish became a matter of humor, and a cause for them to help.

Parent Involvement from a Systems Perspective

It is at the boundaries between and among complex systems that we must work: complex and dynamic systems and boundaries cannot be clearly represented in this static, printed page. Critical transformations can occur across the boundaries. Enhancing the information flow within, between, and among students, teachers, parents, faculties, neighborhoods, and policy makers makes opportunities for transformative feedback, systemwide self-organization, and the kind of learning that leads to constructive and responsive action.

Within, between, and among these complex systems, both inquiry and conversation are critical. In a Funds of Knowledge project, teacher researchers go into the community—students' homes—and through inquiry and conversation learn more about the families. This process releases the potential for information flow across boundaries to encourage responsive self-organization and new systemwide behaviors. In the Funds of Knowledge project, several conditions work to do just that:

- Teachers become learners, seeking out new information and questioning old assumptions.

- Teachers reach out and invite parents and students to share information about home, family, and cultural practices.

- Teachers are welcomed into homes where parents, students, and other family members are the experts and teachers.

- Teachers make plans and take new actions together with families based on conversations that provide multiple opportunities to explore common experiences and values.

- Teachers document systematic inquiry—field notes, interview transcriptions, debriefing sessions, and written reports—keeping the learning available to others for future reference.

We are confident that inquiry and conversation are essential to a Funds of Knowledge project. They encourage individuals to make themselves more open to the new information and energy generated when complex systems are brought together in new ways. Enough of these small transformations will trigger systemwide changes. Movement will not be steady or predictable. We have come to expect surprises along the way.

Making Instructional Changes

We had expected home visits to prompt curriculum content changes. Our actual changes were much more subtle and far-reaching, related more to the conditions necessary to support learning than to the informational content of the curriculum. Teachers' instructional changes fall into complex combinations of two simple shifts: more use of students' background knowledge; and more focus on relevance and student inquiry.

Liz, the middle school English teacher, reports how her participation in this project changed her teaching. Now she

. . . tweaks writing assignments to be more responsive to students' potential funds of knowledge. . . . By doing this Funds of Knowledge research . . . I specifically have some ideas about where students may be coming from . . . and

as I continue this and visit more students' homes, I will build a better . . . and fuller picture of what my students come to school with so I can exploit that in the classroom and make an environment and assignments that will foster their learning.

During her family visits, Shelia learned that the children were spending four nights a week and several weekend hours at their church.

My attitude before was that they are spending so much time at that church . . . not getting their homework done. I don't look at it that way any more. That is their social life as well as their spiritual life. And it is an important way for them to adapt to this whole new way of life."

Shelia stresses that she now wants to know about her students' lives. "I want to know if they are working and when; who's in the home; if and when the parents are working; the importance of the church in their family's life."

In response to the visits, Shelia reframed a culture studies unit so that students would assume the role of ethnographers within their own communities:

. . . after I visited the family a couple of times and heard from them about the differences in the states in Mexico, the differences in dialect, and certain traditions, and the way they prepare food and all that kind of thing, . . . I changed the approach I had planned to use, to inviting them to be like cultural anthropologists, so to speak.

Jennifer, the second grade teacher, noted the importance of the relationship between Delores and her mother.

It also motivated me to make an effort to speak daily to students who might not be interacting with adults in the home. Seeing how much care, love, and attention surrounded Delores at her home, I also realized I have an obligation as a teacher, to the best of my ability, to duplicate that environment in the classroom.

Jennifer mentions the effect that neighborhood safety has on the children's opportunity to play outdoors and the impact that knowledge has on her teaching.

Seeing how students' parents frequently kept them indoors, I began to schedule daily recess time during which students play freely on our safe, outdoor playground. Subsequent to my visits, I place more emphasis on educating the whole child, instead of focusing on cognitive skills alone.

Kindergarten teacher Deb learned of a real difference between her own and the family views of gender roles. Deb also realized that reading each night at home was not part of the lives of most of her children. Rather than blame or put down the family, Deb adapted her instruction:

I felt I needed to give the children, particularly the girls, an opportunity to stretch their visions a little, and we had some talk about making choices. These were difficult conversations, because, while the boys chose to be a firefighter, a police officer, an astronaut, or whatever daddy does, the little girls were mostly silent or responded with wanting to be a mother. . . . I have some hope that while "What do I want to do when I grow up?" was clearly an empty set at the outset of the conversation, there is at least a schema now to be filled.

She extended the time she read to her children beyond the fifteen minutes she had scheduled at first. She noted, "Their progress was remarkable!"

In the Vietnamese community second-grade teacher Pat learned that

teachers in today's culturally diverse communities need to assess more than the academic knowledge of students. Ongoing assessment of family situations, backgrounds, culture and relationships would complete the picture of the whole child. . . . My expectations and my instruction in this class changed. . . . Almost all instruction is now given in small groups and cooperative learning is used in almost every situation. . . . Understanding the . . . family has eased my stress in trying to push the children into a faster level of development than I would have expected of them prior to this research.

Pat bases homework assignments on her knowledge of family strengths and challenges.

. . . Because I know of the limits for assistance in their environment, I have seen that all my students' homework must be limited to creative exploration with the parents in Science or Math and basic review sheets that cover language topics that the children have studied many times. Even directions throw the parents and students off balance when worded differently than the children have heard during class.

Reaching Beyond the Classroom

This Funds of Knowledge project prompted us to reach out and work with students and families beyond traditional classroom boundaries. Ruben's experience with his family took on more of a collaborative relationship. His dual role as Juan's elementary teacher and Cub Scout leader placed him with the family in a range of settings. Juan, a good student, had occasional problems with conduct during the school year. His mother worked mornings in the school cafeteria. At home, she was the one who administered discipline. Ruben and the mother regularly discussed Juan's behavior. One incident involved the father and Juan at a Cub Scout event:

I noticed him driving up towards me with Juan. He told me that he was going home because he didn't like the way that Juan was disciplined by another scout leader. He didn't feel that anyone had a right to discipline his son. I . . . talked to the scout leader and found out that Juan was in an area that was prohibited for all scouts.

Ruben talked it over with the mother, who was able to discuss it with the father and Juan.

Liz created her own opportunities to take her new understandings beyond her classroom when she was asked to present the Funds of Knowledge project to her middle school faculty. In addition to reporting her findings, she invited the entire faculty to participate in a Funds of Knowledge project the next year. Eight of her colleagues responded and Liz worked to facilitate that project for the following two years.

Deb's plan for our second project year was to visit her students' families early and often, to "have an early-in-the-year party in my home to get to know and be known more quickly."

Shelia's participation caused her to question school policy decisions concerning students in her English as a Second Language (ESL) classes. She has become an outspoken advocate for the ESL students. She asks tough questions.

I questioned why ESL students had never been tested for the Gifted and Talented program. . . . No one ever suggested it . . . we tested thirty-nine students of which sixteen would be evaluated for GT placement.

She also took a critical look at sheltered instruction classes at her school.

We created sheltered classes because so many ESL students were failing mainstream classes, not solely because of limited English proficiency but because of the lack of knowledge on the part of teachers on teaching to the diversity in their classrooms.

At Shelia's school sheltered instruction had become, "a kind of tracking, isolating ESL students from the mainstream" students and teachers. ESL students were assigned to sheltered instruction regardless of their level of English proficiency. In addition, many mainstream English teachers viewed both the ESL and the sheltered classes as "remedial."

Carolina called my attention to problems with sheltered classes. "I don't like it because everyone is speaking Spanish trying to help one another . . . It was better when we were in regular classes. Some students in sheltered classes speak English very well." I shared her objections with my colleagues . . . we re-evaluated our placement policy."

Our Funds of Knowledge project has pushed and pulled us far beyond our old notions of parent involvement. We now understand that we do not control parent involvement. We are merely participants in these amazingly complex, self-organizing systems. We are beginning to understand that we can open boundaries to enhance the information flow in all directions. We are beginning to understand that, through inquiry and conversation, we can invite everyone to participate in these interdependent, self-organizing systems called "home" and "school."

Here are some emerging notions about what we plan to do from now on:

Rather than:	We will:
• Teach parents how to be "involved" in school activities	• Focus on the potential for collaborative and reciprocal learning between and among teachers, parents, and students
• Plan and control parent involvement in activities	• Invite parents to join us • Relax and let the exciting possibilities emerge
• View school as the only learning place	• See homes, schools, and neighborhoods as overlapping learning communities

Rather than:	We will:
• Tell parents what they should know and do	• Enhance the information flow among and between all members of the learning communities
• Talk so much	• Take time to watch and to listen
• Be "the teacher"	• Become "the learner," inviting parents to teach us how to help their children and our students
• Expect parents to be the only advocates for their children	• Work together to help students negotiate the institutional constraints that often block students' academic progress
• Assume that school is the only path to success	• View school way as one of the many paths learners take to build productive, happy lives at home and in the larger community

What we learned from our inquiries and conversations with parents and with one another is that we are all engaged in overlapping and interactive cultures—systems of thinking and doing—as individuals, as families, as neighborhoods, as campuses, and as classroom learning communities. From a systems perspective, we want to help all these separate and sometimes isolated systems come together into larger, more complex systems that respond better to changing needs and to new circumstances.

To do that, we must focus on opening the boundaries between systems while respecting the differences that make each interacting system coherent, whole, and unique. Across these open boundaries, we must see that information is available and that we all feel comfortable asking questions, sharing our views, and working together toward common objectives. That is what this Funds of Knowledge project accomplished for us.

Our learning holds the promise of transformation or self-organization across the systems. That can mean dramatic changes in the ways parents and teachers work together. It can mean a growing sense of trust between parents and teachers. It can mean a powerful sense of reassurance and confidence in the future as students see their parents and their teachers learning together.

References

CAPRA, F. (1996). *The Web of Life. A New Scientific Understanding of Living Systems.* New York: Anchor Books, Doubleday.

EOYANG, G. H. (1997). *Coping with Chaos: Seven Simple Tools.* Cheyenne, WY: Lagumo Corp.

GELL-MANN, M. (1994). *The Quark and the Jaguar: Adventures in the Simple and the Complex.* New York: W. H. Freeman and Company.

GONZALES, N., MOLL, L. D., FLOYD-TENERY, M., RIVERA, A., RENDON, P., GONZALES, R., and AMANTI, C. (1993). *Teacher Research on Funds of Knowledge: Learning from Households.* Tucson, AZ: National Center for Research on Cultural Diversity and Second Language Learning.

GUADARRAMA, I. (1997). "Discovering our Experiences" *Studies in Bilingual/ESL Instruction 4,* 6–12.

Houston Chronicle, March 14, 1996.

MOLL, L., AMANTI, C., NEFF, D., and GONZALEZ, N. (1992). "Funds of Knowledge for Teaching: Using a Qualitative Approach to Connect Homes and Classrooms." *Theory Into Practice 31,* 132–141

10

The Wheel of Advocacy: International Students in Middle America

Ann Edmonds

The tree-lined streets of Clayton, Missouri, are filled with apartments and houses, shops and office buildings, a community center and schools. Several universities and international businesses adjacent to the town provide an economic base for families and a school system. While the majority population is upper-middle-class white professional, bussing from the city and non-English-speaking university families have brought diversity to Clayton.

Over the past decade, Clayton classroom populations have shifted from one or two non-English-speaking children who "visited" for a year or two at most to the current 21 percent who speak languages other than English in the home and tend to stay for several years. Students from the city of St. Louis bussed into Clayton form 20 to 25 percent of each school population.

Differences are multiplied when cultures are mixed. Cultural and linguistic differences can become mountainous. Parents, teachers, and children, ignorant of each others' experiences and expectations, may feel frustration and disappointment. The child is squeezed between the parent—separated from the child's new environment—and the teacher.

The first non–English speakers in the district needed only beginning-level English instruction. As the length of stay for international students increases, access to curriculum and to more English becomes essential. As they stay longer, the international children and their families interact with more people from Clayton. New situations arise within the school community, situations that may create culture shock.

More than language differences challenge school family relationships. Parents and teachers often have different role definitions. Some cultures expect the parent to "leave the child" to the teacher. The family nurtures the child. The school teaches the child. Some cultures expect the school to do only rote teaching and expect their children to bring home pages and pages of homework. Some parents are horrified that the teacher is loved by the students. Children shouldn't be happy at school: "I wasn't and I learned."

The Wheel of Advocacy

In Clayton, multicultural education addresses culture, language, and curriculum. Awareness of differences as well as systematic, respectful teaching of similarities and differences around the world is embedded in the teacher-written content area curricula. Yet teachers identified this concern: having a multicultural curriculum was not enough. Merely teaching English to the international children was not enough. School learning was suffering and the students were losing out.

Teachers working with international students posed a solution: the Wheel of Advocacy, visualized as a bicycle wheel (Figure 1). The student is the axle around which everything revolves. The parent/family are the hub, connected to the child and interacting with more of the community. The spokes are the various aspects of the school and community; the school principal, the nurse, the teacher, other students, even the custodian form spokes of the wheel. They all pull at the child and parents in many, varied directions. An advocate serves as the wheel rim, connecting the different spokes, keeping them all in balance.

We call "the rim" the International Resource Advocate. The goal of the International Resource Advocate is to teach and connect the

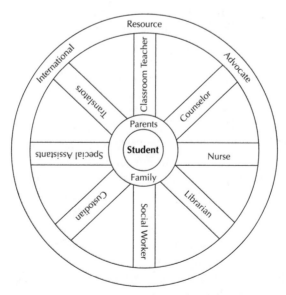

FIGURE 1 *Wheel of Advocacy (by Ella Davan)*

various segments of a child's learning world, home and school, and to positively and actively involve families; to empower parents as full participants in the new life around them so they may learn and grow with their children. The advocate facilitates a more comfortable and powerful learning experience for our children.

In Clayton today, parents and staff recognize the responsibility, difficulties, and deeper joys and strengths in a multicultural, multilingual population.

School Curriculum and Culture

The impact of multicultural information empowers learners in Clayton. It surrounds them. It is constantly accessible to them. The general curriculum is expected to carry the greatest impact. Far more than special events, visiting artists, or immigrant fairs, daily, intentional noticing differences and similarities is a powerful tool for multicultural learning. Teachers weave information about many cultures, many peoples, and many languages into the daily work. For example, biography is in the science classes as well as the social studies classes as children learn about famous inventors from all cultures. When students explore how percussion thrives on all the continents, they learn about artists from all cultures. Each elementary year, students study cultures around the world via an ecosystem, noting similarities and differences. These studies are contemplated through the specialists as they emphasize the music, art, and games from a specific region or culture. When third grade studies grasslands, they focus on Argentina's pampas, Kenya's savanna, and the North American prairie. Students explore the characteristics of each, a bit about the contemporary culture and the similarities of a grassland ecosystem on three continents. Libraries and classrooms have made a concerted effort to provide good literature from and about a multitude of cultures, family systems, perspectives, and physical or personal situations.

The program is dynamic. Professional development emphasizes the subject of diversity during all staff meetings. Teachers' book groups, field trips, guest speakers, storytellers and musicians, and special parent events create a districtwide sense of celebration of diversity. Student curriculum and professional development acknowledge the value of multicultural understanding and education. The infusion of questions and discussions around issues of racism, of diversity, of personal understanding empowers all members of the school district. It makes for a strong layer in the foundation of multicultural education for the whole community.

International Resource Advocate: Instructional Support

The International Resource Advocate works to see that children from diverse backgrounds find themselves represented in the school. National flags color the hallways. Culture Boxes are used in classrooms. Storytellers enhance understandings. The daily sight and sound of flags, stories, artifacts, and information embedded into the schools' atmosphere faster for a multicultural community.

The International Resource Advocates create Culture Boxes containing artifacts and books that help anchor specific multicultural education concepts. The Culture Box is a vehicle for instruction and discussion. It may contain a fragile painted egg, a delicate fan, a sturdy drum, colorful dolls, an elaborate mask, or books in scripts other than English. Parents use Culture Boxes when they come to share about their background as part of the curriculum or at the annual Storytelling Festival or whenever they volunteer in the classroom. Each Culture Box opens conversations.

Storytellers, often parents or older children, tell tales from different times and places. While adults and children laugh and stare, similarities and differences are noticed. Common plots, characters, values, and lessons infuse stories. Small, brave persons succeed against large, rich ones. Tricksters (coyote, rabbit, raven, and more) ply their trade across the continents. Tales of courage and humor, of brains and beauty reach a common human core. Student tellers research and share stories with other classrooms, using this ancient art to communicate within the school culture. A Chinese student, learning from her parents, proudly tells a Chinese folktale, complete with traditional gestures and shouts. An African American student tells about his grandpa's adventures and how he learned the story himself. These stories tie family to school and student to family.

Specialists, working with the International Resource teacher and classroom teachers provide additional opportunities for all students. The specialists enrich the instruction in their discipline by utilizing techniques, attributes, and examples from other cultures. The technology specialist supports access to the rest of the planet through the Internet. CD-ROMs in other languages support the new international student and intrigue English-speaking classmates. This allows the non–English speaker to be the teacher to an English-proficient peer.

The music teacher plays tapes of many different kinds of music. She stresses attention to differences and similarities in pitch, tone, and harmonies. She introduces her students to instruments and songs from many different countries. At the annual concert, students perform songs in many languages. The art teacher extends classroom multicultural studies into the area of art. World art is studied for difference and similarities. Art concepts are taught with various media—clay, paper, paints—using authentic models from many cultures.

Even the physical education program becomes involved. Rather than just a field day, Clayton students participate in a mini-Olympics. Small multiaged teams study the flag, geography, and culture of their assigned country. Flags "borrowed" from the hallways are used in the Opening Ceremonies.

School Culture and Curriculum

School in the United States is different from school systems of other nations. State and federal funding and guidelines help shape individual school districts' standards and curricula. Clayton district manages its own goals and procedures. Parent-teacher organizations have a different role than in many other countries. Not only do they run school parties and raise money for equipment, parents volunteer in classrooms and serve on district committees. They may even serve as elected officials on school governing boards.

Within the school itself, teacher-student roles are often very different. Where parents might expect to see teacher-directed lectures, teachers and students work together to form a "learning community." And where parents might expect rows of desks, classrooms are arranged differently. There may be tables for small groups or study centers, or even children sitting on the floor! Parental experience and expectation may include rote memorization of key facts, while teachers value independent student work and inquiry. Even enlightened international parents who recognize and approve of changing roles are apt to fret that their children are not learning enough or not developing the study habits required for success, especially when their kids like school, treat learning like play rather than work, and when they don't receive more than two hours' worth of homework daily.

International Resource Advocate: Culture Broker

When an international student first arrives, the first person they encounter is the International Resource Advocate, who meets with new families, helps to determine the level of services needed, and gets the children settled in the school. Issues such as immunizations, school supplies, and registration are often bewildering. The International Resource Advocate may do the initial registration, ESL placement testing, a home visit, and a school tour. The whole family can see the location of classrooms, bathrooms, water fountains, and cafeteria area. The parents can thus relieve anxiety before leaving the young one alone at school. Often the child will confide, "Oh, I like to draw" or "I can play basketball real good." The family has an opportunity to confer and ask questions or make personal observations: "Where do you buy the lunch ticket?" "We don't eat pork, what to do?" The parents can visualize their child in the new environment. At home, the family can talk about where to sit at lunch, when conveniently to go to the bathroom. The tour provides a welcoming, personal invitation to the child and to the family. Time spent at the beginning lays a foundation for the child-family-school relationship.

When a youngster enters the school alone for the first time, the International Resource Advocate checks to make sure all bathroom, lunch, and other questions have been resolved. Children adapt quickly to a welcoming space. During the first weeks, the advocate visits the classroom and attends lunch and other recesses. Recess time provides opportunity for networking with other staff and students, a chance to chat. Teachers may reveal concerns: "He just sat and cried this morning, what should I do?" or "She copied off another child's notebook. She doesn't do any work herself?" The International Resource Advocate explains and encourages a realistic positive relationship between a teacher and new student. The International Resource Advocate may call or write a note to tell the parents that the first day has gone well or that the child contributed in class.

The Axle: Children

Clayton currently has three International Resource Advocates. Two serve approximately 75 elementary students. The other serves about twenty-five secondary students. The three advocates work closely with Clayton's English to Speakers of Other Languages (ESOL) teachers. The program is developmental and works within individuals schools and classrooms to best support all the international students.

As the number of international students has increased so has the number of ESOL teachers. As the length of stay has increased, the ESOL teachers have become aware that their roles are more complicated than just teaching beginning language. Language development is a developmental, constructive, and personal process. It involves the whole child.

Young children learn a second language in much the same way as the first. They need support in getting comfortable, in learning basic vocabulary, and particularly in widening and deepening their understanding in their second language. At the elementary level the children study content and language with their classmates. The International Resource Advocate helps empower the learner by connecting the student with teacher, with family, and with the curriculum.

At the high school, English and social studies are taught in a "supported" environment by an ESOL teacher. He also has an English class where students are taught basic English and offered academic support for other classes. The small classes and the personal connection of the ESOL teacher provide a "home base" for international students in the secondary program. The International Resource teacher at the high school works with other staff to help the students flourish. Social as well as academic skills are attended to. As international students become both more proficient in English and more comfortable in the school setting, they attend mainstream English classes. They still have the International Resource Advocate as advisor for support. Even in high school, the families depend on the International Resource Advocate for information, interpretation of school culture, and personal connections.

Without parent connections, the child stays separate. Without connecting to the school, the parent is separated from the child. The gap between home and school cultures expands and, too often, family life falls into the crevasse. Students can become a problem at home or at school or both. Teachers may become frustrated and blame the parents. Cultural and linguistic differences can become mountainous. Everyone feels powerless.

The Hub: Parents and Families

The International Resource Advocates run an American School Program where parents come to district buildings to learn the culture of the American school, to celebrate American holidays like Halloween and Thanksgiving, and to enjoy time to meet for social and educational events. There are both small and large meetings: some are for parents only; others are family-centered events. The program has two special components: a weekly International Coffee Party and the monthly, district-funded, American School Program.

The weekly International Coffee Party is an informal meeting. It is a time to chat, to practice English, to meet with other parents, and to talk through events in the culture or the school. The format includes self-introductions so that each person speaks at least once during each "party." A teacher/leader does a quick information update on school events. School Picture Day or the PTO Book Fair are odd cultural events to many international families. Items on the monthly lunch menu provide good discussion topics on "comfort food" or nutrition or cultural or religious dietary practices. Occasionally one or two participants share a food or presentation from their own family culture. This often leads to further sharing on marriage or birthing customs. The International Coffee Party provides a simple way for families to become accustomed to the school setting and activities. Participants are more willing to attend other school functions. A call from the principal or classroom teacher is far less intimidating when parents are part of regular school-based activities. Many participants stay after the coffee party to volunteer in the school library or their children's classrooms. Others continue the discussion at each other's homes. Parental issues, cultural quandaries, and the isolation international families face are discussed. Friendships are nourished.

The American School Program monthly meetings are held in the evenings. These are divided into parent discussion groups on subjects such as math curriculum, peer pressure, summer programs, or raising a bicultural, bilingual child. District curriculum coordinators and outside speakers participate with these groups. Parents and teachers learn from each other and many big problems are ameliorated or prevented through these discussions.

Family parties are also part of the American School Program. They serve to teach American customs and to provide a welcome place for the international families to learn about the holidays. Scheduled around United States holidays, families come and participate in American traditions like carving pumpkins, eating turkey, or making Valentine cards. The final party is held in May at a park or zoo to give families a community experience. The American School Program establishes intentional time and space for families of many cultures to meet, to learn, and to play together in their new "common" culture. As one mother remarked, "This is the most like a family party since we came to the USA. All the children are running around playing together and the parents are talking together and everyone is eating and laughing."

Parent Ownership

Through the American School Program, international parents created the "Taste of the World"—an international food bazaar, a successful PTO fund-raiser, and a treasured part of the school calendar. The parents wanted to contribute to the school community. At various

American School Program activities, parents shared their concerns, including a major concern over the lack of library books in languages other than English for students. Many of the library books about other countries, home countries to some of these families, were old and out of date. The international parents decided to raise money and educate the local community about their home cultures.

The first Taste of the World was scheduled in conjunction with the annual talent show. More than sixty families brought foods. For fifty American cents a taste, the consumer could sample foods including borscht, fried rice, spinapika, strudel, meringues, empanadas, sushi, and chocolate chip cookies. It was sold out in twenty minutes! The Taste of the World recipe book the parents made is a cherished memento for all.

The second year, with more planning, more space, and more tastes, there was even greater financial success. The library purchased more than seventy-five new books and a new bookcase! As international parents worked together, sharing space, planning, going to committee meetings, and editing the cookbook, they felt like part of the school. For many parents, this was a new form of connecting. Discussion spilled over into the community as cooks discussed grams or cups or "How much is a taste?" It led to many cross-language friendships.

It is important to note that the whole community, not just international families, participated in the Taste of the World. At the first one, multigenerational Americans shared foods like Texas chili and challah. By the third year, families were pairing up and bringing in grandma's specialities or grandpa's barbecue. Children raced around touting their own home foods. With just a "taste" one's meal could truly be multicultural, with a plate filled with continental cuisines of Africa, Asia, Australia, Europe, and North and South America.

It's always fun to share food, to celebrate, to talk, to watch the excited children within a school building. Everyone enjoys tasting but the deeper gift comes by openly recognizing and sharing family heritage. These gifts help connect the international families to the school community and to the larger neighborhood community.

The Future

The Wheel of Advocacy, with child and family at the center and an International Resource teacher as the rim, is a metaphor with ramifications for other populations and other settings. It makes for a powerful program empowering teachers and all students.

As the wheel rim, the International Resource Advocate reaches all sections of the community. The spokes connect the rim to the parents and child at the hub. The International Resource Advocate balances and integrates curriculum, language, and culture, resulting in multi-cultural education for a whole community. Connections from home and school build and strengthen a community foundation. Children who become part of the learning community, with strong connections from school to home, help each family thrive. Students, families, staff, and faculty who carry experiences of learning through working together, see a working, living vision of the future. With respect and delight, children learn, work, and play in a diverse community: a glimpse of the 21st century filled with home and possibilities.

11 Affirming Difference While Building a Nation:

Teaching Diversity in Neo-apartheid America

Owen van den Berg

I was born and raised in South Africa, and for all my adult life until recently (1995) I worked as a teacher and teacher educator in that society. The policy of the minority *apartheid* regime throughout those years was to emphasize difference; to attempt to keep the members of each ethnic or racial group separate in all aspects of life; and to work to divide the country into several ethnically distinct "nations" in a way that left the "white" minority in a dominant and privileged position.

Those of us who worked to oppose this policy attempted to bring together people from different groups, to oppose inequality and authoritarianism, and to work towards a common South Africanism in which national unity could be forged alongside respect for difference. From 1982 on I was a professor of education in the historically black University of the Western Cape, and much of what we did was to try to create an island of integration and awareness within an ocean of segregation and authoritarianism. I used action research to help me and my students reflect on the pedagogical and political dimensions of teaching with a view to transforming education and society. In many ways the struggle against *apartheid* was the struggle of opposing views of culture.

It is hard to describe my emotions when, on a rainy April day in 1994, I was able to participate in a democratic election that included all my fellow citizens, and not just those of the dominant "white" group, of which I was a member. The time had come (we hoped) when one could work, with the support of the state, for national reconstruction—the forging of an all-inclusive nationhood within which different cultural, ethnic, and religious traditions would be respected and affirmed. Against the legacy of *apartheid*, which had been a nation-*destroying* policy, the challenge now was to promote a nation-*building* policy that would honor and affirm diversity.

At the start of 1995, when I married an American citizen and moved to St. Louis, Missouri, I was by no means a stranger to the country. Coming to live permanently in the St. Louis metropolitan area—and the United States—proved to be a bigger shock than I had anticipated. American sanctions had hastened the fall of the *apartheid* regime, but the America to which I moved seemed to be heading in the exact directions for which it had boycotted South Africa! I saw increasing residential segregation; growing public and legislative resistance to equal opportunities for all and to the elimination of poverty; and the increasing desire to impose a dominant culture and language on all the people of the country.

While the rhetoric of multicultural education suggests that Americans will increasingly find themselves in culturally diverse school and work settings, I found myself often teaching groups of students that were more segregated than those I had taught in South Africa, and where knowledge and tolerance of people from other traditions and societies was often minimal, if not nonexistent. To be sure, teaching diverse groups of students or workers to coexist and respect one another is one challenge America faces; but teaching multicultural respect to people living in increasingly segregated and isolated—*neo-apartheid*—settings (such as the St. Louis metro area) is another matter altogether.

Course Intentions and Design

In 1997, I took an appointment in the Department of Educational Studies at St. Louis University (SLU). When I heard that I was to teach an undergraduate course in cultural diversity, I was somewhat bemused about how to go about it. I suspected, given what I knew about the Greater St. Louis area, and about the university, that the students who would likely end up in my class would come from pretty *undiverse* backgrounds. I decided, therefore, that, in teaching the course, I should not focus so much on the cultures of faraway and exotic places, or try to teach "techniques of multicultural education" to people who were not yet teachers, but rather that I should concentrate on encouraging the students to explore their own cultures, to identify the levels of difference and diversity that exist within their group, and to proceed from there to deep discussion of key issues of diversity—race, gender, social class, language, disadvantage and giftedness, and so on.

I hoped to generate rich discussions about equity, equality, the culture of schools, and the role of the United States in the world (and the way it is perceived by Americans). I did not see myself as delivering a body of knowledge about diversity, but rather as the facilitator of discussions. I saw the class not as the *resource for our learning* rather than a *target for my teaching*—an easy position to adopt if one does not believe that there is a crucial canon of knowledge that has to be taught and learned. In the course syllabus I set out my intentions. (See Figure 1.)

In addition to seeing the class meetings (seventy-five minutes twice a week for fifteen weeks) as discussions rather than lectures, I viewed the assignments as crucial to the achievement of my purposes. As there was no "knowledge" or "content" that I wished to test, I set a rather heavy load of five lengthy assignments, to be handed in at three-week intervals. (See Figure 2.)

In teaching this course, I also knew that my practice would speak more loudly than any intentions or slogans. I wanted the students to understand that, as teachers their classrooms would develop a culture that affects their students in a variety of ways. I wanted them to be critically aware of my teaching strategies and the atmosphere that prevailed in my classroom. I attempted to write regular reflections on the progress of the course and invited anonymous, written course evaluations from the students. I made these available to the students for comment. Near the end of the course I wrote a long reflection on the course as a whole, and had the students read and respond with specific or general comments. I edited the student

---

It is often hard for us to imagine that we have a culture, or what that culture might be. In this course I will try to engage you in *discussion about what a "culture" might be,* and what our individual and group cultures might be, with a view to thinking about appropriate attitudes for us to take up towards people and groups that are different from us. I will also attempt to encourage you to think about the *school curriculum as a selection from the culture*—the totality—out there, and about how you might think of teaching as inevitably a multicultural activity within which the teacher has a great deal of power. Finally, I will attempt to make the course as "personal" as possible, within the constraints of people's rights to privacy, so that each participant, myself included, might feel that by participating in it we have come to *a fuller understanding of ourselves as persons who have been socialized and acculturated in very particular ways,* and how that affects the way we think about ourselves, our future careers, and our relationships with other people and institutions within society. . . .

FIGURE 1

THE ASSIGNMENTS

The first assignment—personal culture

Reflect on your own life and the way in which you have been socialized or educated into a particular "culture," and attempt to describe what the keystones of that personal culture are.

The middle three assignments—cultural explorations

- Report on a cultural activity in which you are a minority, or where you feel that you are "different" in significant ways from the participants.

- Choose a person from a different "culture"—someone with a different sexual orientation, a recent immigrant, an elder citizen, a street person, a person from another racial group, etc.—and meet with this person in order to write an oral history of a particular event that the person participated in or experienced, or an oral biography of a phase in or aspect of the person's life.

- Do one of three things in self-constituted small groups:

  1. Read a book together, written by a person different from your group in terms of culture, race, age, ability, class, or gender, and write a report on the experience.

  2. Develop and maintain a scrapbook of newspaper clippings or themes related to multicultural issues and/or the way people who are deemed to be "different" are treated in this society, and write an accompanying report.

  3. Select a key issue of international concern or attention over the last year, search out some writings that present a view strongly critical of the U.S. position, and prepare a paper on the issue.

Final assignment

Revisit the first assignment in the light of your change or lack of change over the course of the semester.

Journals

Keep journals to submit three times over the semester.

FIGURE 2   *Course assignments*

comments into my original text, presenting it for class discussion, both in small groups and in plenary discussions. As a reflective practitioner, I need to investigate my own teaching and treat my students as partners in that endeavor. If I expect my students to trust me and do some significant personal sharing, then I have to demonstrate a willingness to take risks.

Some Key Features of the Course

The Importance of Getting to Know Ourselves as a Group

After working through the syllabus with the students at the first class meeting, I had them provide me with certain information about themselves, which I summarized and typed up for circulation at the next meeting of the class. I included my own personal information to each question in the typed-up copy that was given to the students.

The discussion of the characteristics of the class, the extent to which we were similar or different, and what implications this had for the members of the group and for the teacher, lasted for several sessions. We had data on a wide range of topics. We found out, for instance, that we had twenty "white" students and five who were "African American" (and an instructor who considered himself quintessentially an African American!)—at a university situated in an overwhelmingly African American part of the metropolitan area. We also discovered from the data that only one of the twenty-six students lived in a single-parent home, that ten had not been outside the United States, that none had been to Africa (or to Delaware, New Hampshire, or North Dakota), that hardly any were fluent in a second language, and that only one person in the room had a mother tongue that was not English.

I shared my written reflections on the data: "The really interesting question . . . is how one could use all these data to promote diversity in one's classroom," and we had some discussions in class about how one might use it to enrich the life of a class. We collected and discussed other information about the group as the course continued. I am confident that this contributed to our sense of how diverse a seemingly uniform group of people can be, and to the dangers of stereotyping people.

In teaching cultural diversity—particularly in supposedly homogeneous settings—we need to start with ourselves as groups of people who constitute very real resources for the task at hand.

The Importance of Personal Explorations

Students had to submit two copies of each assignment, and each person in the class was required to read, comment on, and grade, the paper of a fellow student. I did this to focus on the "culture of grading" so prevalent in schools, and for students to reflect on the impact of grading on their decisions about completing assignments. Students met in small groups to return assignments and talk about them, after which I had plenary discussions about the assignment and issues that arose in it. Generally they were uncomfortable about being graded, or having to grade, and I hoped they would remember that emotion as teachers.

The first assignment required the students to reflect on the ways they had been socialized or educated into a particular "culture." Many students commented favorably on the first assignment. Kari Olson, in her end-of-course reflections, wrote:

> The first paper that was assigned to us was probably the most difficult one to write. I have never had the chance or need to sit down and evaluate my own culture and aspirations for the future. I have always had firm values and beliefs, but did this make up my culture and how others viewed me as a person? . . . this paper forced me to have some serious conversations with my mom and dad that would never have taken place if it wasn't for this paper. Even after I was done with my first paper, every so often they would ask me how this class was going and we would again engage in conversations about their views on subjects like racism, growing up in today's society versus when they grew up, etc. I feel that this was an amazing benefit from this class that I was not expecting at all.

The final assignment called on students to look back at what they had written in their first assignment and write a reflective essay on how their thinking had changed or remained the same over the course of the semester. Many of them spoke of having a more nuanced sense of the diversity of people. Paula Washington, for instance, wrote:

> The most important thing that I have learned this semester is that people are not always what they seem because of stereotypical judgements I have previously conceived from things such as their religion, race, profession, and public attitudes. Learning from one's own judgmental flaws through the process of eliminating stereotypical attitudes, in my personal opnion is what education is all about.

Amy Brenner wrote in a similar vein of the teacher's dilemma:

> I can't take what little I know about my students and make assumptions based on those few facts that I know. On the other hand, I have to take what I know and make assumptions from there on how I can best help each student individually. . . . I realize that I will need to account for all of the possible combinations of cultural variance that may be present in my classroom.

Encouraging students to share from their own personal experience is a powerful approach when one is trying to develop respect for cultural diversity. But it is also a risky business (given the power the teacher has over the students), and one that can easily violate individual rights to privacy. What is more, as one student put it, was I not "grading people's lives rather than their assignments?"!

The Importance of Cultural Explorations

We spent quite some time in class discussing the middle three assignments, first in small groups and then in plenary sessions once I had the chance to work through all the assignments. My sense was that this combination of cultural exploration and discussion was the most powerful aspect of the course. Let me provide one or two examples of the students' experiences and reflections.

For the second assignment—attending a cultural activity in which you are a minority or different—many of the students chose to attend religious meetings. But Barry Williams, an African American, chose to go to Incahoots, a line dancing "club" in St. Louis. He writes wittily about his prejudiced anticipation of this outing:

> My preliminary expectations were strictly based on what I had seen on television and in the movies. My expectations were also based on some of the literature about western expansion. I visualized a smoke filled room with a putrid smell of stale beer. I thought I would see pictures of rebel army officers and political portraits of people who had opposed the old Northern concepts. On the parking lot I expected to see plenty of pickup trucks with gun racks in the rear window. I also expected to see confederate flags. Even though moon shine is outdated, the low, fast contraband carrying vehicles, to me, are synonymous with country western music. I was anticipating seeing pool tables, and wrestlers, and mechanical bulls. . . . I also expected to hear that world renown sound of steel guitars, harmonicas, banjos, fiddles, mouth harps, and scrubboards. . . . I know in any given situation there may be some neanderthal remains of a long time past, but the attitude toward our party was not what I expected. It was receptive and pleasant. . . . You will have to take my word for this, but the cowboy hats were outnumbered by baseball caps. I found it hard to believe that any self respecting cowboy would be seen with a baseball cap on.

Erin George was one of a group of several students who chose (for assignment four) to read children's literature from or on a variety of cultures and to see what stereotypes or differences they revealed.

One book, supposedly giving brief glimpses of different cultures, really struck Erin:

> The book titled *People*[1] portrayed Americans to be living in mobile homes and tepees and participating in activities like horseshoe throwing and rodeos. I quickly became aware of the likelihood that things I had been taught about other cultures weren't necessarily untrue, just did not give the whole truth.

In teaching cultural diversity it is hard to imagine how we can have a significant impact on our students' sense of the richness of the world if they are not required to interact in significant ways with parts of that world that are alien to them.

The Importance of Deep Discussion

I used a small-group format for discussion of controversial topics, such as affirmative action, Ebonics, the notion of educational equality, inequality between the sexes, and racism in American society. Sometimes, to promote discussion on a particular issue, I gave the students a brief reading on the topic, or showed them a video. Every day's news brought topics for discussion—from atheists in the Boy Scouts to American foreign policy towards Cuba—and all these could be handled in terms of attitudes towards people whose beliefs and lifestyles are different.

Usually the small group discussions were followed by whole group discussion, but I did not require the small groups to report back to the larger class, because I feel that this interferes with the quality of the discussion in the small groups and that by leaving the small group discussions "private," students do not have to engage in the art of pleasing the teacher. Yet by respecting the "privacy" of the small groups, I also was less able to gauge how effective their discussions were. When I wrote in my end-of-course reflection that "I was not always convinced that there was widespread participation in the discussions," one student responded in writing, "Not every student in class will offer their opinions in class, not due to uncomfortability as much so as habit, perhaps."

A major problem I encountered with small-group "deep discussion" was the frequent struggle (or was it unwillingness?) to enter into meaningful discussion on serious, controversial topics. The sound-byte approach to public debate in American society is a profoundly

---

1 Spier, Peter. (1988) *People.* New York, NY: Doubleday

antidemocratic tendency that teachers need to strive hard to counteract. I found it difficult to have both sides of an argument fully heard and explored, and students often confessed to being *angry* when others disagreed with them. As an "outsider" I often took very unpopular positions, particularly in terms of American foreign policy, in order to provoke discussion by taking up, with passion, the "foreign" perspective.

As I wrote in the end-of-course reflection that I shared with the students:

> I was quite surprised—even discouraged—by the attitudes of many of the students regarding certain basic inequalities and biases in the society. It seemed that several of them, for instance, were far from sympathetic towards homosexuals and their rights; also, many of them had no sympathy for affirmative action, and seemed to believe that merit was the crucial way to choose between people, even as they acknowledged that merit was an extremely slippery concept. Many, I suspect, were also uncomfortable when I painted a picture of the role of the United States in the world in a less-than-glowing way.

Deep discussion can make a major contribution to students' sensitivity to difference and diversity, but appropriate and adequate background materials and resources need to be employed in such a way that the students are driven to respect alternative viewpoints and lifestyles, even if they do not accept them. Teachers need also to respect the student's right to remain silent.

The Importance of Recognizing Tension and Friction, and Dealing with It

The previous discussion leads quite naturally to the issue of tension and friction dealing with diversity. I was unnerved to read the following journal from one of the students after I had shown a video on hate in American history, *The Shadow of Hate: A History of Intolerance in America,* produced by the Southern Poverty Law Center:

> To me, it was the same basic movie as I was forced to watch year after year in gradeschool. I hated them . . . I was always the bad guy. Viewing these tapes at such a young age gave me many insecurities about my race as a child that I have since had to deal with. I resent these movies now so my judgement of this one is clouded to say the least . . . I think another reason I was bothered was because I feel as if the professor/teacher is expecting me to react to the film as if it is the first time I've seen this type of treatment. It's not . . . it has been drilled into my head through years of history classes in the St. Louis Public School District.

Why this response to the video shook me as much as it did, I think, was because it made me wonder whether I, in the name of promoting diversity, was not simply pushing my own, undiverse, line in the classroom. When I included the above quotation in my end-of-course reflection and added the comment, "Is what I'm doing nothing but a repetition of stuff that has been thrown at these students time and again?" it drew a wide range of written responses from the students. These ranged from "I agree but no one can forget the horrible things that people have done in the past, so why attempt to" to "This is mine [i.e., the student is acknowledging that she wrote the original comment], the other students are not coming from the same place as me so they wouldn't share the same opinion."

I brought issues of classroom conflict or individual statements of anger into the public domain. Much of the institutionalized intolerance of diversity in American society stems from a mixture of ignorance and fear. Too often issues are avoided rather than dealt with. I felt that, by finding an appropriate way to share the angry journal comment from an anonymous individual student, I could engage the whole class in the discussion and have them reflect, as prospective teachers, on the complexities of creating a challenging classroom where people also can feel safe. One student, in her final evaluation comments, wrote that "most importantly I have learned not to fear writing papers that express my personal feelings about controversial topics."

We do our students a disservice if we ignore, avoid, or gloss over conflict situations. Conflict is a real and necessary part of modern societies, and we owe it to our students to give them experience in dealing with the emotions that conflict generates. Conflict, carefully handled, is a powerful teaching tool.

The Importance of Understanding the Culture of the Classroom, and Reflecting on Practice

Teachers play a huge role in determining the culture and climate of our classrooms. Yet we are often unaware of the basic feelings of our students or of the currents within the classroom. As I said earlier, I knew that in teaching this course "my practice would speak more loudly than my intention or slogans." I therefore tried to reflect on my work on a regular basis, to share my written reflections with my students for their comments; to give them frequent opportunities to give me feedback; and, via the journals, to engage them in discussions about whatever issues they chose to raise.

With these strategies I learned a great deal about the dynamics of my class, about my teaching, and about myself. I have already discussed the "hate" video issue, which caused me to reconsider carefully what I was doing. Another instance was the fairly conclusive evidence from the students' responses that I required the discussion of certain topics to drag on too long. One student, in her final evaluative comments, referred to the discussions and assignments before adding the following the sage words:

> You cannot necessarily change people's views with one course. It takes time. That, if nothing else, is something I know all too well. The papers made sense; they had some effect. Maybe that effect was less than you'd hoped for . . . but any amount of change is good.

One priceless advantage of obtaining student feedback on your teaching is that students often affirm what it is you set out to do, but phrased in ways that are novel to your thinking, and which thus contribute to your reflections about your work. Kari Olson's final evaluative comments resonated with my ambitions for the course in very real ways:

> I have learned from this Cultural Diversity class in a different way than I thought I would learn. This class was different from all the other classes I have taken here at SLU in that it focused on learning about yourself and not book learning. I think this was shocking to me at the beginning because it was a different set up. I did not want to talk about myself and others' experiences in life. I thought it would be difficult to share in class and tell the other students my feelings about touchy subjects like racism and feminism . . . This class has taught me more about people and society and myself than I ever expected it to . . . Without each other, we would never have a chance to discover what lies within our heart and mind. These ties with others are what makes us shape our own cultures and beliefs.

If we allow ourselves to become fascinated by the culture of the groups that we, teachers and students, come to create, and if we investigate the impact of our actions on that classroom culture, then we shall be better equipped to build student solidarity and affirm and explore diversity.

Postscript

Americans are very isolated—from the rest of the world and, increasingly, from other Americans who think and act differently from them. Americans typically have little grasp of how the rest of the world perceives their country, and of how they are perceived by other inhabitants of the United States who happen to be different from them.

The task of overcoming this isolation and cultural encapsulation, I believe, is best pursued not by attempting to teach about the cultures of faraway places (nor am I convinced that one can do this in any meaningful way) but rather by starting with a group of students, and the context within which they find themselves, as both the resource and the curriculum. The cultural goal we need to seek with our students is that they come to a richer understanding of themselves, of the people in their world, and of the structures and institutions of the society. Such cultural learning may well make them better citizens and defenders of democracy. One student, Christine LaClear, said of the Cultural Diversity course, " . . . I've learned more about life without traveling far." We should want our students to learn more about life without necessarily having to travel far.

This requires what is first and foremost a *political* commitment—to the acceptance of other people and other ways as legitimate, even as we affirm that for which we stand. This commitment was beautifully expressed by Katie Yock in her final evaluative comments on the Cultural Diversity course:

> When I think of the United States I can't help but focus on our diversity as a whole. Year after year, we become more diverse, frequently changing with the times. We pick up new customs through those we meet, like I have in the past semester, and it makes us better people. I have no doubt that diversity is wonderful for us as human beings. It adds to our lives, raises our awareness, and stimulates our sense of becoming united as one.

We all need to learn how to open our eyes a little wider to the world around us.

References

Spier, Peter. (1988) *People*. New York, NY: Doubleday.
The Shadow of Hate: A History of Intolerance in America (1995). Southern Proverty Law Center. Montgomery, AL.

12

Becoming a Multicultural Educator: Talking the Talk and Walking the Walk

Dean Cristol

Several years ago, I had the opportunity to spend an extended and intensive period of time with a group of learners in Greensboro, North Carolina. I asked them, "What is a multicultural perspective?"

Edith said that she "thought it was about learning about black people, and Hispanic things, something that is really out where you can see the differences . . . "

In Ivy's view, "whether it would be middle class whatever, white or Hispanic or black whatever, or male/female, you can't just hit one group. If you have different sides or views in your material, multiculturalism means a lot more people."

These two beliefs were typical in this class. My view was typical, too. Confident in my ability as a teacher and researcher, I knew that what I provide through teaching and field experiences is enough to change a person's perspectives toward another person, especially when the other person's background is ethnically and culturally different.

It didn't matter that the students in my group were all women in their twenties, college seniors, in their last year of a two-year teacher education program that emphasizes "Teaching as Inquiry" and reflective practices.

I was confident that the answer to my own question, "Do preservice teachers who experience multicultural issues in their professional studies become multicultural educators?" would be yes. I was going to help these beginning teachers become multicultural thinkers in the classroom. I would seek the answer to the question by discovering their multicultural perspectives and documenting their teaching from a multicultural perspective. I held the belief that what we were teaching at the university, would translate to good multicultural teaching during their field experiences.

I was sure they would multiculturally "talk the talk and walk the walk" in their classrooms. What I discovered was not what I expected.

Setting

My relationship with this group of 19 preservice teachers began at the University of North Carolina at Greensboro in my last year of doctoral studies as part of the Professional Development Schools (PDS) program. The central mission of the PDS program is to advance the profession of teaching. Embedded in this mission is a key tenet in the pursuit of a multicultural education curriculum: the belief that all children can succeed in school. Students in this program worked in inquiry teams with other preservice teachers beginning in their junior year and continuing through their student teaching.

It was apparent that it was going to take awhile to get some of the women to trust me. Halfway through their two-year program, I had replaced their first supervisor; she'd just completed her doctoral studies. She was a positive influence on their development, someone whom they entrusted with their fears, ideas, and beliefs about teaching.

Multicultural Teaching

In order to understand the experiences of the preservice teachers and earn their trust, I first had to define multicultural education for myself.

Multicultural education is an approach to empower all students through teaching and learning. Empowerment validates the experiences and identities of students, promotes equality and equity by nurturing cultural pluralism, and incorporates a process for social justice (Cristol, Hoover, and Oliver 1994).

This definition is based upon the work of Geneva Gay (1997), who maintains that all teachers, including preservice teachers, must acquire the knowledge concerning ethnic and cultural groups' histories and heritages, life experiences, and interactional styles to bridge the gap between the cultural values and behavioral codes of themselves and their students. As preservice teachers become knowledgeable about their students' cultural and ethnic identities, both the teacher and students will experience a sense of liberation from the customary constraints practiced by traditional educators. Traditionally, education placed the teacher as the controlling source of knowledge and the students were the passive recipients of that knowledge. Educators who practice multicultural education in their classrooms often shift their roles as teachers to become students in their own classrooms. Multicultural educators see themselves in a constant state of learning about and providing for the needs of their students. Multicultural learning and teaching creates an educational culture that is constantly reacting and changing to meet the needs of all students.

During the semester prior to student teaching, they took courses together in reading and social studies methods and interned at one of two magnet schools in Greensboro. One half of the children at each school came from the surrounding neighborhood and the other half came from all over the city. One school was located in a predominately African American neighborhood, while the other school was located in a predominately white neighborhood. One school was in an integrated middle-class neighborhood, while the other was in an African American middle-class neighborhood. Teachers came from diverse sociocultural backgrounds from all sections of the city. Our group wasn't quite as diverse. We had three African Americans and one Latina. The rest of the group considered themselves to be white.

For this semester, they were to: (1) continue individual and small group instruction including planning, carrying out, and evaluating remedial and enrichment activities; (2) increase their experiences in planning, carrying out, and evaluating instructional activities for the whole class; (3) participate when possible in noninstructional activities such as school-based assessment committee meetings or staff development activities; (4) bring in a multicultural perspective to the curriculum; and (5) attend internship seminar sessions focusing on multicultural education.

At our first meeting, I explained that I was to have two roles working with them, as their university supervisor and as researcher. My role as supervisor was to facilitate their success as teachers. My role as researcher was to observe and analyze evidence of their growth as multicultural educators.

A sign that I was gaining their trust was when several women began to seek my advice to improve their teaching practices. As the trust between us became stronger, I no longer had to inform the women when I was acting as their supervisor or as the researcher. As the year progressed, in fact, my roles as researcher and supervisor began to blur. It was at this period that several of the women began to share their beliefs openly without feeling like I was judging them. They knew I would not jeopardize their growth at the expense of my research. Eventually, most of the group viewed me as a person who cared deeply about their progress as teachers. Yet, I was never able to gain the complete trust and confidence of a few members of the group.

Prior to the student teaching semester, our university students and the cooperating teachers participated in deciding student teaching placements. Most, but not all, preferences were accommodated. Some of the women were assigned to schools and grade levels that were not their first choice. Each woman had interned at least once at her student teaching school. For some women, their assignment caused some uneasiness early in the semester, but most of the women quickly adjusted to their student teaching placements.

The internship seminar played a strong role in the program. Three questions guided the seminar: what is a multicultural perspective, why should we teach from a multicultural perspective, and how should we teach from a multicultural perspective?

Students in the seminar during the semester read Sonia Nieto's *Affirming Diversity* (1992) and Vivian Paley's *White Teacher* (1979). They also read *Roll of Thunder, Hear My Cry*, a children's book by Mildred Taylor (1976). Seminar discussions were structured around the following concepts: (1) key concepts of multicultural education; (2) struggle between traditional versus multicultural approaches to education; (3) aspects of ethnicity; (4) learning style; and (5) ethnic identity development. The three guiding questions and five key concepts framed our group's dialogue and reflections, as well. Throughout the year, I challenged the preservice teachers to reflect on the role teachers need to demonstrate in a classroom with a diverse student population.

The seminar sessions allowed for open, safe, and reflective discussions on difficult issues. A major focus of the sessions was to help the preservice teachers see how individual group affiliations affect the ways teachers interact, especially the students in their internship schools.

Three Preservice Teachers

Following my year's experience with the group, I found three general outcomes. I will present a detailed illustration of three members of the group who each exemplify one of the outcomes. Ivy's experience represents members who developed high levels of multicultural understanding through the university portion of the program and had difficulty practicing those perspectives during their field experiences. Edith's experience illustrates those members who had minimal understanding of multicultural education upon entering the program and left the program with a high degree of confidence in their understanding and competence with issues of diversity in school. Terry's experience is an example of members who entered the program with a partially developed multicultural perspective and left the program with a highly developed perspective on multicultural teaching and learning.

Ivy

Ivy is a petite, well-spoken woman in her early twenties with bright eyes, dark hair, and a deep sense of curiosity. She identifies her ethnic/ cultural group as Hispanic. Her mother is from a Latin American country. Ivy loves to speak Spanish and uses her bilingual abilities in classroom settings. She has lived in various parts of the United States and expresses interest in teaching in another part of the country or possibly in another country. She consistently questioned ideas and concepts presented in university courses, questioned her teaching abilities, and questioned my decisions for the group in a mature manner. Although she was one of the most outspoken members of the group, Ivy rarely socialized outside the school setting with her university classmates.

Ivy wrote in her journal that the multicultural content in the seminars was helpful in understanding how and why children behave differently. She wrote, "Teachers must become aware of the ways the children react or behave in class or interact with students or even with the teacher." From this knowledge, Ivy believed that the content of the lessons "has to be geared where they (children) come from, and what their experiences are at home and that could be ethnic, or can be economic, or the stability in the home."

> The times that Dr. Wilson came for seminar sessions, I thought that was really helpful for me and, I think, a lot of people. It helped a lot. What she did was good as far as having you think about how we view ourselves and about our ethnic groups and also taking that into teaching and helping students with it.[1]

Later, Ivy wrote, "We saw a video about discrimination that was shockingly frightening, so many people in America still harbor so much prejudice. To deny a person the right to rent an apartment, solely because that person has a different color skin." She began to see one of her roles, as a teacher, was to combat prejudice and discrimination: "It was my duty as a teacher to help students understand and

---

1 Personal journal entries are not written with other readers in mind. In this chapter, some journal entries have been edited for clarity.

appreciate different cultures and people who are different from themselves." For Ivy, the multicultural seminar sessions were a catalyst to help understand and develop her own multicultural perspectives. Few of the group members internalized these concepts at the same level as Ivy. She understood how teachers' group affiliation can affect the way they perceive and interact with their students.

A major focus for Ivy's journal writings was that many of the teachers at the internship schools utilized and presented multicultural materials, but rarely dealt with the issues that concerned the students. Near the end of her studies, when Ivy finally experienced a cooperating teacher who challenged students' perceptions and beliefs about others, Ivy wrote "that even young children were able to discuss some hard issues."

At the conclusion of the semester before student teaching, I asked Ivy what teachers must do to create a classroom atmosphere that emphasized respect for all people.

> If you let them talk about something that means something to them, they will listen to each other, it means so much more to them. I can stand here and talk forever and let them say one or two things and that is fine and they will get something from it, but if they get a chance to express what they are feeling it will mean something more to them. I learn from the kids when I am watching them. I think the teacher should respect the different ethnicities and different races, and respect and acknowledge the differences not just looking at them, but acknowledge and work with them. With children if you identify some of the differences and play on that, have them work from that.
>
> I see multicultural education as educating the students about other experiences, it gets hard because you have so much to do and I think you have to do it in a way, not necessarily specifically sit down and teach this, you have to make it part of your teaching. . . . You have to reach different children different ways.

Ivy's multicultural awareness levels seemed to fluctuate between two extremes. She was able to articulate her multicultural perspectives in a clear and concise manner during the seminar and in her journal entries, yet she had difficulty translating these perspectives into language elementary children understand.

During several of Ivy's student teaching observations, I observed that Ivy was often surprised at the different academic and social levels within her classroom, and had difficulty adjusting her teaching to meet the many needs of the students. When I asked her about this difficulty with the students, she responded, "Some students exceeded the objectives in their assigned grade level, while other students could not do those very basic things, which made teaching to a diverse classroom a difficult task." Her multicultural perspectives were philosophically developed. However, her ability to put them into practice remained at a superficial level. She did not complete student teaching with a heightened awareness of how to teach from a multicultural perspective, but rather a sense that she has the ability to teach from a more traditional perspective. During an interview at the end of the program, Ivy stated: "One of the big things that I learned in student teaching was how much you really have to adjust the assignments and the lessons for each child."

Edith

Edith did not follow the traditional path to become a teacher. She continues to live, with her husband and young daughter, in the same all-white, rural town where she grew up, sixty miles from the university. Edith describes her neighbors as having very conservative social, political, and religious beliefs. Generally soft-spoken, when she speaks in class it is after giving the topic a lot of thought. Edith is careful not to insult people, yet was honest in expressing her beliefs. She has a pleasant, disarming way when disagreeing with people, by smiling when speaking as a way to alleviate the tension.

At the beginning of the program, Edith's perspectives toward teaching and learning were based upon her own monocultural experiences. As Edith began to spend more time in the two culturally diverse schools, she began to realize that learning and teaching are a complex process.

Edith wrote in her journal that the multicultural seminar discussions helped her to better understand the African American experience. She was grateful for the interactions with the members of the group who presented an African American perspective. From the seminar and internship experiences, Edith's perspectives toward society and specifically the students at the two schools began to change. Her writings revealed how her appreciation and respect of people's cultural and ethnic differences increased. She wrote in her journal about a required seminar reading, *The Education of Little Tree* (Carter 1990), which focused on the unfair treatment of Native Americans. The book forced her to reexamine her own perspectives toward people who are different from her:

> I have never thought about Native Americans being treated badly, this book gives the reader an insight to the injustices in society

toward many people . . . it was interesting to see how Little Tree, the main character, viewed people's actions toward him before he knew what discrimination was.

I don't think you can separate a multicultural perspective and education. It is so interwoven into people, I don't think you can separate it; not when you want to do the best you can for the kids and try to get them to be learners, productive citizens. It is not just whether they can do math, but if they are going to vote, what kind of educational background, what they would look at, if they are law abiders. Education was so concrete when I was younger, math, English, but it is not so simple anymore.

Edith was better able to define multicultural education because of the multicultural seminar and internship experiences.

Edith told me about an incident in one of her internships that demonstrated the pervasiveness of prejudice and discrimination in elementary schools.

I heard a couple of girls, one little white girl made a very bad comment about black people's hair, their smell, you could tell it was coming straight from home and she told some stories, it didn't surprise me . . . it starts in second grade, with the white-black racial thing and by fifth grade you can see little sets inside the classroom."

She believed a way for teachers to combat these negative beliefs systems was to make learning relevant for every child.

I see multicultural education as not only teaching other kids about the other ethnic people. Teach about *themselves and* other people around them.

She provided an example of how her exposure to different ideas changed her perspectives about American society. During one multicultural seminar session, the group viewed a video about the exposure of a group of rural white children to discrimination in a teacher-directed activity. Edith wrote:

A video *A Class Divided* [Peters 1986] served its purpose by exposing the children to discrimination and they seemed to carry this knowledge with them throughout their lives. I think it's important to note that the exercise took place in an all-white rural farming community. This exercise would have been more harsh if the class contained people of different races. I think the kids would have been more threatened because the seeds of discrimination have already been planted through their life experiences.

This video forced Edith to redefine her own perceptions of the teacher's role. She believed multicultural education will not naturally occur in classrooms, but teachers must provide opportunities for children to question and explore different perspectives.

> The internships have been in a lot of different places. The range of kids you have; I never really thought about it until last semester. It is something that you really have to have someone bring it up to you before you think about it because so much of it is unconscious. I found myself picking up on comments that are said when I am at home or out in a social area that made me think and to say let's really think about this. I have really seen a change in my attitude. I never intended to have any kind of different attitude. I think it is subconscious . . . until it is brought out. I saw a difference in me. I am different than I would be if we never discussed any issues.

Edith's experiences during the internships made her wary of offending people. This concern created a heightened awareness of how one's own ethnicity affects the way they teach. Edith wrote in her journal about a cooperative teacher who was very aware of how a teacher's own perspectives can sometimes offend students. "There were some things that she changed in my lessons, things that may offend some people. That helped me more. I think not all the classrooms are like that."

Edith was beginning to understand the effects of prejudice and discrimination were not issues for others to solve, but had direct impact on her own life, especially her professional life. Following a student teaching observation, she described how her teaching experiences forced her to confront her beliefs about children whose experiences were different from her own.

> Some of the stories they tell me, gosh, you saw that right in front of your house, I really felt sorry for the children. I would be horrified if my daughter had seen things like that. They told me matter-of-factly, like no big thing, it just happened. I want to hug them all. I think about it a lot at home, it is nothing that you can get away from.

When I asked how her perspectives toward education changed, this was her response: "I believed the school must educate children in justice and integrity. If we all were more caring, we would help those who are less fortunate."

During our last interview Edith discussed how the success of all students was intertwined with the teacher's ability to provide an open and safe atmosphere where the children could express their feelings and opinions. Edith said:

> I care about how the kids have been feeling at school, so I try to let them know that at least at school somebody in their classroom cares about them and wants them to be there.

Terry

Terry was a petite white woman in her early twenties from Greensboro. She was a regular contributor during large group discussions, but she was never perceived as a leader by her peers. Terry appeared to enjoy her experiences working with the children and never discussed being overwhelmed with the cultural and ethnic differences she encountered. One of her endearing traits was to take chances in the classroom. If something did not go as well as expected, she never let it get her down, usually blaming it on her own lack of experience.

During the second semester of the program, Terry began developing an understanding of the importance of learning about a child's experiences and how that impacts the teacher's approach to the individual child's learning style. She worked closely with a child who lived in a homeless shelter. Several people in the school told her that he had many behavior problems, especially speaking at inappropriate times in the classroom. After spending several weeks working with this child, she wrote in her journal: "Biographies about African-Americans would be a good choice to help him begin to like school." During our last interview, I asked her to elaborate on this belief: "This boy had very little self-esteem and I believed reading this type of material would make him realize that there are African Americans who have succeeded in this society." Terry felt that working with him made her aware of the importance of learning about the total child, in order to teach the child.

During the intern semester, Terry began making multicultural connections with her own teaching and learning process. Her lessons introduced differences among ethnic groups and showed concern for the individual needs of the students. During her student teaching semester, she tried to connect her multicultural education perspectives to her teaching practices. At times she reverted back to more traditional concepts of teaching, but the majority of her lessons included multicultural concepts.

Terry became interested in how her students selected each other as friends. "If the children get to choose with whom they want to play, they play with people of their own race, I guess what is familiar."

She asked the children if they play with certain children outside of school. These children were from different ethnic or cultural groups and they would often answer with statements like they "really don't play outside of school with each other very often." These types of statements led Terry to ask two of her students who frequently played together, if they were friends outside of school. One girl was African American and the other white. She observed that these girls frequently played together in school. The African American girl said they were "Not really that good of friends" and the white girl said that the African American girl "doesn't like me." Terry concluded: "I was really amazed because when they said we are not really friends, what can you do to make them friends, you can't."

During our last interview, Terry discussed how she selected multicultural education materials and the role of the teacher. She said, "There should be no sign of stereotypes in these materials, students should be exposed and taught to learn to appreciate other cultures that are different than their own." I asked her about a book she used in a student teaching lesson, *No Good at Art:*

> I chose the book not only because it was multicultural, but because it also talked about how everyone could do well in art or anything they choose to do, no matter what their ability. That book was multicultural because it had different groups represented. It talked about males and females, had different races, girls talking about what they wanted to do when they grow up, and it had different occupations, no stereotypes of males and females, it also had a kid in a wheelchair.

She believed materials must help the children understand that people were not alike. She emphasized that even if you teach in an environment where there is only one ethnic culture, it is the teacher's responsibility to discuss and expose the children to different perspectives in the classroom.

> If you are talking about folktales you can bring in a lot of multicultural things, folktales are from everywhere, so you can bring in stuff and talk about different people who wrote folktales, that tells a lot about different cultures. I can spend hours looking at books. I read everything before to make sure the information is correct. And because book, from a long time ago may have stereotypings. I look at the dates.

Terry held that teachers must practice respect for all the members in the classroom, by learning and teaching about their ethnic and cultural identities. I asked if she had experienced a conflict of beliefs, values, or attitudes during her professional studies, and she by described an incident that occurred several times during the entire program.

> How to get through to some children? The kids that have a home environment that is a big challenge to get the parents involved, or those who are coming from environments where they are going to be distracted or kids who do not going to bed on time and that just floored me.
>
> Find out what is important, what children think, that is a matter of respect. If I didn't care about what they thought I wouldn't be here any way. They have personal knowledge to pull from that shows they have something important to contribute. I show confidence in their ability, that they already know some stuff—especially with informational things—I usually talk about what they already know, before I do anything else. To me if I do that then it makes my lesson more important and they listen more. The kids have to get along and respect each other and help each other and teach each other: There needs to be respect between the kids and me and the kids in all aspects, the group.

Conclusion

As I return to my original question: do preservice teachers "talk the talk and walk the walk" regarding multicultural education issues, I realize that the answers can never be a simple yes or no. Being a multicultural educator is dependent on more than having a very good teacher education program. These three women's experience suggests that preservice teachers culture and ethnic identity influence their multicultural decision-making. The Ediths and Terrys of the group are closer to yes. They are headed in the direction Gay envisioned for a multicultural educator. What remains challenging are the Ivys who understand what a person needs to become a multicultural educator at the theoretical level, but have difficulty putting their perspectives into practice. I wonder if, like Ivy, I have difficulty transferring concepts outside of the multicultural spectrum from the university into classroom practice, or is there something unique about becoming a multicultural teacher?

Clearly, this work demonstrates that exposure to cultural differences through various experiences, even with structured supervision, does not necessarily lead to good multicultural teaching. Teacher educators need to design ongoing programs that address multicultural issues in order for good multicultural teaching to begin during and continue after the teacher preparation program. The success that Edith and Terry experienced should remain the goal for teacher educators. As a teacher educator, I must remember that multicultural education is complex and must be first understood by the educator before integrating it into any educational system. Developing preservice teachers' multicultural perspectives is an intricate undertaking, which involves more than course work, internships, and student teaching. Perspective development is an evolutionary process that incorporates the historical, developmental, ethnic, and cultural identities of any person.

References

CARTER, F. (1990). *The Education of Little Tree*. Albuquerque: University of New Mexico.

CRISTOL, D., HOOVER, K., and OLIVER, D. (1994). "Constructing Multicultural Middle School Classrooms through Teacher Education Programs." *Transescence: The Journal on Emerging Adolescent Education 21*, 7–15.

GOODENOUGH, W. H. (1963). *Cooperation in Change*. New York: Russell Sage Foundation.

GAY, G. (1997). "Educational Equality for Students of Color." In J. A. Banks and C. A. McGee Banks (Eds.), *Multicultural Education: Issues and Perspectives,* 195–228. Boston: Allyn and Bacon.

NIETO, S. (1992). *Affirming Diversity: The Sociopolitical Context of Multicultural Education*. New York: Longman.

PALEY, V. G. (1979). *White Teacher*. Cambridge, MA: Harvard University Press.

PETERS, W. (1986). *A Class Divided*. Alexandria, VA: PBS Video.

TAYLOR, M. D. (1976). *Roll of Thunder, Hear My Cry*. New York: Dial Press.

13 International Students, International Teachers: A Multicultural Dilemma

María Angeles Fernández Castro

An International Challenge

International schools face the enormous challenge and responsibility to provide students with worldwide recognizable passports and credentials that enable mobile students to transcend geographical frontiers; work in multicultural societies with an appropriate corpus of knowledge; and also to understand, tolerate, and perhaps adopt unfamiliar values, perceptions, and attributes. International schools are as numerous as they are varied in structure, student and staff composition, setting and environment, educational standards and evaluations, purposes and objectives. These schools' policies reflect different models, which reflect specific philosophical views of external and internal needs, expectations, and demands. The Directory of the European Council of International Schools (ECIS) provides a broad description in terms of these institutions' varying size, organization, facilities, and curriculum (Matthews 1989a, 10–11).

Despite complex diversity, efforts have been made by some international schools' associations to create a true "system of international schools." International educators envision a common core of knowledge and skills that are transferable, adaptable, and multicultural. Such educators work in unison toward the fulfilment of a single ideal: the molding of the international learner into a multidimensional, multifunctional, and multiflexible trans-language learner (Jonietz 1994, 43, Barter 1994, 34). Therein lies survival as social creatures in an alien milieu—indeed, a truly Darwinian experience, "that students should be able to adapt easily and rapidly upon transfer . . ." (Matthews 1989b, 24).

Many difficulties are encountered on the way toward homogeneity. Multicultural schools suffer varying degrees of isolation due mainly to the distances between them. Other more subtle obstacles can be found in the analysis of the schools' educational policies, and how and why they come into being. Comparison of these policies may show differences between them that may seem irreconcilable—how to cater to four different pupil nationalities within the same classroom? Or, how to reconcile national and international curricula standards within the same school? The fact that these educational policies show marked differences is quite understandable, since they are the concrete embodiments of philosophies, and these in turn have been elaborated, curbed, and influenced by a variety of social and individual, economic and ideological, institutional and communal, national and international drives. The values permeating each international school are not identical: the educational policies behind these organizations, whether external or internal, mandated or democratic, politically, socially, and/or economically inspired, necessarily reflect each school's ethos, which is "as intangible as that of any other school system, but is nonetheless real" (Matthews 1989b, 33).

How can an educational policy reconcile forces that clash, compete, or overlap with provisions for crisis, change, and continuity? An answer is hidden in the past, as the desire to understand, to pass along, and to teach. It is hidden in the definition of culture as societies that preserve their past.

Educational policies then must encompass certain attributes in order to be effective:

- They have to be rigid and specific enough to be contained in a written record.

  "If it isn't in writing, . . . it doesn't exist" (Matthews 1989b, 33).

- They have to be flexible enough to be altered or modified at any time, when conflict arises.

  "Effective policy making is the cohesion and acceptance of objectives, and not waste energy in conflict" (Newton and Tarrant 1990). (LISA-Quote OK? Sense?)

- They have to reflect the wisdom acquired through a past history.

  " . . . the absence of sustained historical input is extremely difficult to justify" (Silver 1990, 6).

- They have to reflect the acquisition of experience in order to accommodate the present, and to move into the unpredictable future with a degree of certainty.

    ". . . a historical input needs to be aware both of the complex web with which it is engaged, and the determinants of its own starting points" (Silver 1990, 15).

- They have to be permeated with the values, beliefs, and attitudes of the communities they serve.

That is to say, they have to be democratic in their nature, and representative of the cultural identity to which they belong (Silver 1990, 213). Educational policy aims to provide "major guidelines for actions" (Silver 1990, 213) and descriptions about a wide range of topics at school (Newton and Tarrant 1992, 120–121). It is a framework, encapsulated in a philosophy of the past and the future. A policy manual contains partial solutions to unforeseen problems. An indispensable attribute of a comprehensive policy lies in its prediction, and therefore, in its prevention quality, ". . . the role of history, not as lessons from the past. . .but as prevention, as warnings against what did not work, what it might be preferable to avoid" (Silver 1990, 30).

School Curriculum

A school level curriculum is perhaps the most technical and transparent aspect of the educational policy. It incorporates a school's purposes and aims, as well as the intrinsic values of the educational organization. Of all the aspects that educational policy covers, it is the curriculum that is most enlightening in terms of cultural descriptions and policy expectations. Learning about the curriculum of each school will invariably lead to the learning of the school itself "at sensitive and revealing points." (Silver, 1990, pp. 140–141). The type, the kind, and the amount of knowledge contained in the curricula marks the differing educators' views in relation to the students' needs for their preparation for adulthood in a highly mobile world.

The International Student

Perhaps the first learning experience students face when they move to a new environment is that of culture shock, which can be more or less apparent (Pearce 1996, 141). Beyond core instruction, the international school curriculum must serve a dual purpose. Some educators see this modern dilemma as a condensation of the international identity itself. It is a compromise between "where we are now, and where we belong"; the essence of building a cultural awareness in students. Through adoption of a culturally diverse syllabus, international students develop a sensitivity to perceive the similarities of their cultures, acknowledge the differences. This should not be "merely a receptive attitude in the sense of showing interest in manifestations of other cultures. It must be of mutual enrichment by the discovery of ways of feeling and thinking that are different from our own" (Renaud 1974, 9–10).

International students should also be able to proclaim their own national identity, harmoniously coexisting with the notion of being a "world citizen."

The International Teacher

International teachers probably face similar "learning" experiences, or some degree of culture shock, when they move to a new, unfamiliar setting. Most international teachers are hired through an agency abroad and parachuted into a cultural warp intrinsically different from their familiar world. How well equipped they are for their new professional commitment greatly depends on their own training and personal traits to cope with innovation. How rich and influential their moment will be in the particular school history depends on the degree of their involvement in the social school community. Successful school policy and curricula largely depend on the practitioners' acceptance and commitment. The key to this is the school's educational policy of rights, duties, and responsibilities, as well as aspirations, visions, and rewards. The schools' administrators are partly responsible for meeting the teachers' expectations, and for feeding their motivations, acknowledging their needs, and offering the degree of challenge they are likely to accept (Fullan and Stiegelbauer 1991, Ch. 8). The teachers' comfort and performance in the new environment are self-fulfilling; it is the school's moral obligation to show the foreign teachers the way to achieve personal success, by making them "feel that they belong" (Pelowski 1994, 33).

A small-scale study was carried out at St. Hilda's College of Argentina, which is categorized as a bilingual school (Spanish (L1) and English (L2)). The school has traditionally hired professionals from abroad, mainly from the United Kingdom and the United States, to teach subjects in English. The focus of the research centered on the beliefs and attitudes of nine practitioners with extensive experience in international schools. All the professionals in the research received general job descriptions with no details of the educational policy of the school before their arrival. Most teachers agreed that a deeper knowledge of some school aspects would have helped tremendously in building expectations more in tune with reality. Curriculum content is a common issue: what to teach, whom to teach, and what time to devote to each subject. Other issues include a description of the student body, especially concerning age-related educational objectives, classroom numbers, duties, and timetables.

Only one of the teachers interviewed would have liked to receive more information about the cultural milieu of the country, "to lessen the cultural shock." The rest of the teachers did not include this aspect of cultural information as relevant to their new jobs. These teachers also have a relatively low degree of involvement with the local social environment. The international professionals in the school group themselves rather tightly within the "expatriate" cluster, where identification with each other is eminently felt as the cultural components (values) they all recognize as their own, such as their native language, their customs (country traditions), and their habits (individual traditions).

Some teachers may choose to remain detached from the broader social setting of the community due to their short-term commitment to the school setting (generally a two-year contract). Perhaps this is a "self-defense technique"; departures are more painful when emotional links become stronger. This phenomenon has been described in relation to mobile pupils (Burleigh 1994, 48–49). Its applicability to adults seems valid.

Another reason for the teachers' limited involvement may be a lack of opportunity to innovate at the level of school policy. They may not share the school vision, but they are expected to adopt it. They inherit the resources, the structure, the syllabuses, and the students. They are directed by established school objectives, aims, and purposes, and they are expected to act accordingly in an amazingly short time.

The question that arises at this point is whether the professionals' value system is consistent with that of the institution, for, if it is not, the school's vision, coherence, ethical context, and moral concern might be endangered (Pollard and Tann 1987, 63; Owens 1995, 306).

If teachers lack influence at the level of policy making, then on which grounds can they exert their immediate influence? Where lies their strength? Which tools do they possess for negotiating transactions and bargaining at the micro political level? Probably, it is from their expertise and international teaching experience that their power emerges (the experts?). If this is the case, their knowledge of the specific subjects they teach, the imported methods they employ, and their familiarity with international educational standards are their main assets. For these professionals, it is through the curriculum content that they can clarify the variations of cultures and establish appropriate norms and objectives for the community's well-being and continuity. Undoubtedly, the vision of these teachers would be enhanced through familiarization with the school educational policy to illuminate the multifaceted reality in which they interact.

Knowledge provides the "newcomers" with the clues to understand the philosophy of the community, the insights to share its mission, and the guidelines to preserve it and develop it. This is true for teachers as well as students!

Conclusion

International school associations now hold a unique opportunity to learn from the qualities of diversity and mobility that the transient teacher and student display; the cultural warps in which they find themselves are, by no means, impenetrable: a multicultural vision built on the need and the will of any particular community, matched with the speed of communications, clearly elevates them to a position that was, only some fifty years ago, quite unthinkable.

> We must utilize these qualities to make significant contributions in such areas as bilingual education, cross-cultural links with the local community and all the other curricular areas where we are admirably positioned to take a lead. (Matthews 1989b, 33)

References

BARTER, R. (Spring 1994). "Multiculturalism and Multilingualism: What It Means in Practice." *International Schools Journal* (27), 31–40.

BURLEIGH, J. C. (Spring 1994). "What Works: A Study of Multicultural Education in an International School Setting." *International Schools Journal* (27), 46–52.

FULLAN, M. G., and STIEGELBAUER, S. (1991). *The New Meaning of Educational Change.* (2d ed.) New York, NY: Teachers College Press.

JONIETZ, P. L. (Spring 1994). "Trans-Language Learners: A New Terminology for International Schools." *International Schools Journal* (27), 41–45.

MATTHEWS, M. (1989a). "The Scale of International Education." *International Schools Journal* (17), 7–17.

MATTHEWS, M. (1989b). "The Uniqueness of International Education." *International Schools Journal* (18), 24–34.

NEWTON, C., and TARRANT, T. (1990). "Objectives for Change in Educational Organizations." *Educational Management and Administration* 18 (3), 61–67.

OWENS, R. G. (1995). *Organizational Behavior in Education.* Boston: Allyn & Bacon.

PEARCE, R. (April 1996). "Kipling's Cat: Learning from the New Student." *International Schools Journal* 15 (2), 23–30.

PELOWSKI, B. G. (Spring 1994). "Developing a School Profile in an Overseas Setting." *International Schools Journal* (27), 15–17.

POLLARD, A., and TANN, S. (1987). *Reflective Teaching in the Primary School: A Handbook for the Classroom.* London: Cassell Educational Limited.

RENAUD, G. (1974). *Experimental Period of the International Baccalaureate: Objectives and Results.* Paris: UNESCO Press.

SILVER, H. (1990). *Education, Change and the Policy Process. Education Policy Perspectives Series.* Bristol, PA: Falmer Press

14

Using Critical Questioning to Investigate Identity, Culture, and Difference

Jill Gladstein

As an English as a Second Language (ESL) teacher I teach classes entitled "American Society" and "American Life and Language" where I am supposed to introduce students to several aspects of American culture. This form of multicultural education, common in the ESL curriculum for older students, has a unique presence in the ESL classroom. The underlying philosophy for these classes is to help new immigrants become American, to help them *blend in*. Traditionally these classes focus on cross-cultural differences, ways to overcome communication difficulties, and isolated facts about American culture or society. The course syllabus typically includes such topics as the American family, perspectives on health, the U.S. court system. It also includes a melting-pot view of American ethnicity.

My unit on ethnicity always brought many interesting—and unsettling—responses. Each semester, with each class, it was as if I had opened a dam on stereotypes and ignorance. After I would explain briefly about immigration trends and what different groups live in the United States, the following conversation would usually takes place:

Jill, what ethnicity are you?

I'm an American Jew.

A Jew, does that mean you are Jewish?

Yes, why?

Well, you must be rich and smart.[1]

---

1 This is a sample of a conversation that took place in many classes. It is not actual data that was transcribed, but rather a synthesis of many conversations that had taken place.

One by one students would tell me or ask me about being Jewish and about all the "horrible" things they heard *my* people had done. There were many times as a teacher in the ESL classroom that I heard negative representations of different ethnic groups in America. When asked where these representations had come from the students replied that they read it somewhere or someone told them and therefore they were true. The students rarely seemed to question what they had heard to see if it was valid.

As a teacher in ESL, I wanted to develop a space to respond to the ideas and experiences I encountered with the students and their views of difference in American society. It is because of these experiences and others like them that I designed a new course. The original course was set up as part of a dissertation research project. I originally wanted to see how the students were constructing their perceptions of people in the United States and how their experiences in the classroom might inform the representations previously held.

In the process of developing the research study, I discovered that before the students could explore their representations of others they had to explore their views of identity, culture, and then difference. Students needed to see how they were defining these terms of identity, culture, and difference as terms themselves and investigate how their understanding of these terms influenced how the students looked at their representations of difference in American society. Therefore, identity, culture, and difference became the three overriding themes of the course.

Theoretical Background

The design of the course involved a complex theoretical framework.[2] One central aspect, which will be briefly presented here, was the notion of *critical questioning*. Questioning is defined as a process in which a person looks at a text and poses questions that may lead to a deeper understanding of that text. A text is defined as more than a written document, but also as a conversation or experience someone has in daily interactions. Questioning helps give some distance so that an individual might be able to look at a situation from a different perspective. The definition of critical questioning used in the course derived from the theories of reflection, metalinguistic critical theory

---

2 For a more detailed description of the overall framework see Gladstein (1999), *Using Literacies to Question Identity, Culture, and Difference in the Intensive ESL Classroom.*

in education. Aspects from many theorists have been combined in order to create a style of questioning that was used to have students look at themselves and their representations of others.

The students were asked to read, write, and listen to a variety of media about the topics and taught to critically question the content of each. It is one thing to read something on the surface without asking questions, but it is another to carefully examine what a reading is saying and what interpretation the reader receives from the document. Critical literacy and language awareness has the potential of being a tool of empowerment for the learner. In the context of this course the empowerment comes from the awareness of the definition and complexity of identity, culture, and difference and their interaction with each other and within the students' lives. As students critically question and analyze the content of course material they become empowered learners.

One of the major tools for this empowerment is of critical reading (Wallace 1995). This idea of critical reading is more than a critical response to the text. It also involves critically looking at how the students read as a whole. Many of my students have expressed that their cultures discourage questioning or challenging that which is said or read in the classroom or written in a newspaper. Many of them have been taught to accept what they hear and read as fact. By incorporating a critical approach to learning about identity, culture, and difference through the use of questioning, I tried to give students tools they might use to question and think deeply about the course topics and issues surrounding them.

Description of the Course

As mentioned, this course was designed around the concepts of identity, culture, and difference using a critical approach to learning.[3] The main goal of the course was to have the students explore their definitions and understanding of identity, culture, and difference in relation to themselves and their interactions in American society. A collection of materials and methods were developed to elicit a variety of responses and perspectives on the topics presented and to encourage

---

3 The course has now been conducted in several intensive English classes at two universities. Materials and activities have also been adapted for use at different grade levels and in different contexts.

students to look at each topic from several angles so that they might begin to see the complexity and challenges of each.[4]

Through the use of critical questioning, the course was framed around the notion of questions. Each topic was introduced as inquiry to aid the students in their understanding of each concept. Key questions provided the foundation for six learning units:

1. What is culture?

2. What is identity?

3. How do others see me in American society?

4. How are identity and culture connected?

5. What is difference?

6. How do identity, culture, and difference exist in American society?

With each unit a variety of materials and activities were introduced. The students' exploration during the units resulted in both learning about the concepts and learning of the language. The course used an integrated skills approach to learning English in which students used the four major skills of language in the context of exploring the course content.

Course Methods

The methods used in this course were many and varied. It is impossible to present them all here. Only some of them will be introduced. Overall, the course used many different literacy practices as well as the use of critical questioning in hopes of getting students to look deeply at the course content and to give them the tools to express the discoveries they had made.

Critical Readings of Articles, Poems, and More

The text for the course was no single bound document. Throughout the course many readings were presented to the students. The readings came from current newspapers, Shel Silverstein poems, excerpts from

---

4 The materials and activities designed for the course are in the process of being prepared for a textbook to be used in the ESL classroom.

ESL texts, and so on. In addition to written documents, the text was also a video of a news program, or the content of the class discussion. As mentioned in the theoretical framework, Catherine Wallace (1995) used several questions in her study on critical reading. I adapted these questions and provided them to my students as a tool to critically examine a text in order to see the many perspectives the text represents. The questions used were:

What is the student's reaction to the article?

What is the author's message? Why was the article written?

Who was the intended audience? Who did the author want to read his/her article?

Are all perspectives represented in the article? If not, whose is missing?

Why do they think the author left out that perspective?

If they could change anything in the article what would it be and why?

Providing these questions has helped the students look at what they read differently. Once I included these questions in my class activities, I found that the class discussions took a different direction and also lasted for a longer time period. For example, I would present newspaper articles on a current issue in the United States such as bilingual education or Ebonics. Wallace's questions have given students the tools they need to not just accept the reading as fact, but rather to question what they are reading and to form their own opinions on the issue presented.

Essays

To see how the students were interpreting the course themes I designed a couple of writing tasks. The most interesting and also difficult for the students was the writing of an essay entitled "Who am I?" The students were asked to answer this question in a one- to two-page essay. The following is an example from one of those essays:

Student Essay: Who am I?

There are many things that explain me, my race, my family, my job, my hobby, etc. All of these things are part of me and to know about these is important to find an answer the question "Who am I?" Moreover, it is also required to combine these things, because these facts cannot exist separately. I am a Korean and I am also a daughter, a sister, a student. And at the same time I like to listening music and watching movie.

Other essays revolved around the prompt of "What is culture?" Or students were provided with a small text and asked to explain how identity, culture, and/or difference were being discussed in the article.

Journals

In addition to essays, journals were used in many ways. They helped the students process the material for the course as well as showed me how they were interpreting the material. With many assignments the students were asked to write a response in their journals in order to better prepare for the next day's discussion. The journal gave students the opportunity to express their thoughts in writing first and also gave them a chance to familiarize themselves with vocabulary that might have been new to them.

Web Page

The more I taught the course the stronger I felt that there was not enough time available in class for most discussions. To continue the discussions (as well as to allow follow-up on my research) I created an internet web page for the course.[5] The web page contained an on-line discussion in which students responded to posted questions about the course and posed their own questions. Other sections of the Web page included, updates on the research project, on-line interview questions, and news from alumni. This Web page was created with ideas from students. As time has progressed each group of students has added something to it.

Interview Project

In order to have students be able to use the tools presented in the course and explore one aspect in depth, the following final project was created: students chose a topic related to the course themes and American society and formed a research question. The students then needed to interview a certain number of Americans in order to get a

---

5 The web page was created from a grant received from the Penn TESOL East organization. Funding was provided for instruction in web page creation and editing. Thank you to Penn TESOL East for its generosity and support of this project.

better understanding of their question.[6] Finally the students conducted library research in order to see if they could reach any conclusions about their question. One purpose of this project was to challenge some of the perceptions the students have made about American society by speaking to a variety of people. In the beginning of the project the students were asked what their expectations for their project were and then they reported in their final presentations whether these expectations were met. Some past research questions were:

- Why are Americans so concerned with race?

- What are Americans' values? Do they believe only in money?

- What does freedom mean to Americans?

- How important is individuality to Americans?

The students have found this assignment to be very rewarding and challenging. Most of the time their expectations were not completely the same as the results of their research and they felt that at the end of the project they had a better understanding of American society. Most reported that they realized how complex the issues were and that the issues were not easy to understand without talking with more people.

This is just a sampling of the methods used to develop and implement the course. In order to get a richer understanding of the course, the following two activities are introduced and explored.

Focus on Activities

As varied as the methods used were so too were the activities. The following two activities come from different units and illustrate the integrated nature of the course as a whole. A description of the activity will be presented as well as examples of how students responded to each.

---

6   In order to make this project more accessible for the students I put out a call on e-mail at the university for volunteers. Most semesters I had thirty to forty people volunteer for a fifteen- to twenty-minute interview. The volunteers would be students, both undergraduate and graduate, as well as staff from the university. In each session I have had a variety of ages, gender, and races represented in the volunteer pool. In a higher-level class I had the students find their own interviewees. Both ways have been successful.

Identity Quotes

This activity was created as a way to integrate several of the ideas the students had been discussing up to this point in the course. Many of the students found the topic of "What is identity?" very difficult for two main reasons. First, the students thought the topic was abstract and difficult to discuss both because of their English and because it is something they had never thought about before coming to the class. The second reason was the personal nature of the topic. In many of the students' cultures they were not encouraged—in fact they were discouraged—from looking at themselves as individuals. The following quote from a student interview sums it up best:

> To know identity is very important in some aspects. If man has his own identity he try to make himself better. To know identity includes recognizing his talent and calling. It makes him the way which he should go and through whole life. To know identity also unique which never is changed to other. I heard that if man knows his worth and value, he acts in different way and feel happiness and makes his effort to be the best. Unfortunately I didn't still have my own identity. Identity could be mainly formed during adolescence. But in my country we had no time to think over our identity during that period. We are only pushed to enter the college, so many college student wandered during period of college. It was same to my case. Because I don't still have a confirm identity, to think of the identity helps me to find and seek who I am and what I shall do through my whole life." (1/14/97)

The "What is identity?" quote activity involved the teacher making posters of quotes that define identity. When I began this activity I used quotes from famous people, but as time went on and I began to gather a collection of student quotes I used instead. Before the students enter the class the teacher posts the individual quotes in various places throughout the classroom. The students are instructed to read the quotes as they enter and sit by the one that they most agree with or wish to discuss. Once the students are settled they are given three questions to discuss in their group: (1) Share why you chose the quote you did. What stood out for you? (2) How is your quote connected with identity? and (3) Each group should create their own quote about identity. Some of the quotes I have received and use to post on the wall for future groups are:

> "If others judge me it will not be correct, they do not know me because I don't know myself."

"You need to love yourself in order to experience yourself or understand yourself."

"If you want to succeed in your life, you have to know about yourself."

"Identity is all the colors of the world."

As can be seen, the students use this activity to begin to look more deeply at the concept of identity and their relation to it. Once each of the individual groups is finished I conduct a large group discussion around all the quotes and the activity as a whole. Students are encouraged to question each other about why they wrote the quote they did and how it helps to define identity. This discussion usually spawns additional questions around the topic of identity and serves as a good introduction into their essays on "Who am I?"

As I used the topic of identity in the classroom, I questioned its use. Do students need to be given an opportunity or place to explore themselves in the new culture? Will this give them a better understanding of the new culture? One student on a midterm evaluation of the course, when students were asked how they would describe the course to a friend, said:

> If you pursue your identity, I mean who you are this class is helpful to you. In the class you will think of many things around you and you will think of their influence on you. This course is a process in which you can find yourself in America.

As a teacher and creator of this course, I'd like to believe that a space can be provided for students to "find yourself in America" and that by providing this space we are helping students gain a better understanding of the new culture and the differences they have with it. In addition, this topic brought some of the students' English to a new level of discussing abstract concepts. Prior to this experience, many of them had only used their English for concrete conversations, and they appreciated the time spent trying to comprehend and discuss this concept. For some this topic of identity was about finding themselves and for others it was about finding the language to discuss identity as a concept. No matter which one was the focus each provided support for why the topic of identity is an important addition to the ESL curriculum.

Culture Museum

The topic of culture is difficult and complex and yet too often it is presented very simplistically. When developing this section of the course, I wanted students to discover the complexity of the notion of culture and provide them with activities and language to discuss this view of culture. Culture Museum is my favorite activity in the course. It has always provided many opportunities for discussion of the complexity of the concept of culture. The initial idea came from an ESL textbook, but as time has gone it has been adapted and incorporated into the following activity.

The Culture Museum takes place over two days. The first part involves the students in small groups illustrating culture. I write on the board, "What is culture?" and ask them to draw their answers. I provide each group with some butcher paper and markers and about twenty to twenty-five minutes to construct their drawings. Figures 1 and 2 are a couple examples of the students' drawings. In the caption I have included students descriptions of their picture.

Many would expect this activity to produce only the visible aspects of culture (food, clothing, and so on) because of its instruction of illustration. I like to use the pictures because it helps some of the students describe an abstract concept without having the English necessary to explain their ideas fully. For some, the pictures give them the focus to describe the concept of culture. As the examples given show, the students created a deeper view of culture than just the visible

FIGURE 1   *Vision of Culture: We want to express all the different things about culture. First is a way of greeting, second is religion, and third is kitchenware.*

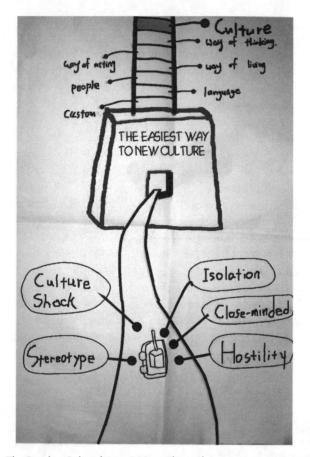

FIGURE 2   *The Road to Cultural Acquisition: The tank is a person. He is trying to learn culture. He has problems that can hurt him from getting culture. If he doesn't have problems he climbs through a small hole and up ladder to get culture.*

aspects. It is with this deeper view that I decided to extend the activity in order to have the students analyze their own as well as other pictures to see how each was defining culture.

Once the pictures were drawn I asked the students to discuss their picture. They were given three questions to answer: (1) How is your picture defining culture? (2) Is your picture defining culture as a noun, verb, and/or adjective? Why? and (3) Give your picture a title. I do this to encourage the students to see culture as more than the visible items or nouns such as food.

The following day, I post their pictures throughout the room, as well as some pictures from past classes. I write a message on the blackboard welcoming the students to the "Culture Museum." In their small groups they are asked to interpret two to three pictures in the museum using the same three questions that they used for their own picture. Once the students have completed their small group discussions I conduct a large discussion around all the pictures. It is through this large group discussion that students begin to see the different views of culture and begin to question their own and others' views in order to get a better understanding of the concept. There is a fascination at looking at each other's drawings as well as hearing how different people had differing interpretations of the same picture.

This activity clearly demonstrates the complexity of culture for the students. It is from this point on that the students ask for clarification on the term *culture* and verbalize the many aspects of it. It is a fascinating experience to be a part of, from the time the students begin their drawings until the museum is closed.

Conclusion

The goal of this chapter was to show the reader how a course can be designed to have students explore the concepts of identity, culture, and difference. I discovered both in my research and practice that once the students began to define and know the complexity of these terms, they began to look at their representations of American society and groups within it through a different lens. The students go through a process of learning about themselves as well as about their views and perspectives of the culture they are trying to learn more about. It is through this exploration that the students learn about themselves, their own culture, and about the culture they are trying to acquire.

References

BENESCH, S. (1993). "ESL, Ideology, and the Politics of Pragmatism." *TESOL Quarterly 27(4),* 705–717.

FAIRCLOUGH, N. (1992). *Critical Language Awareness.* London: Longman.

FAIRCLOUGH, N. (1989). *Language and Power.* London: Longman.

FREIRE, P. (1970). *Pedagogy of the Oppressed.* New York: Continuum.

GIROUX, H. (1988). *Teachers as Intellectuals: Toward a Critical Pedagogy of Learning.* South Hadley, MA: Bergin & Garvey.

LANKSHEAR, C., and McLAREN, P. (1993). *Critical Literacy: Politics, Praxis, and the Postmodern.* Albany: State University of New York Press.

PENNYCOOK, A. (1994) "Critical Pedagogical Approaches to Research." *TESOL Quarterly 28(4)* 690–693.

PENNYCOOK, A. (1990). "Towards a critical applied linguistics for the 1990s." *Issues in Applied Linguistics 1(1)* 8–28.

PEYTON, J. K. (1991). *Writing our Lives: Reflections on Dialogue Journal Writing with Adults Learning English.* Englewood Cliffs, NJ: Prentice Hall Regents.

RICHARDS, J. C., and LOCKHART, C. (1994). *Reflective Teaching in Second Language Classrooms.* New York: Cambridge University Press.

WALLACE, C. (1995). "Reading with a Suspicious Eye: Critical Reading in the Foreign Language Classroom." In Cook, G., and Seidlhofer, B. (Eds.) *Principle and Practice in Applied Linguistics: Studies in Honour of H. G. Widdowson.* Oxford: Oxford University Press.

15

Sparking the Conversation:
Teachers Find Cultural Connections and Communities of Learners

Nancy P. Gallavan

"I n two weeks I want you to bring something to class that reflects you and your cultural heritage," the professor announced the first day of our university multicultural education course. "Be prepared to talk about your artifact for three minutes."

One student reflected in her journal:

What does she mean by "my cultural heritage?" What in the world would I bring to share with this class? What will I say for three minutes? I am a "typical American." I don't really have a culture of my own. I am a white, middle-class, thirty-two-year-old, married, female, elementary school teacher. My family has been in the United States for many generations. We don't have any unique cultural background. I don't feel like there is anything special or different about me!

Several weeks later from the same student:

Sharing the cultural artifacts in our class was one of the most wonderful experiences I have ever had in a university course. I had spent days agonizing over my decision to select just the right thing representing me and my culture. I spent an evening with my parents talking about our family background, who we were, and where we had come from. This assignment sounded so easy at first, yet it consumed all of my thoughts and energy for weeks.

After I shared my family photograph and told the class about my ancestors (and I could have talked for an hour or longer), I realized the power of this seemingly simple exercise. In merely a month, I had reflected at length about who I am and my family's background. I had listened intently and learned so much from the people in my class—people I barely knew, people I had not anticipated getting to know. Many values and beliefs that I previously held about other people had been challenged in a comfortable and informative manner. The professor prompted me to think about the deeper meaning of culture in ways I had never allowed myself to think before.

This student's reflections summarize reactions to the first assignment in my graduate Multicultural Education course. The task is not intended to be arduous or stressful; however, most students begin their time to share by affirming how unexpectedly difficult it was for them to define the term *cultural artifact,* how personally challenging it was to select items that ideally represented their own cultural heritages, and how insightfully revealing it became when preparing to speak knowledgeably and articulately, describing the importance of these items for themselves and their families.

Sharing the artifacts yields one of the most rewarding sessions of this course by creating awareness for cultural connections and establishing an open community of learners. Students speak from both their heads and their hearts as they show their cherished artifacts and relate their personal stories. Their powerful stories capture their various and deeply held values and belief systems, which are indeed the true definitions of multicultural education (Buchen 1992; Cole and Wertsch 1996).

It is obvious how the students have dedicated much time and attention to their selection of both their artifacts and their words. It is a time of joy and celebration—a class session of reflection, inquiry, and insight. Compelling learning occurs as students realize the importance of every artifact to each owner as told through the individual's voice (Jackson and Meadows 1991).

After we brought our cultural artifacts to class, I felt like everywhere I went I was seeing the world for the first time, and it was filled with cultural artifacts—valuable treasures that symbolize incredibly important yet diverse meanings for the people who own them. I learned so much about so many different things in just one class session. I was amazed at the wealth of knowledge readily available from the other students in this class. I now know that this is true about the students in the high school math class that I teach.

And another student shared:

Someone commented how quickly our class bonded the day we shared our artifacts. I felt like I truly knew these people and suddenly realized that I don't take much time to get to know or care about the people around me. I also became painfully aware that I harbor a variety of feelings, sometimes strong and not-so-comfortable feelings, about other people, people who are different from me and "my kind of people." Sometimes I have already decided what kind of person someone must be before I actually get to know them as an individual based on their race, religion, gender, or how much money they seem to have. When the other students brought in their artifacts and talked so passionately about their cultural heritages, they provoked many strong feelings within me. The sharing of our artifacts was an astounding and eye-opening exercise.

Defining and Understanding the Concept of Culture

I have incorporated the Cultural Artifact assignment into my multicultural education courses to achieve several goals. First and foremost, I want to create an opportunity for students to explore and understand their individual cultures (or perceived lack of culture). Second, I want them to define "culture" independently rather than my imposing an "expert's" definition upon them (Linquist 1996). Most of the students enrolled in my teacher education and graduate courses tend to be white, female, and middle-class; frequently tell me that they have no culture other than being a "typical American." They seem unaware of their own rich and individual cultures, the diversity of cultures that thrive in the people around them and how to value cultural diversity in their own students. Focusing on self-reflection, inquiry, and discovery offers a safe, but challenging, learning experience for each student to construct a personalized meaning and deeper connection with the concept and existence of culture. This exercise provides students with a place to express and build upon that new knowledge and awareness (Wood and Wilson 1996). Third, I want them to challenge the students' previous ways of thinking and believing in how they interact with others.

Introducing the Cultural Artifact Assignment

This assignment is introduced during the first class session. Only brief instructions and a few examples are given as I want students to delve openly and freely into this assignment. Students are encouraged to ask themselves and one another provocative questions, to seek information from their families if possible, and to reflect deeply about their own individual cultural heritages. It is essential for them to consider how culture is represented or manifested as a cultural artifact within their personal lives (Havas and Lucas 1994).

I sure was glad when someone asked the professor to explain more about this assignment before we left class on that first day. Initially I was bothered that she would not tell us specifically what to bring. She told us "it could be a family heirloom, a photograph, or a contemporary item that defines who we are." She gave a smattering of ideas, but I just wanted to be sure that I would be selecting the right thing. Finally, as I was driving home, I realized that if had to be my own Cultural Artifact—it had to be about me and my family background. There was no "right thing" to bring to class!

Another student remarked:

Immediately I knew what I was going to share. As a child, my family instilled in me a strong sense of belonging through my religious beliefs and active participation. I would bring a symbol of my faith. I couldn't wait to talk to my family about this activity and then share it with the class.

Students in every multicultural education course describe walking through their homes actually looking at the items that hang on their walls and sit on their shelves—the things that represent who they are. The students talk about seeing these artifacts as if for the first time in their lives and questioning why they have chosen these specific items to represent their histories, their lifestyles, their journeys. They reflect upon the artifacts that their parents and grandparents have passed along as family keepsakes representative of their backgrounds and heritages. Students talk about digging in old boxes and storage areas, calling their parents and lifelong friends, and spending time with both their childhood and adult families to help them select the one artifact that best defines them. These stories reflect the essential need for this assignment and the rewarding opportunities that such an investigation promotes for families and friends to spend time together talking about themselves and who they are. The assignment compels students and their families begin to make powerful cultural connections (Taylor and Lambert 1996). Students candidly share the challenges they encountered while defining "cultural heritage" for themselves and the formidable tasks they wrestled with in selecting their cultural artifacts.

One student reflected:

I have always felt deprived of having a culture. Although I respect and enjoy listening to others speak about their ancestors through their heartfelt tales and treasured relics passed down through generations, I feel that I have no stories of this kind to share. I find my childhood accounts and family traditions equally important, but they do not seem to offer the same significance as those I hear from other people. I have been envious of people who have a special ethnic background to share and define their lives.

Another student added:

Heritage was rarely an issue in my family. I never spent any time with my grandparents or other relatives, nor did we ever discuss our background. My father was in the military; we lived in many places around the world moving every few years. I did not feel as if I had roots or belonged to any one cultural group. In fact, sometimes I didn't even feel like I belonged as a U.S. citizen.

Students describe the assortment of experiences they encounter when talking with their families.

I called my mom right after class and told her about this overwhelming assignment. I exclaimed that our family had no unique culture; we were not members of any particular ethnic group. She laughed at me and started telling me all sorts of fascinating stories like how my great, great, grandparents had immigrated to the United States. She invited me to come over to look at some photographs and relics that she had saved in a trunk. I couldn't wait to see these thing and to hear the stories. Yet, I wondered why it had taken this long in my life to hear about my own cultural background. I felt lucky that a university class assignment was sparking all this conversation.

Reflecting Upon the Cultural Artifact Experience

The Cultural Artifact assignment has a second requirement previewed during the first class session. Students are asked to record their reactions to each of the first three class sessions beginning with the initial description of this assignment and continuing through the class session where we share our cultural artifacts within the large group setting. They are requested to journal their thoughts, conversations, and actions related to selecting and sharing their artifacts. This companion assignment culminates with students submitting a two- or three-page synthesis and analysis of the entire Cultural Artifact assignment process.

Their journals reveal the students' growth and powerful insights for valuing cultural diversity gained over a short time period. A student's reflection:

To share my culture by bringing one artifact would be impossible; there is so much that I consider to be representative of me, my heritage, my people, my values, my beliefs. Yet I fully understood the professor's need to limit each of us to just one artifact. How would I select just one?

During the second week of class as we explored stereotyping in society and schools, I suddenly knew exactly what I wanted to share. I realized that I was probably the only practicing Jew in our class, and it has been my experience that few students understand Judaism. I would share my Ciddur given to me at my Bat Mitzvah. This would be perfect!

The day we brought our artifacts was exciting. I was anxiously looking forward to presenting my Ciddur. In fact, a few hours before class I shared my artifact with my coworkers (who are not teachers and are intrigued with my assignments in the graduate program). They were fascinated with the beauty of the Ciddur, the writing, and how my people use it. I explained it to them, as my father had explained it to me. They asked the same questions I had asked of him. I realized that most people never take the time to learn about themselves nor the people around them. If we had more conversations like these, there would be less stereotyping and prejudicial behavior in everyday life. People would be more understanding and accepting of one another. This university class assignment was far more than I could have ever imagined.

Creating a Community of Learners

An equally valued goal guiding this assignment is to create a community of learners who begin to think, construct, and express their personalized understandings of culture and individual voices through story. By design, students are not provided specific examples or told what is "the right thing" to bring or to say in class. A safe and open forum is established for them to listen carefully to their own voices and to one another as they discover the meaning of culture within themselves and this new community of learners. To enhance sharing the artifacts, the second class session is devoted to concepts of stereotyping and acceptance. Students begin to connect the concept of culture as encompassing characteristics far beyond race, ethnicity, nationality, and religion. They start to link other cultural attributes such as social class, gender, sexual orientation, ability, size, interests, and so on, as valuable aspects that define who we are, what we value, and how we operate within classrooms and society (Jackson and Meadows 1991).

One student reflected:

I was confused how some students knew immediately what to bring to class and others were not concerned at all about speaking openly among our peers. They seemed to know clearly who they were, and they were so proud of their backgrounds. My family had always kept to ourselves. We had to; I grew up in a poor family. I had few opportunities to own things, to go places, or to do many things—particularly things I could tell to my friends. I was sure other students in this multicultural education class wouldn't understand. I don't think they understand their own students of poverty. How would they understand me?

I was a bit intimidated thinking that my "cultural heritage" was not defined as much by my ethnic background as my life of poverty. I wanted to share about living in poverty, but I would need to find the right artifact to help me communicate this difference visibly. The more I thought about this assignment, however, the easier it became—especially after we talked about stereotyping and prejudice. I knew I could tell this class about my unique cultural background. They probably had never met a teacher who had lived in a homeless shelter as a child. This might be a shocking experience for the students in my university class, but I felt willing to take that risk and share that part of me and my culture.

Sharing the Cultural Artifacts

The day students bring their artifacts the atmosphere is electrified. The adult university students are behaving just like young children during the holidays. They arrive eagerly with their artifacts wrapped carefully in a variety of bags and boxes, and conversations abound.

From one student:

I was concerned about this assignment from the beginning. When I came into the classroom, I was so relieved because other people around me also were worried; they were comparing the things that they had brought with one another. I had so many thoughts racing through my mind. Maybe I should go early and get this over. I opted to wait, and I forgot all my anxieties once the sharing began. Soon I felt more and more comfortable with what I had brought. Everyone else was sharing something much like my artifact, and I was surprised how quickly I began to feel an attachment to the members of our class.

And another student wrote:

The discovery that provoked the most thought for me was how similar other people are to me, and how the same events occur for most of us regardless of the family configuration. Although I knew I am not the only one who experiences a specific event, it is nice to hear others talk about getting cookies in a shoe box, families going to church or on trips together, or parents disapproving of boyfriends, etc. Our cultural backgrounds may be different, but the conversations are similar and the emotions are the same.

Students bring all kinds of treasures, which seem to fall into one of three categories: religious icons, global connections, or personal interests. Many different religious icons such as Bibles and books of prayer representing various religious institutions are shared in class. Religious icons include symbols that students hang inside or outside of their homes and symbols they wear as jewelry. Students speak passionately about the meanings of these icons to them and their families. These are powerful soliloquies that at times are in direct opposition and hostile disagreement to other students' belief systems. However, students behave appropriately as their peers describe the importance of not just the icon but the religious belief systems that the icons represent within their daily lives. Frequently students ask probing questions that help them to acquire more information or to clarify misconceptions they have related to the particular religious organization. Likewise, students enjoy finding peers who believe as they do. They have never had this type of opportunity within a university class (Pinsker 1994).

A wide variety of international connections are shared in class. Students bring food, clothing, jewelry, accessories, maps, passports, sayings, and so on. Everyone enjoys sampling tasty treats from around the world, and students joyously show their global roots on the large world map I display in this classroom particularly for this assignment. The questions focus on global beginnings and international travel. These conversations tend to be more casual than the discussions related to religious icons and beliefs. Students seem appreciative when speakers explain various international customs. All these conversations help students to understand the importance of making the learning relevant and meaningful. Everyone learns more about others and the world, since the descriptions are framed within one person's individual experiences.

Students also bring a variety of cultural artifacts representative of the facets of their personal lives such as politics, recreation, music, art, and a plethora of social affiliations. Some of the artifacts connected with special talents, hobbies, or organizational memberships have been passed down through generations. Other interests extend to contemporary family lifestyles such as those related to music or sports. Students speak strongly about these artifacts and their families' connections with these diverse interests and affiliations.

Again, these connections may be in direct conflict to another students' participation and belief systems. Usually a student remarks about how similarities and differences in our society have been the "justification" for disagreements ranging from neighborhood battles and gang fights to international conflicts and world wars. One student remarked:

> It's too bad some world leaders including religious leaders couldn't take this class so they could learn to listen to one another and begin to tolerate and accept differences. I guess that would be too simple.

Successful Orchestration of this Assignment

It is important to schedule sharing the Cultural Artifacts carefully. I meet in a classroom with detached chairs so I can arrange the chairs in a large open circle allowing all the students to see and hear one another easily. It is essential to ensure that all the students join the circle and no one self-selects to sit back or behind the rest of the group. All students need to feel welcomed and valued. This arrangement not only provides a safe and open forum for these university students, it models and reinforces the importance to include all students in every classroom discussion—an essential component of teacher education.

Time must be scheduled carefully too. All students must be provided the opportunity to share during the same class session. I allow each student to talk for three to four minutes. This limitation produces one of the most revealing discoveries. Initially most students react fearfully to the idea of talking about their culture for even three minutes. However, on the day we share, many students disclose that they have much more to say than the time allows them. If a safe and accepting environment has been established, students will no longer be concerned with talking or how much to reveal. These common responses often link the class members as they identify their tremendous growth and deepened understanding with one another as a community of learners. Although some students may be reluctant to share, each student is anxious to complete the assignment at that time. No student wants to prepare for this class session a second time. More importantly, the electrified feeling tends to be limited to this one class session. Powerful observations and insights will be ignited at this time as students share their cultural artifacts and heritages; all students will be ready to write their personal reflection summaries.

Extensions into Pre-K–12 Classrooms

One semester a second-grade teacher replicated the Cultural Artifact assignment in her own classroom incorporating some important modifications. She began by showing her students the video of the children's book *Molly's Pilgrim*. Building upon the concepts of personal culture and self-confidence, her class discussed how people are alike and different in their individual lives. Within a story circle, the teacher guided her students to create a list of examples on a large sheet of paper. Students quickly contributed many specific illustrations; they categorized these items into larger groups such as types of homes, food, clothing, vehicles, recreation, and so on.

The teacher skillfully eased the conversation into an exploration of race, religion, gender, social and economic status, size, and ability by asking to students to look at the similarities and differences among the students in the room. These characteristics also were added to the list. She told students that most of their families originally had moved to the United States from another country over a long period of time accounting for our international heritages and backgrounds. The teacher also explained that people have many different religious beliefs and value systems, which define who they are and how they act.

The teacher culminated the story circle by sharing her own personal cultural artifact, the same cultural artifact that she brought to our university multicultural education class. She shared with the students that it was now their turn to bring something to share with the class. The teacher read aloud a letter that her young learners would be taking home to their families explaining the purpose and procedures of this assignment. The letter carefully detailed the goal of showing personalized meaning for valuing cultural diversity among her young learners. It expressed the importance for families to help their children in selecting and understanding their individual cultural artifacts so the young learners could share comfortably and competently with their classmates.

Later that week all of the second-graders brought their cultural artifacts. The teacher told our university class that her students behaved exactly as the university students had behaved. Their treasures were carefully wrapped, and the students seemed equally anxious about their selections and unsure of what to say. The second-grade teacher dedicated an entire afternoon for her students to share their cultural artifacts. She was amazed at the reactions of her young learners. They spoke knowledgeably and proudly of their cultural artifacts; they listened carefully to one another; they asked intelligent and insightful questions. They suddenly seemed to know and understand one another better—just as the adult students had discovered in our university multicultural education class.

Following the group sharing time, the teacher displayed a blank "big book," in which students would draw pictures of their selected cultural artifacts. The students also wrote one or two sentences describing their cultural artifacts and the importance of the artifacts in their families. As with our university class, the second-grade teacher was attuned to organizing the sharing and drawing within one afternoon to capture the same electrified excitement and understanding. The second-graders were changed, and the teacher watched it happen quickly. The teacher readily acknowledged that the families of her students were responsible for the overwhelming success of this rewarding response. Obviously, time and attention had been given to prepare each student. Many families contacted the teacher to thank her for integrating this powerful learning experience into their children's and families' lives. The second-grade teacher had no idea that this exercise would make such a positive difference for so many. The university students were equally impressed with this experience and in viewing the second-graders' big book of cultural artifacts.

Summary

Most teachers want their students to achieve by participating actively in specific learning experiences, to construct a personal understanding of the learning, and to apply the learning to their individual lives. Teachers design classroom experiences to help students connect with one another as a community of learners striving to work together as a caring, sharing, and productive team. These connections provide authentic experiences in preparation for real life.

The Cultural Artifact assignment exemplifies one successful approach used in my multicultural education course with both preservice and inservice teachers as well as a second-grade classroom to achieve these goals. Students not only engage actively in a personalized learning experience, they begin to construct an inclusive and useful definition for the meaning of culture. They explore their own rich and individual cultural heritages and histories; they discover and enrich their understandings for the range of cultural diversity that thrives in the people around them. As teachers, they start to value cultural diversity and the importance for creating cultural connections among their own students and communities of learners within their own classrooms (Csanyi 1992; Singh 1996).

From one student's journal:

> I cannot fully explain all of the emotions that I felt when we were sharing our cultural artifacts in my reflection paper. As we shared our treasures and passed around our artifacts, I was flooded with childhood memories that I have not revisited in a long time. There were many similar experiences shared by other students causing me to

realize that I have never related my cultural heritage to my daily life of today. I know I have not considered the power of culture in the everyday world around me.

Now I have taken the time to reminisce with family members and friends, and it has challenged me to think about my upbringing and personal belief systems. Some of my thoughts are reassuring, others are a bit painful and reveal the kind of person I have become as an adult and as a teacher. I am beginning to better understand the importance for valuing cultural diversity in all students, in everything I teach, and in how I teach. I am afraid that I may be leaving out some of my young learners. I can't believe how little I know about my own sixth-grade students, which means they probably know nothing about one another. This Cultural Artifact class exercise has made me more aware that our students come to school representing many different cultures and belief systems that may or may not match the school and the teacher. I am going to find a way to incorporate this type of learning experience into my own classroom soon. The students will learn so much about themselves, each other, and the world around them!

References

Buchen, I. H. (1992). "The Politics of Race, Gender, and Sexual Orientation: Implications for the Future of America." *Equity and Excellence 25(2–4),* 222–228.

Cole, M., and Wertsch, J. V. (1996). "Beyond the Individual; Social Antimony in Discussions of Piaget and Vygotsky." *Human Development 39(5),* 250-257.

Csanyi, V. (1992). "The evolution of culture." *World Futures 34(3–4),* 215–224.

Havas, E., and Lucas, J. (1994). "Modeling Diversity in the Classroom." *Equity and Excellence in Education 27(3),* 43–48.

Jackson, A. P., and Meadows, F. B., Jr., (1991). "Getting to the Bottom to Understand the Top; Understanding Culture and Its Implications on Multicultural Counseling. *Journal of Counseling and Development 70(1),* 72–77.

Lindquist, T. (1996). "Solving Culture Mysteries; Understanding Diverse Cultures through their Artifacts." *Instructor 105(7),* 28–30.

Nagel, J. (1994). "Constructing Ethnicity: Creating and Recreating Ethnic Identity and Culture." *Social Problems 41(1),* 152–177.

Pinsker, S. (1994). "What Americanists Talk about When They Talk about Culture." *The Georgia Review 48(1),* 154–162.

Singh, N. N. (1996). "Cultural Diversity in the 21st century: Beyond E Pluribus Unum." *Journal of Child and Family Studies 5(2),* 121–137.

Taylor, D. M., and Lambert, W. E. (1996). "The Meaning of Multiculturalism in a Culturally Diverse Urban American Area." *The Journal of Social Psychology 136(6),* 727–741.

Wood, J. A., and Wilson, B. (1996). "Teacher Inservice Training for Cultural Sensitivity." *NASSP Bulletin 80(582),* 113–115.

16 Finding the Freedom to Teach and Learn, and Live

Joan Wink

O nce we had as much freedom as we wanted. A quick glance at my previous syllibi would show that my students and I used books by Jim Cummins, Bonnie and David Freeman, Paulo Freire, Ken and Yetta Goodman, Herbert Kohl, Steve Krashen, Tove Skutnabb-Kangas, and Lev Vygotsky. Rigor and joy were central to our classes. We made books; we read books; we reflected on books. We loved each other; we loved our class; and we loved our learning. We loved our freedom to teach and learn.

However, that has changed drastically on a global scale. Micromanagement, mandates, and military metaphors are eroding our freedoms. Where I live, bilingual education has been outlawed, explicit English phonics has been legislated. I started teaching thirty-four years ago. I have seen difficult times in education before but I have never experienced anything like this. Never. Ever. I am now living in a scripted English-only world.

Martin Luther King once gave a speech on creative maladjustment. He talked about how we all eventually have to adjust to many things. However, there were some things he could never adjust to: for example, racism. Today we would add sexism, classism, and xenophobia.

In addition, I cannot adjust to the dogma underlying the current climate in education. Therefore, I will have to find creative forms of maladjustment to survive and thrive. Incidentally, if you would like to join me in creative maladjustment, you will find that a sense of humor is very handy. It also helps to be a bit nimble.

Changing Times Are Changing Education

It started very simply. A colleague came to our graduate class to discuss culture. She asked us to empty purses and wallets to see what could be learned about each student's culture. It was amazing how much we learned about the social, political, and cultural institutions that represent the various cultures among the group. Before she left, the professor explained to us that there are many definitions of cultures, but essentially they all have two commonalties: cultures are learned and they are shared.

When she left, I spontaneously shared with the class some of the things I could remember learning from my own culture. When I left home to attend college, I met my future husband. I remember our initial conversation because he told me several things about himself that bothered me. I remember the discomfort I felt when I learned he was from Iowa. I was from South Dakota, and you know how *those people from Iowa* are. He added to my anguish when he said that he was from a farm. I was from a ranch, and you know how *those farmers* are. He further told me that his family belonged to the Farmers' Union. Horrors! My family belonged to the Farm Bureau, and you know how *those Farmers' Union people* are. I didn't ask any more questions because I was afraid of what he might say about his home culture. However, I very clearly remember wondering what his politics and religion were. You know how *those Democrats* and *Catholics* are!

The class and I laughed about the things that I had learned from my own culture: ranchers were good, and farmers were bad; Republicans were good, and Democrats were bad; Protestants were good, and Catholics were bad. As we were laughing together, a young grad student slowly raised her hand and shared her culture with the class.

"I went to private Catholic school for 12 years," Heather said.

"And, you know how *those private school kids* are," one of her friends said, which relieved the tension we were feeling. The class and I nervously laughed.

"Do you know who I learned to hate when l was in private school all those years?" she asked us.

"No," we answered, curious.

"Public school kids and teachers," she quietly and seriously told us.

"That's us," someone blurted out.

"You know how *those public school kids* and *teachers* are," another student offered weakly.

A third student responded to my initial comments, "And it wasn't the Democrats who were bad either. It was the Republicans. I learned they were only interested in making the rich richer and the poor poorer."

This sudden outburst about Protestants versus Catholics and Democrats versus Republicans made the class and l realize that we were on a slippery slope. We were entering new territory. It was exciting and dangerous—ripe with potential and this was not a part of our prescribed curriculum; this was not on the syllabus. I was not transmitting knowledge; we were generating ideas together; we sensed transformation could not be far behind. However, the truth is that we raced up that learning curve with reckless abandon. Everyone wanted to share; we all wanted to learn. This conversation of our lived experiences mattered to us. It was real. For the remaining six weeks of the semester, we wrote, read, reflected on the "other," which was new and disturbing language for many in the class. Not every moment was wonderful. But, in the end, we all learned far more than was on the original syllabus.

Today, in our era of scripted, prescribed—and proscribed—curricula, I could get into trouble for allowing that to happen.

Since our English-only mandate, my students now have to pass a sound-centric test before they can even get their teaching credentials. We drill in English. We read the prescribed books in English. We worry in English. The students memorize, in English, for a test that has very little to do with being a good bilingual teacher. They learn to do what this test dictates they must do. Some would say that it is a phonics test. I would say that it is a test of dogma and ideology. I would fail this test—if they would let me take it. They will not; nor will they let me see the test. It is a secret. And, they check my syllabus to see if I am teaching in the prescribed, correct way (I would be ashamed to show you my syllabus). And, if my students do not pass this test, they will not be able to teach. My dean and chair will ask me why my students did not pass. The list of passing and failing students is readily available throughout my department for all to see.

The same thing is taking place in the world of literacies. Whole to part? Part to whole? What in the world is the right way to teach reading? The literacy wars have much in common with other wars: friends turn against friends; families turn on other family members; incumbent and wanna-be politicians take sides whether they know anything about it or not. We are all a tad paranoid and worry about who is on whose side. As I write, I wonder, who is my audience. If I am completely honest, what will the repercussions be? Will I be "targeted?" Will it hurt my students? Will it hurt my university?

Politics are now a public part of our pedagogy. How can it not be? Schools are filled with people, lots of people who all bring a diversity of thought, perspectives, opinions, and experiences. Schools are social, schools are cultural, and schools are political environments that reflect the world around them.

When you choose curriculum, it is a political act. When you make a decision about who will learn what and how, you are taking political action. And even if you choose not to act, your passivity is also a political action.

We live in a time when everyone is suddenly and passionately interested in education. Are we on a historical path that leads us to a time when politicians and/or the public choose curriculum, programs, and methods? The American fight over bilingual *or* English-only; the fight over whole-to-part or part-to-whole pedagogy; the fight over sound-centric literacy or meaning-centric literacy are, I think, designed to hide the real war, which is really over the future of public education. We must not be lulled into fighting so hard for the parts that we miss the whole.

Some polls demonstrate that the public has about had it with educators. This newly acquired interest in education from politicians and the public has made teachers an easy target. The public blames teachers for low test scores; for bad manners; for outrageous behavior; for violence; for lack of morals.

Teachers are blamed because the public and the politicians are frustrated and don't know what to do.

Teachers are blamed because it is always easier to blame teachers and kids than it is to acknowledge the fact that schools reflect the community.

Teachers are blamed because that is easier than it is to go to a neighborhood school, and volunteer on a regular basis, and learn to know teachers and students, and to seek solutions collaboratively.

The blame game is easier than positive actions and interactions.

My Own Struggles

Out with Freire; in with phonemes. Out with meaning, in with minutiae. Out with schema, in with the schwa. Out with the whole, in with the parts. This is how I felt when I sat down one September to update my Bilingual Language Arts course syllabus to reflect emerging state mandates. As new guidelines dictate that I must prepare preservice teachers with a knowledge of fricatives, phonemes, and phonology, the truth is that I find myself feeling philosophically frustrated. This would be funny, if it weren't fact.

In my first class under the new regulations, there were thirty-three teacher credential candidates in my bilingual reading/language arts class. The majority spoke Spanish as a first language; many were from migrant labor families. One such student described himself this way:

> I am a second generation Mexican-American whose parents were farm laborers. My parents bought a small two bedroom house and raised five children. My dad worked for a farm labor contractor, and he worked six days a week from sunrise to sunset. My mother stayed home to raise the children and eventually went to work in the canneries when we got older.

I allowed myself the first couple of weeks the pleasure of not worrying about the requirements of state mandates. I wanted the students to reflect on their own reading before we set out to learn to teach others to read. The first night of class I asked students to write mini–case studies of themselves as readers. How did they learn to read? What did they read? How did they feel about reading? The majority of the students said they loved to read. Some described themselves as avid readers; passionate readers; even merry readers. Yet it was those who said they hated reading who had a special place in my heart. One of them wrote, "Me as a reader. What a concept! I've never thought of myself as a true reader."

I divided the case studies into simplistic categories. Twenty-three loved to read. Their comments were very revealing about what really matters in how to teach reading.

> I was very fortunate to have a fantastic history teacher who exposed his students to wonderful books. He did something that no other teacher had done before—he invited us to his home to see his incredible home library. Have you ever seen the movie *Beauty and the Beast*? In the movie there is a part where the Beast shows Beauty his enormous library with books from wall to wall. That is what his library looked like to me. I have never forgotten any of these books. One day I hope I can do that for my students.
>
> My mother never wanted me to lose my Spanish so, anytime she had a little extra money, she would buy books in Spanish. She read to me right before bedtime.
>
> For as long as I can remember, I have always enjoyed reading. I remember my mother taking me to the library on a weekly basis.
>
> One time I went to the library and checked out 12 books and had to carry them home 15 blocks.

In the stack of ten case studies of those who hated to read, comments were equally revealing about how not to teach reading.

My teacher in junior high would use reading as a punishment. I always behaved so that I would not be punished and have to read.

We didn't have books of any kind in our home. Once I went to live at my uncle's house and was overwhelmed with all the children's books my little cousin had. I can remember wanting to read those books. I asked my uncle to let me go to school, but he did not grant permission.

The truth is that reflecting on the literacies of these students gave me hope. The vast majority of my students had overcome obstacles far greater that a state mandate just to be in a teacher education program at the university.

For the rest of the semester, I taught as I had been directed. I placed the emphasis on sounds and the relationship between sound and letter. We did phonemic awareness in English and Spanish. I quizzed them on phonemics, phonology, and phonetics.

Be honest: could you pass a text asking you to define phonetics, phonemics, phonology, and fricatives? Does that mean you are not a good teacher? Can all your students pass the high-stakes tests? Does that mean you are not a good teacher? My students passed the tests. Does that mean I am a good teacher?

At the end of the semester, it was clear what these students had learned. It was equally clear to me what they had not learned. I did not turn them into passionate readers. I didn't implant a thirst for knowledge. I did not help them see themselves as intellectuals and scholars who will continue to grow and learn and read; who have a perception of themselves as powerful professionals. They can teach phonemic awareness but I never equiped them with ways to cope with the next (unreasonable) local, state, or federal mandates.

This raises difficult questions. What is an educator to do? What is a bilingual educator to do? What do I, as a critical pedagogue do? Let me share how I tried to find some answers for myself.

My Exploration of Pedagogy

Any discussion of education is ultimately grounded in pedagogy. I could not work through my own teaching struggles until I returned to my understandings of pedagogy, critical pedagogy, literacies, and critical literacies. I am reluctant to print definitions. I fear that someone somewhere will memorize them—or someone else somewhere else will make *another* someone memorize them. As if there were the one true definition! If you memorize my defininition, you'll soon forget it for you don't own it. Keep this in mind as I share with you—I made them up! I encourage readers to use my words as a starting point and to discover their own definitions.

Pedagogy

When I first started teaching, in 1966, I thought I knew exactly what pedagogy means. This is what I thought: "I will teach and they will learn." It all seemed so simple, pure, and clean. In my preparation to be a teacher, I was never taught that politics is a part of schools. (Imagine my surprise!) In fact, I was taught to believe the opposite. I was taught that somehow we teachers were *above* politics, that we worked on some pure plain of pedagogy.

Gradually and painfully, I began to recognize that my assumptions of thirty-two years ago were wrong. Maybe they weren't wrong for thirty years ago, but they certainly don't reflect my experiences since then. Nor do they reflect the incredible changes since that time. My early definition of pedagogy was not only simple, I think now it was simplistic. It now reminds me of the old saying: For every complex problem, there is always a solution that is obvious, easy, and wrong.

I now think that pedagogy is the dynamic, reciprocal (and often times, barely controllable), interactive relationship we develop with students as we teach and learn together. One time in a graduate class, my students had been teaching and learning with such rigor and joy that I suddenly heard my mouth saying, "Stop this learning, I want to teach!" I find it to be true that the less I teach, the more they learn.

The Legacy of Teachers

I find courage in pedagogy. I look to the legacy of those who have gone before me. In the history of time, I am just a tiny speck. It's true: I am not the most important person in the world. I try to see the big picture. At my computer, surrounded by my books, I think of all the work that others have done and how my life is enriched because of their contributions. They have worked, and I have benefitted.

Let me introduce you to some of my distant teachers who give me hope and courage.

Lev Vygotsky

I look up at my bookshelf, and I see my Vygotsky books. He lived only thirty-four years during a very painful time of history, the Russian Revolution. Food and heat were luxuries. He suffered with poor health and died far too young. When he died, his works were censored; no one could even read what he had written for decades. Now as a new century begins, we see his immense contributions to collaborative and dialectical teaching and learning. One of his favorite lines from poetry testified to the fact that, no matter how difficult it is, we can all still "live, think, feel, love, and make discoveries." This line of poetry gave him hope—and, now it does the same for me.

Paolo Freire

I look up at my bookshelf and see my Paulo Freire books, and I think how he was driven from his native Brazil for seventeen years because he would not give up his claim to the freedom to teach and learn bilingually. Translated from Portuguese, Paulo Freire defines critical literacies: "reading the word and the world." Critical literacy involves knowing, lots of knowing. It involves seeing, lots of seeing. It enables us to read the social practices of the world quite clearly. Critical literacy reveals the zone of "all-this-learning-really-isn't-so-great." Critical literacy means that we understand how and why knowledge and power are constructed. And by whom. For whom.

And, from Freire, I remember his *Pedagogy of the Oppressed* that turned into his *Pedagogy of Hope* near the end of his life. I see his books, and I remember *rigor* and *joy*.

Tove Skutnabb-Kangas

I look up at my bookshelf and see my books by Tove Skutnabb-Kangas, and I hear her words, "Language rights are human rights." I hear her telling me "Joan, think wildly; think of your utopias; dream big." I hear her extolling the virtues of creative chaos. I am reminded to see the potential and the possibilities and transform these to creative chaos.

Herbert Kohl

I look up at my bookshelf and see my books by Herbert Kohl, and I am reminded of his concept of "hopemongering." Kohl writes about affirming our and others' hope for an equitable and just future even in the midst of contrary evidence. A hopemonger does not give false hope; a hopemonger keeps hope alive, even during difficult times. As a teacher educator, I see that as some of our most important work.

Ken Goodman

I look up at my shelf and see my books, and my T-shirt, by Ken Goodman. I read the shirt, "Banned in California: freedom to teach, freedom to learn, social justice." His courageous work vigorously defends our freedom. He has written extensively for the freedom of all of us to turn our theory into practice; to turn our beliefs into behaviors. I am indebted to the strength and honesty I have found in *Call to Courage*, a call for unification of our shared knowledge about languages, literacies, and cultures, and our freedom to live our personal and pedagogical beliefs.

Living Your Beliefs

We all need to reflect critically on our own experiences and those of others, and then to connect these new thoughts to our own lives in new ways. Those who do not come from a tradition that encourages critical reflection are often so busy *doing* that they fail to take time for *thinking*. Thinking about important ideas needs nurturing. And it takes time.

Paolo Freire teaches us that critical pedagogy is to name, to reflect critically, and to act. My daughter, Dawn, found critical pedagogy her first day of teaching. Returning home from her kindergarten classroom she burst through the door, "All the toys are old, broken, and dirty. The last teacher left boxes and boxes for my kindergarten students. It's just junk. I snuck out to the garbage and threw it away. There were even teaching materials from the 1950s."

In this case, Dawn *named* it, junk. She *reflected critically* as she decided the value of the junk and snuck outside to find the garbage. And she acted. She tossed it. Critically pedagogy helped Dawn to know that forty-year-old English materials would not meet the needs of the Spanish-dominant children in her bilingual kindergarten.

We're so busy fighting, defending, educating, sharing with others that, certainly, it must be affecting our teaching. I know that it has affected mine. I try to live authentically and honestly based upon my own knowledge and experiences, too. I must be able to live with myself and my pedagogy. Others have worked their entire lives for the freedom to teach and learn. They may not even know me, but I am blessed because of their work. It is in their legacy that I find hope.

Do not deny the politics of education. Do not be frightened by it. Jump in. Share your knowledge, your perspectives, your experiences. Write and speak and act. Do not stick your head in the sand.